THE CHURCH

A DIVINE MYSTERY

THE CHURCH

A DIVINE MYSTERY

by

Abbé Roger Hasseveldt

Translated by William Storey

Fides Publishers, Chicago, Illinois

57313

LIBRARY OF CONGRESS CATA-
LOG CARD NUMBER: 54-11023

NIHIL OBSTAT:
Rev. Joseph Cavanaugh, C.S.C.,
  S.T.D.

IMPRIMATUR:
✠ John Francis Noll, Archbishop-
Bishop, Fort Wayne, Indiana

NIHIL OBSTAT:
Eugene Masure, C.D.

IMPRIMATUR:
P. Duthoit, v.g.

Bx
1751
H313

Manufactured in the United States of
America by American Book–Stratford
Press, Inc., New York
 55

Published originally by Les Éditions
de l'École, 1953, under the title, *Le
Mystère de L'Église*, Paris, France.

Table of Contents

v

CONCLUSION

PREFACE

A study of the Church which appeared in France under the title, *In Christo et In Ecclesia,* was in great demand in seminaries in France. At the request of many professors of religion, Catholic Action chaplains, and lay members of Catholic Action, Abbé Roger Hasseveldt re-issued the book in revised form in 1953, under the French title, *Le Mystère de l'Eglise. The Church: A Divine Mystery* is a translation of this revision.

In the author's mind, a study of the mystery of the Church cannot be undertaken without constant reference to Holy Scripture. He recommends that the reader have a copy of the New Testament handy when he reads this book. The New Testament will also be essential for the additional research which the author suggests at the end of each chapter for the serious student. So far as the Old Testament is concerned, substantial texts have been included at the end of various chapters.

The Church: A Divine Mystery has a two-fold use. Because of its simplified, almost outline presentation, it offers a complete and easily grasped development of the Catholic Church. On the other hand, the book has been designed as a workable instrument for the classroom, with a systematic (though not scholarly) treatment, accompanied by projects for work at the end of each chapter.

Both the general reader and the student of theology can acquire not only an exact vision of the mystery of the Church, but also a profound religious conviction, a real apostolic zeal, and the firm will to participate actively in the mission of the Church. Abbé Hasseveldt has destined his book for a learned faithful and particularly for lay apostles anxious to enlighten their faith and support their action.

In answer to those who question today, *Why the Church?* Abbé Hasseveldt looks at the Catholic Church from within, as a believer who seeks to discover all the splendor and challenges of his faith. He is particularly concerned with the connection between Christ and the Church and the need for going through the Church in order to reach Christ, the need for being in the Church in order to live by and in Christ.

The reader shall see from this study that the Church is the Mystical Body, the Communion of Saints, and that it includes the whole of history from the beginning of the world, especially that portion of history which extends from the first Coming of Christ until His return at the end of the world.

Chapter 1

THE CHURCH IS A MYSTERY

"Christ, yes; the Church, no." This slogan expresses well the thought of many of our contemporaries and the temptation of even some Catholics.

This separation of Christ and the Church brings about a certain indifference in regard to the Church or the various churches: "One religion is as good as another; Catholics are not any better than anybody else, and there are sincere people in every religion."

It is an evil characteristic of our times.

—In the IV and V centuries, during the discussions of St. Augustine and the Donatists,[1] the faithful asked: "Which is the true Church?"

—At the time of the Protestant Reformation,[2] in the XVI century, the faithful asked: "What is the Church?"

—But today the faithful are asking: "Why the Church?" It is the very fact of the Church which is brought into question, not only by our contemporaries generally, but at times even by Catholics themselves.

What are the sources of this evil?

—It stems, on the one hand, from the progress of *individualism*. Generally speaking, we are rather respectful of personal value, but somewhat indifferent in regard to institutions. While formerly those institutions which were universally respected threw a halo of prestige about the persons associated with them, today the persons supply an institu-

---

1 "Quaestio certe inter nos versatur, ubi sit Ecclesia, utrum apud nos, an apud illos." *Ad Catholicos epistola contra Donatistas* (vulgo: De Unitate Ecclesiae), c. 2; P.L. 43, 391. See the whole of this letter: P.L. 43, 391-446.

2 "Est ecclesia congregatio sanctorum, in qua evangelium recte docetur et recte administrantur sacramenta." *Augsburg Confession*, art. 7.

1

tion with its value and prestige. We have only to think, for example, of the varying fortunes of present-day royal families, according to the personality of the ruler.

—But in regard to the Church, the special source of this error lies in the *ignorance* of the true nature of the Church and of its connection with Christ. Even Catholics often know only the exterior make-up of the Church. They have viewed it only from without, as they would view a stained-glass window from the outside, and they are surprised when they do not understand its meaning.

There are, indeed, two ways of looking at a **stained-glass window**.

1. It can be looked at *from the outside*. From that position it reveals a few of its features, but as a whole appears meaningless. The fact is that the stained-glass window is not designed to be seen from outside but from within.

2. There is only one way to understand it, and that is *by going inside* the building. Then there are no more problems, everything is lit up, and even the leading and the dark patches of the window appear as integral parts of its beauty.

Similarly, there are two ways of looking at the Church.

It can be looked at **from the outside**, either in its history or in its organization. As in the case of the stained-glass window, the Church reveals a few of its features: it appears as a religious society founded in former times by Jesus Christ and today spread throughout the world. But it is composed of both saints and sinners, and its history is not always edifying. Consequently, when seen from without, and by the light of reason alone, the Church might appear as an enigma, even as a mass of confusion, if not a scandal.

The Church, like a stained-glass window, must be looked at **from within**, that is to say, **by the light of faith**, for it is not only a complex and mysterious reality, but a true *Mystery*, like the Incarnation, for example. The remainder of this book will demonstrate this fact.

We shall therefore look at the Church as "believers" who seek, not so much to justify the Church to unbelievers, but, above all, to discover all the splendor and all the challenges of their Faith.

We shall discover that the Church, as seen from within, that is, with the eyes of Faith, appears as a harmonious whole: the paradoxes and oppositions become reconciled on a higher plane.

But we must understand that such is not the case for unbelievers. When the opportunity presents itself, we should even tell them that we understand their difficulties, that they are unavoidable, given the point of view they take. But we can invite them to pick a better point of view, namely, that of contemplating the Church from within as we do and in our company.

The stained-glass window will then show up in all its glory, and before such splendor our words will be but little needed.

Thus, at the end of this study, we shall understand the connection between Christ and the Church, and the need for going through the Church in order to reach Christ, the need for being in the Church in order to live by and in Christ, Christian life being a life in Christ and in the Church: *"In Christo et in Ecclesia."* We shall then understand that page of Bossuet's Catechism [3] which says:

"Why do we put these articles: the Communion of Saints, the forgiveness of sins and life everlasting, after: 'I believe in the Holy Catholic Church?'

"*Answer:* In order to show that there is no holiness, no forgiveness of sins, and, consequently, no salvation nor life everlasting, except in the Catholic Church.

"And why do we put all those after: 'I believe in the Holy Ghost?'

"*Answer:* In order to show that it is the Holy Ghost who gathers together and animates the Church in which he has deposited all His graces.

"And is the resurrection of the body also among those

---

3 *Second Catechism*, second part, lesson XII. (Oeuvres complètes, Louis Guérin Bar-le-Duc, Paris, 1863, t. XI, p. 474.)

graces that we receive in the Church through the Holy Ghost?

"*Answer:* Yes, the resurrection for life everlasting.

"Where do all the graces of which we have been speaking come from?

"*Answer:* From the Holy Ghost who gives them to us in the Catholic Church.

"Is there then no salvation outside the Church?

"*Answer:* No, there is no salvation outside the Church."

PROJECTS

In order to measure the place that the Church holds in your life, try to imagine what would be changed in it if the Church did not exist: in your day; in your week; in your year; since your birth.

Chapter 2

THE COMPLEXITY OF THE MYSTERY
OF THE CHURCH

The word **"Church"** often only recalls to our mind the visible society founded by Jesus Christ. We readily set it in opposition to other apparently richer realities, such as the Mystical Body, the Communion of Saints, etc.

We shall see better at the completion of this study that the Church is the Mystical Body, the Communion of Saints, and that it includes the whole of history from the beginning of the world; but, nevertheless, for us it signifies especially that portion of history extending from the first coming of Christ until His return at the end of the world.

In this way we shall rejoin the language of the whole of Tradition:

"By the Church, brethren, we must understand, not only those who began to be holy after the coming and birth of our Lord, but all those who were holy at any time whatsoever, because they all belong to the Church. So it is that our father Abraham belongs to us, despite the fact that he lived before Christ was born of the Virgin" (St. Augustine).[1]

"The Church is simply the *community* of all the saints. All who from the beginning of the world were or are or will be justified—whether Patriarchs, like Abraham, Isaac and Jacob, or Prophets, whether Apostles or martyrs, or any others—make up one Church, because they are made holy by one faith and way of life, stamped with one Spirit, made into one body whose head, as we are told, is Christ (Col. 1:18)" (St. Niceta of Remesiana).[2]

Let us notice first of all that we continue to use the term

---

1 *Sermo* 4, c. 11; P.L. 38, 39.
2 *Explanatio Symboli* 10; P.L. 52, 871. Trans. G. G. Walsh, Writings of Niceta of Remesiana (The Fathers of the Church VII), N. Y., 1949, p. 49.

"Church" (Church Triumphant) for what will remain of God's plan when the visible society, as we know it now, will have disappeared. It will then be easier for us to designate the religious society of the Old Testament by this same term "Church."

In order to orientate our mind toward such an extension of the notion of the Church, we shall successively study what will exist of the Church at Christ's return, and what already existed of the Church before the coming of Jesus.

I. The Church at Christ's Return

Some components will change; others remain.

The components which will change:

—The present governmental hierarchy of pope, bishops and priests will no longer exist. It will be replaced by the equality of the children of God, or rather, this hierarchy will be replaced by another hierarchy, that of holiness. By that very fact, there will be no more laws, nor any obedience corresponding to those laws.

—There will be no more Sacraments, since divine life will exist in all the elect.

—Faith will disappear in order to give place to the Vision of God.

—Hope, likewise, will give place to the possession of God.

—The present mixture of Good and Bad in the Church on earth will come to an end by the final separation of the Bad from the Good.

—Similarly, sin and death will have definitively disappeared in the risen elect.

Thus, certain component elements which appear to us as essential to the Church, such as the hierarchy, the Sacraments, will disappear, and yet the Church will continue. The fact is that the Church is not limited to these component elements, and that its definition is richer than we thought it was at the beginning.

The components which will remain:

And yet it is really the same Church lived here below which will last forever after the return of Christ, despite the preceding modifications.

—The risen **elect** who will make up the Church after Christ's return are the very ones who will have made up the Church in its earthly condition here below.

—And the essential reality will remain absolutely the same in both conditions, namely, **charity.**

"In their calumnious manner the Donatists claimed that the Catholics recognized two Churches, the present one containing a mixture of good and bad, and another which is to come after the resurrection containing only the good, just as if the saints who will one day reign with Christ were not the same as those who now live justly and put up with the wicked for His sake" (St. Augustine).[3]

II. The Church before Christ

There was already a People chosen by God, one which bore the Hebrew name of "Church." This people already had the promise of the Saviour and of Salvation. God had already made a covenant with this people, the "**first covenant.**" It had its Temple, its Law, its Sacrifices, its Feasts, its sacred persons: priests, kings, prophets.

It was Jesus who saved all the men who had hoped for His coming and who had believed in the promises of God and in the religious realities of this first covenant. It is the same Faith which saved the righteous men of the Old Testament and which now saves us: for them it was Faith in the Christ to come; for us, Faith in the Christ who has come.

But the great innovation is precisely **the coming of Jesus.** Henceforth, because of His coming, we no longer have promises, but reality; no longer merely the first covenant, but the new and eternal covenant; no longer the blood of the paschal lamb, but the very blood of Jesus, the true pas-

---

[3] *Breviculus Collationis cum Donatistis,* Collatio tertii diei, c. 10; P.L. 43, 634.

chal Lamb. It is this presence of Jesus which causes all the reality and efficacy of the new People of God and of His new Sacraments.

✕ Thus, the notion of the Church becomes more precise with the coming of Jesus, but, at the same time, we see that it extends well beyond His coming and includes the whole history of the preparation for Jesus.

"Before the coming of Our Lord Jesus Christ, when He came in humility in the flesh, righteous men preceded, believing in the same way in Him who was to come, as we believe in Him who has come. Times vary but not faith. For verbs themselves vary with the tense, when they are variously conjugated. The expression, 'He is to come,' has one sense, but the expression, 'He has come,' another. There is a change in meaning between 'He is to come' and 'He has come,' yet the same faith unites both—both those who believed that He would come and those who have believed that He is come. We see that both have entered, although at different times, by the one doorway of faith, that is, by Christ... Under different signs there is the same faith... All those who believed at the time of Abraham or Isaac or Jacob or Moses or the other patriarchs or the prophets who foretold the coming of Christ, were sheep and heard Christ. They listened to His voice and not another's" (St. Augustine).[4]

It is probably as difficult for us to understand these things as it was for the Jews to whom Jesus explained: "Abraham your father rejoiced that he was to see my day. He saw it and was glad." The Jews therefore said to him, "Thou art not yet fifty years old, and hast thou seen Abraham?" Jesus said to them, "Amen, amen, I say to you, before Abraham came to be, I am" (John 8:56-58).

III. Conclusion: The Complete Church

The Church of the New Testament, in which we now find ourselves, is therefore neither a beginning nor an end. It

---

4 *Tractatus in Joan. Evang.,* 45, 9; P.L. 35, 1722-23.

lies between the Old Testament which it fulfills and the heavenly Church which it prepares and anticipates. It is one stage in the over-all plan of salvation.

The complete Church is the whole of this scheme of salvation which includes three principal phases:

—a preparatory phase (Old Testament)
—a phase of earthly realization (New Testament)
—a phase of heavenly fulfillment (Apocalypse)

The particular difficulty of the mystery of the Church lies precisely in the fact that the Church is at once a reality which is **identical** and yet very **different** according as we consider it at one or another moment in the history of salvation, that is to say, in God's eternal plan: "He chose us in Him (Christ) before the foundation of the world" (Ephesians 1:4);—in the Old Testament;—in the present stage of history until the return of Christ;—and, finally, after Christ's return and the resurrection.

There is an **enduring element**, even an eternal one, since the Church existed in the eternal plan of God, and because it will endure forever after the return of Christ.

But there are also **transitory elements** which change according to the phases of the history of salvation, and which are, nevertheless, essential during that phase, for example, the sacraments and the hierarchy at the present time.

In its enduring elements the Church is in some way the very terminus of salvation, and in its transitory elements it is the means of salvation. That is why the Fathers depict the Church as **Paradise** itself into which we enter through baptism: "The Hebrews after having passed through the Red Sea arrived in a desert; but we, after having passed through Baptism, arrive at Paradise" (St. Zeno).[5]

But at the same time, they depict the Church as the vestibule, the **gate of Paradise** "opened by Christ on Easter day: through which believers alone may pass" (St. Augustine).[6]

—In the first part of this work we shall study the enduring

[5] *De Exodo,* lib. 2, tract. 43; P.L. 11, 519.
[6] *Sermo supposit,* 159; P.L. 39, 2059. (Cf. Glossa Ordinaria, lib. Levit., 6, 16; P.L. 113, 312.)

elements in the Church, namely, the plan of God to "re-establish all things in Christ" (Ephesians 1:10).

—Then in the second part we shall study the various stages of this plan, that is, what changes in the Church.

—In the third part we shall consider in a special way the stage in which we now find ourselves, that is, in the Church of the New Testament.

—Finally, in an important conclusion we shall try to understand better what makes up the Mystery of the Church and our Faith in this Mystery.

PROJECTS

Find in your missal at least a dozen different titles which are given to the Church. Say which one you prefer and why. (Look, for example, in the mass for the Dedication of Churches, and in the Vigils of Easter and Pentecost.)

First Part

THE PLAN OF GOD:
THE CHURCH

(What Endures in the Church)

Chapter 3
A PANORAMA

Hermas, an early Christian writer, relates a vision in which the Church appeared to him under the aspect of an elderly woman: "Why is she elderly?" I asked. "Because she was created **before all things**," he said. "For this reason she is elderly and for Her sake the world was erected." [1]

Indeed, St. Paul tells us that the plan of God is from all eternity:

"Blessed be the God and Father of our Lord Jesus Christ, who has blessed us with every spiritual blessing on high in Christ. Even as he chose us in him before the foundation of the world, that we should be holy and without blemish in his sight in love. He predestined us to be adopted through Jesus Christ as his sons.... And this his good pleasure he purposed in him to be dispensed in the fullness of the times: to re-establish all things in Christ, both those in the heavens and those on the earth" (Eph. 1:3-10).

In Christ, God **calls us all together,** that is to say, into a Church, in order to make us His children, for the English word "Church" comes from the Greek *"Kyriakē"* meaning *she who belongs to the Lord*. The Church is *the gathering together of all the children of God in Christ*. In the Church each member is personally a child of God, but not in an isolated fashion, for he is a child of God within the family of the children of God. Each one is personally summoned to enter into communion with Christ, with the Holy Trinity, and with all the children of God.

---

1 *The Shepherd,* vision 2, part 4. Trans. J. M.-F. Marique (The Fathers of the Church I), N. Y., 1947, p. 240.

In this part of our work we are going to consider this great mystery under the following three headings:

1. In Christ the Church shares in the life of the Trinity.
2. In Christ the Church is the image of the Trinity.
3. In Christ each one of the faithful personally enters into communion with the Trinity and with the entire Church.

In order to avoid going astray, here is a summary of the road we shall traverse:

—The Life of the Trinity is one of knowledge and love. The Church shares in this life of knowledge and love.

—The Trinity is itself a communion of Persons in the unity of a single life and a single nature. The Church is the image of the Trinity because it is, like the Trinity, a communion of persons in union with Christ. The Church is, therefore, made up in some way of the following two dimensions:

(a) its sharing in the Trinity is its "vertical dimension";

(b) its being the image of the Trinity, that is, by our participating in the Trinity, not in isolation, but together in mutual communion with one another, is its "horizontal dimension."

—Eternal happiness will consist in our knowing God together, in our loving Him together, that is to say, "in the Church."

—In this enduring and eternal aspect the Church is truly "the Family of God," "the People of God," "the Communion of Saints."

—By defining the Church as we have just done, we shall entirely escape the most common danger that Catholics incur, namely, that of reducing the Church to its exterior, juridical or transitory elements, or even of reducing the Church to its function: the Church is not merely the organ of salvation, or the collection of means conducive to salvation; basically it is **Redeemed Humanity.**

—Thus it is that all the wealth of Grace, which is still only too often studied in a separate treatise, enters into the mystery of the Church, as its enduring and eternal element.

PROJECTS

By examining the epistle to the Ephesians, or the epistle to the

14

Philippians, or the epistle to the Colossians, try to discover how St. Paul presents and characterizes this plan of salvation:

—the absolutely gratuitous and eternal initiative of love on the part of the Father;

—who calls us to be His adopted children in His incarnate Son;

—and the role of the Holy Spirit in this plan.

Chapter 4

IN CHRIST, THE CHURCH SHARES
IN THE LIFE OF THE TRINITY

Sometimes we have difficulty in understanding how there can be any relation between the Trinity and the Church, because, more or less consciously, we consider Christ as separate from the Trinity, and the Church as separate from Christ. Somehow or other, there would be God; then below Him and in some way separately, Christ; then, still further down and also separately, the Church.

With such an outlook, it becomes impossible to understand either Christ or the Church.

Christ Is in the Trinity

First of all, we must understand that Christ is in the Trinity. Indeed, God is a Trinity: Father, Son, Holy Spirit. The Son and Christ are not two different persons. Christ is just the eternal Person of the Son become incarnate in human nature.

Because the mystery of the Incarnation is an accomplished fact, the Trinity is:

—the Father,
—**the Incarnate Son,** that is to say, Christ,
—the Holy Spirit.

It is here that we should recall the great insights of St. John: "God so loved the world that He gave His only-begotten Son..." (John 3:16). "And the Word was made flesh..." (John 1:14).

Notice that in the Creed we do not say "I believe in the Father, I believe in the Son, I believe in the Holy Spirit, and I believe in Christ," as if there were four persons, and as if Christ were something other than the incarnate Son. Rather, there are only three terms:

I believe in the Father
I believe in Jesus, who is the Incarnate Son
I believe in the Holy Spirit.

"It was the Son alone in the Trinity who assumed the form of a servant, a form which in His case was fitted into the unity of His person, or, in other words, that the one person, Jesus Christ, should be the Son of God and the Son of Man; and so that we should be kept from preaching a quaternity instead of the Trinity, which God forbid that we should do" (St. Augustine).[1]

Similarly, throughout the whole liturgy, the only-begotten Son of the Father is always called "Jesus Christ," meaning that He is always envisaged in the mystery of His incarnation.

The Church Is in Christ

But we must continue and add that the Church is in Christ.

When the eternal Son became incarnate, it was precisely in order to become in his human nature:

—the *Vine,* of which we would be the branches (John 15:1-8);

—the *Body,* of which we would be the members (I Cor. 12:27);

—the *Firstborn,* whose divine life and heavenly inheritance we would share (Romans 8:29).

It was in order to communicate to us His divine life as Son, just as He lives it Himself in His human soul. What we call grace, for lack of better term, is nothing more than divine, filial love in the human soul of the Incarnate Son.

He becomes **one with us** in His human nature in order to make us **one with Him** in His life of divine sonship. "God becomes man," says St. Augustine, "so that man may become God."

---

[1] *Tract. in Joan. Evangelium,* 99, 1; P.L. 35, 1886. (trans. M. Dods, Edinburgh (1874), vol. II, p. 388).

The liturgy even speaks of a mysterious exchange between Jesus and Humanity:

"O wondrous exchange! the Creator of man, having assumed a living body, deigned to be born of a Virgin, and having become man without man's aid, enriched us with His divinity" (Antiphon of the Vespers of the Circumcision).

"Grant that by the mystery of this water and wine, we may be made partakers of His divinity who deigned to become partaker of our humanity, Jesus Christ Thy Son, our Lord" (Offertory of the Mass).

Thus, as St. John so often repeats, Jesus abides in the Church, and the Church abides in Jesus: "Abide in me, and I in you" (John 15:4).

The life of the Church is truly a life "in Christ." St. Paul repeats this formula "in Christo" around 170 times.

The Church Is in the Trinity

Since Jesus is in the Trinity, all those who are united to Jesus are themselves also in the Trinity. Jesus is in the Trinity because He is the very Son of God; but this Son gives us His divine, filial life, that is, grace, and He presents us to the Father as His adopted children.

Jesus is the Father's sole object of love: "This is my beloved Son, in whom I am well pleased" (Matt. 17:5). But since we are united to this beloved Son, we are also the object of the Father's love. "He has loved us in His beloved Son" (Eph. 1:6).

Yes, Jesus is the only Son of God, but all those who are united to Him by grace, that is, the Church, are in Him—like Him—with Him—truly Sons of God.

He introduces the Church into the Trinity, that is, into the bosom of His own family, just as a bridegroom brings home his bride (Eph. 5:22-30).

"The Father celebrated the marriage feast of His Son when He united Him to Holy Church through the mystery

18

of the Incarnation. The womb of the Virgin Mother was the bridal bed of this Bridegroom" (St. Gregory the Great).[2]

Consequently, the Church is *by marriage* everything that He is by nature. Christ is God's heir, but because of this nuptial union with her Spouse the Church shares in this inheritance.

"But if we are sons, we are heirs also: heirs indeed of God and joint heirs with Christ (Romans 8:17).

PROJECTS

Pick out everything concerning the union of God—Christ—and the Church in chapters 14, 15, 16 and 17 of St. John's Gospel. Then, with the help of these texts, show how the union of the Father and Christ is the model of the union between Christ and the Church.

---

[2] *Roman Breviary*, homily of the 19th Sunday after Pentecost.

Chapter 5

IN CHRIST, THE CHURCH IS THE IMAGE OF THE TRINITY

What Is God?

It sometimes happens that we think of God as a solitary, isolated being, turned in upon Himself in sterile contemplation and everlasting boredom. Corresponding to this picture of *an individualistic God,* there is sometimes a similar picture of *an individualistic salvation.* This individual God creates men according to His own image as just so many isolated individuals. To each man individually He offers an individual salvation: "I have only one soul and I must save it...." Each individual, being responsible for his own sins, and relying upon his own merits, receives from God individual reward or punishment according to his merits. This individual God creates other individuals in His own image. All this is a logically consistent way of looking at things. Fortunately, it does not correspond to reality.

"Let us beware of conceiving God as an old man of venerable appearance.... Do you want to see God? Then think of this saying: 'God is Love.' What does Love look like?... No man can say" (St. Augustine).[1]

God Is Love

God is not this powerful, solitary and isolated being; rather God is a Trinity: in Him three distinct persons love one another so completely that we find realized in them what all human love desires, namely, to become one heart and soul, and even nature, with the person loved.

---

[1] *Tract. in Joan. Epist.,* 7, 10; P.L. 35, 2034.

God is a **Communion of Persons** within the unity of a single Life. And the work of God is in the image of God:

—Since He is love, all His work will be a work of love: out of love He invites us to participate in His life of love, as sons, in His incarnate Son.

—Since He is a Communion of Persons within the unity of a single life, His work will be one of Communion and of unity: He summons us to share in His life, not as isolated individuals, but together, as a family, as a communion, as a "Church."

The Church, as the image of the Trinity, *is a communion of persons within the unity of Christ.*

"That they all may be one, even as thou, Father, in me and I in thee; that they also may be one in us" (John 17:21). Here we should recall all the images of **unity**: the Church is a single Vine;—a single Building;—a single Temple;—a single Spouse;—a single Kingdom;—a single Body;—a single Flock; —a single People of God.

Person and Community

—Each one of us is personally known and loved by God, as we shall see in the following chapter. But it is *as a member of Christ*, at a given place, in a given vocation, that God has thought of us and loved us.

Grace, that is to say, the life of Christ, is given to each one of us, not as isolated individuals, but as **members of one body,** both for ourselves and for the sanctification of all the others.

Consequently, there is no conflict possible between personal development and the service of the Community, since each person is placed by God in a given location, for a particular vocation, and is personally endowed for this vocation: personal development and the service of the Community become identified in Charity.

—However, we should notice that God began by revealing the mystery of our unity and of our Communion before revealing our value as persons. In the Old Testament, it was first of all *the People as a whole* that was considered as the son of God: "Israel is my son, my firstborn" (Exodus 4:22). "The Lord thy God hath carried thee as a man is wont to carry his little son" (Deuter. 1:31).

Later on it was to be learned that within this people *each member* is personally a son of God. Only the Church can resolve the antinomy of the two great contemporary currents of thought:

(a) the *communitarian* current (which in Communism ends up by despising the person);

(b) the *individualistic* current (represented, in its most extreme form, by Existentialism).

For the Church is a Communion of *persons,* not anonymous individuals, nor mere numbers in a series; and because of this fact, the Church can take to itself whatever may be of value in the present personalist current of thought. But these persons are in *Communion* and can only develop through love and mutual service; and from this point of view, the Church can take to itself whatever is of value in the communitarian current.

Filial and Fraternal Life

Our unity as a family does not hinder the intimate relationship of each person with God. As in a family, fraternal love does not impede filial love, but on the contrary, filial love is all the stronger when shared by many brothers. Thus the life of the Church is at once filial and fraternal, in Christ who is both **the Son of the Father and the Brother of men.** Eternal happiness will not only consist in participating in God's life as sons, but also in participating in it as brothers in mutual communion. Eternal happiness will be made up of this double love: filial love towards God;—fraternal love towards men.

"We shall be wholly occupied in singing Amen and Alleluia. What do you say, brethren? I see that you have understood and are in joy. But do not allow this carnal thought to sadden you, namely, that if any one of you were to stand all day long singing Amen and Alleluia, he would quickly grow weary, would fall asleep pronouncing such words, and would soon wish to keep silence; and perhaps it would enter his head to despise this life rather than to desire it, saying to himself: 'How could I ever stand going on saying Amen, Alleluia, forever?' . . .

"In their exultant joy the citizens of this celestial city, burning with love for one another, and above all for God, mutually encourage each other to praise Him by forever saying Alleluia, just as they say Amen" (St. Augustine).[2]

PROJECTS

By using the first epistle of St. John show:
—that God has made us to His own image of light, holiness and love.
—that the life of the Church is a life of Communion with God and with our brethren (love is both filial and fraternal).

---

2 *Sermo* 362, c. 28; P.L. 39, 1632-33. Read the whole last part of this Sermon.

Chapter 6

THE COMMUNION OF SAINTS

This fraternal unity of all the children of God is set forth in the Creed: "I believe in the Communion of Saints." This means both the Communion of *persons* and the communion of *spiritual goods*. To these we must add a Communion of *action*.

I. A Work of Unity

All of God's work, because made to His own likeness, is a work of unity, not only in the order of the divinization of the world, but also previously *in the order of the creation of the world*. Our supernatural communion in the life of Christ rests upon a primary **natural communion** of the human race, in the order of persons, of action, of goods.

The modern world, because of its mastery of space, is becoming more and more aware of this unity:

—unity of the human race,

—unity of the material universe,

—close unity of man with the universe.

Grace is the fulfillment in Christ, the incarnate Son, of this primary unity of creation. There are not two different planes in God, a natural plane (creation) and a supernatural plane (divinization). The God who creates is not a different God from the God who sanctifies. The God who divinizes the world is the very one who created it. God created men in order to make them His children in Christ, and He created *the universe for His children*.

Thus, all is orientated toward Christ. God thought and created all things in Him: "All things are yours, and you are

Christ's, and Christ is God's" (I Cor. 3:21). "A great invitation has been extended comparable to that of the parable in which the Father invites us to the marriage feast of His Son. The table is laid and the order for communion with God is sent in all directions.... A communion of all men with one another.... A communion of man with nature.... And a communion of all nature with itself and with its Creator" (Paul Claudel).[1]

II. A Communion of Persons in Christ

All those who are united to Christ are also united among themselves.

Communion in the Natural Order

Even in the natural order this communion is already a very close one. By our fleshly birth we belong to the human family and to the universe. The human race has often been likened to a single man: "All men born of Adam may be considered as one man" (St. Thomas Aquinas).[2] "The entire series of men ought to be considered as one single man who always exists and who learns continually" (Pascal).[3]

Communion in Christ

Christ is the only Son of God and all others only become sons of God by their incorporation in Christ, their insertion in Christ, their participation in the life of Christ.

Thus all the sons of God also enter into communion with one another within the unity of one same life, within the unity of one same living being. In consequence, this Communion of Saints extends to all those who live in Christ whether in their *earthly existence,* or in *heaven* in the Church Triumphant, or in *purgatory* in the Church Suffering. The same Christ who lives in me and who divinizes me, also

---

1 *Conversations dans le Loir-et-Cher,* p. 263.
2 *Summa Theol.* I-II, q. 81, a. 1.
3 *Pensees et Opuscules* (ed. Brunschvicq), p. 80.

lives in the Blessed Virgin and divinizes her. I thus communicate with all the saints across all the boundaries of time and space.

We all live the same life within the same living being, Christ. "But God, who is rich in mercy, by reason of His very great love wherewith He has loved us, even when we were dead by reason of our sins, brought us to life *together* with Christ...and raised us up *together,* and seated us *together* in heaven in Christ Jesus..." (Eph. 2:4-6). "For you have died and your life is hidden with Christ in God. When Christ, your life, shall appear, then you too will appear with Him in glory" (Col. 3:3-4).

One same life, one same living being links together time and eternity. St. Thomas even goes so far as to say: "As regards our participation in beatitude, that is, in the life of Christ, there is a closer union between our soul and that of our neighbor than between our soul and body." [4]

This Communion of Saints must extend to all mankind since every man is invited to enter into this Communion; God is at work even upon sinners in order to have them enter into this Communion. Only the damned, because they have definitively excluded themselves, have no share whatsoever in this Communion.

III. A Communion of Goods

In the Natural Order

There is already a communion of goods of the natural order for mankind. Indeed, life consists in exchanges, in reciprocal gifts. The more life there is, the more there are exchanges. This fact distinguishes the more evolved living organisms from the simpler types. The same thing goes on in society as regards all the various goods and services which men exchange for their mutual benefit.

The *modern world* is becoming more and more aware of the universal extension of these exchanges. Every acquisi-

---

[4] *Summa Theol.* II-II, q. 26, a. 5, ad. 2.

tion of science, thought and technology is of universal interest, e.g., the international control of atomic energy, the various services of the U.N. and of U.N.E.S.C.O.

Our actions affect the whole of mankind in one way or another.

"Each one of the acts that we insert into the course of events is diffused, so to speak, to the whole of mankind and prolongs its good or bad effects to the limits of time and space. Each virtuous action, each conquest of freedom is capitalized as it were in the individual by habit, in society by opinion and custom, in posterity by heredity, and thus concurs in the moral progress and happiness of all men. Likewise, any act of cowardice or vice entails an incalculable series of difficulties, faults and wretchedness" (D.C.R., t. VI, col. 414).

This is a real communion both as regards good and evil, but it appears to us as more striking in regard to what is evil, for example: world wars, general economic depressions, heredity.

"For a child to be born healthy, whole generations of virtuous ancestors are necessary. But one sin of one man suffices to poison the wellsprings of subsequent generations of his descendants" (André Fayol).[5]

Since the natural communion in good and evil is so strong, it will not be surprising to discover an even closer communion of goods in the domain of grace. This latter communion is simply the transposition of the whole human order to the supernatural realm.

In the Supernatural Order

As we said above, life consists of exchanges. The divine life is one of exchange. The Trinity is formed by the mutual Exchange of the three Persons. Each person exists only in order to give Himself and by giving Himself. They are called "subsistent Relations." It is this divine life that we share in Christ. Our Christian life will, therefore, be essentially a life of love, or reciprocal self-giving, of exchange.

1. A Communion in sin.—Humanity's first communion is in sin.

---

5 *Notes sur l'amour humain.*

(a) The mystery of original sin is not so much that of the solidarity of humanity with an individual called Adam, as the mystery of the solidarity of the whole human race in itself. It is because this **human family is one and interdependent** that the first sin had such universal repercussions.

(b) Consequently, we must not cast all responsibility on Adam, nor merely consider the solidarity between Adam on the one hand, and the whole of mankind on the other. **Adam, the "first sinner,"** has a special responsibility, and his "first sin" has a graver and more universal repercussion, since it is this first sin alone which accounts for the absence of grace in other men. Adam bore within him, so to speak, the responsibility for the destiny of his race, and by his deliberate choice gave it an orientation which was necessarily to influence his descendants.

But he only began the series; certainly he laid a heavy debt to humanity's charge, but each one of us has increased this debt by our personal faults. What Christ came to repair was not only the original sin, but also all our personal faults, in short "the sin of the world."

Obviously, we are directly responsible only for our personal sins, but we must realize that our sins, too, have their repercussions in other and on future generations: by the influence of example, of word, of action or of physical and moral heredity, or through lack of development. Our actions thus have an immense influence, not only on the vertical plane of eternity, but also on the horizontal plane of humanity.

"Christ will give you the clear understanding of what you are: an immortal soul, not one living in isolation, but one surrounded by a great many other souls over whom you exercise power for better or for worse. When grace diminishes in you, it diminishes in a great many others who depend upon you. If you are a friend of Christ, many others will warm themselves at this fire, will share in this light. The darkness of sin in you will cast its shadow over those whom you now enlighten. And the day when you no longer burn with love, many others will die of the cold" (F. Mauriac, *Message aux Jeunes*).

(c) The problem is, therefore, not: "why are we all punished for the fault of one man (Adam)?" but rather: "why this solidarity of mankind?" There would be injustice involved if we were associated in evil, without being so associated in redemption. But since through redemption we are at one with Christ and the whole Church, then the question is this: "why this pattern of solidarity and of communion, rather than an individual pattern?"

When confronted by the fact, we can discover its religious meaning and harmonious lines. This communion of humanity in sin and this communion in Christ's redemption show us the love of God Who became incarnate in our sinful family, Who shouldered the burden of our human heritage, even unto death. It makes us aware of our unity: God preferred to have us "united" rather than "isolated." It also permits a greater love among us in Christ: salvation is everybody's business; our life is to be a personal collaboration in a collective work—the salvation of the world.

2. **A Communion in Redemption.**—There is in a special way a communion of all mankind in Redemption.

(a) By His sacrifice Christ merited the pardon of sin and the gift of divine life for us. "Neither is there salvation in any other. For there is no other name under heaven given to men by which we must be saved" (Acts 4:12). We receive everything from Christ and without Him we can do nothing as regards our salvation. "Without me you can do nothing" (John 15:5).

(b) But Christ gives us the power to **collaborate in Redemption.**

Christ did not want to save the world without us: our personal participation is necessary, not only *for ourselves,* because we are free and conscious persons, but also *for the rest of men* by reason of our communion in Christ.

The total sacrifice which saves the world is the sacrifice of Christ as shared by the Church. How can we merit for other men? We are persons and not unconscious cells. Love can only well up from within a person, that is, from within a conscious and willing being. Our personal merit can never dispense another person from this personal act, nor do it for him. This would be a contradiction in terms. What we must bring about is rather **the opening of a person to love:** we have to help him to take this personal step by himself.

What means are at our disposal for this? Not just the exterior apostolate of personal witness and persuasion, but also the interior means, such as prayer, the invisible radiation of our holiness and our merits, go to obtain from God more abundant help which will aid the will of the other person to lay itself open to love. By increasing our own holiness we somehow enrich and foster the environment in which this will is bathed. If we are unfaithful to our vocation, to our call to holiness, this environment will be less nourishing, and our neighbor will perhaps lack that help which would have permitted the awakening or development of a personal love.

This also explains **the invisible repercussion of our sins:** they do not directly influence persons, but they diminish and impoverish the fostering environment from which these persons draw their strength. In this sense: every soul that falls, fails the world, and every soul that rises, raises the world.

(c) Let us try to clarify what we mean by this communion of goods.

On earth all participate in this communion of supernatural goods, but not all on the same grounds:

Those who are in the state of grace pass on to others the help of their prayers, merits and satisfactions. These prayers and merits dispose others to receive grace according to the way we have defined above. Satisfaction expiates the temporal punishment due to sin. The Church disposes of this "treasure" and applies it under stated conditions both to the living and the dead in the form of indulgences.

They are enriched by the holiness of the whole Church. "Everything good which the saints ever brought about is imparted to those who live in Charity, because they are all one." [6] "The work of those who are one with me in charity is also in a certain way mine." [7] "What one seems to possess individually, all possess in common to a certain degree, in as much as, through perfect charity, each one considers the good of the other as his own." [8]

---

6 St. Thomas Aquinas, *Explanation of the Creed.*
7 St. Thomas Aquinas, *IV Sent.,* d. 45, q. 2.
8 *Ibid.,* d. 49, q. 5.

Those who are not in the state of grace, the useless branches of the Vine (John 15:4), can contribute nothing. But they *receive* the benefit of the prayers, merits and sufferings of those who are in the state of grace. These aids dispose them to conversion.

The Souls in Purgatory (the Church Suffering) can no longer merit either for themselves or for others. They must expiate the temporal punishment of their sins and cannot themselves hasten their liberation. But they receive the aid of our satisfactions which help them to expiate more rapidly.

In heaven (the Church Triumphant) the elect can no longer either merit nor satisfy. But they can intercede, precisely because of the merits they acquired on earth. This intercession is more efficacious than that of those living here below. "The Saints co-operate with us in obtaining our salvation. By their help they obtain from God what we ask of Him. It is more glory for them to be able to help others: in this they are co-operators with God" (St. Thomas).[9]

They hope for the beatitude of all those who are still on earth, "not properly speaking by the virtue of hope, but rather through the love produced in them by charity" (St. Thomas).[10] Our salvation increases their eternal joy.

The Blessed Virgin Mary holds a privileged position. She is both Christ's mother and ours. Consequently, she participates more closely than anyone else in the work of redeeming the world.

(d) What is **the religious meaning** and the love-value of this communion of goods?

We have not only to give to others, but also to receive from others. Whence there follows:

—**Respect** for each man. Each one possesses his own particular worth, and his personal contribution is irreplaceable. This is already true from a human point of view in that each man is my superior in some fashion. How much more so then from a Christian point of view in that each one reveals to me a particular aspect of Christ and contributes a particular grace to my formation. It may well be that I shall

---

9 *Ibid.*, d. 15, q. 4.
10 *Summa Theol.* II-II, q. 18, a. 2, ad. 3.

never be aware of such help, but in the communion of saints his action and his influence will be of real value.

—Stemming from this there is an **attitude of acceptance,** docility and also thankfulness towards every man.

—**Giving** to others consists in inviting them in their turn to blossom forth so that they can both give and get. In this we imitate God who loads us with His gifts until we too are enabled to give in our turn.

—There is also an invitation to **develop all the gifts** of both nature and grace that we have received: we enrich ourselves in order to give, and we enrich ourselves in giving.

—We are so bound together by our union with one another in Christ that anything that concerns any one of us has its repercussions in the others, visibly or invisibly. As in the case of the growth of the members of a body and of a body itself, the growth of each Christian and the growth of the whole Body of Christ mutually condition one another. Each person is **responsible for the** growth of this Body of which he is a living, free and conscious member. We should be haunted by this thought of total growth for which we must work in every way possible; and first of all, by fully corresponding ourselves to the love and call of God, so that we can build up this Body of Christ by our own personal holiness.

—We owe the divine life which is ours to the sacrifice of Christ, but to this sacrifice as participated in by each one of His members, that is, to the **total sacrifice** of regenerated mankind. This fact permits greater love among us and mutual thankfulness—perhaps not necessarily here below, but at any rate in eternity.

IV. A Communion of Action

It is in this communion of action, in this mutual cooperation in the work of building up the Body of Christ, that we become more aware of our profound communion in the order of being. All those who are united in the life of Christ collaborate in this work of construction, but in diverse ways. In some manner, every man, no matter who he may be, collaborates in this work, at least by his contribution of creative activity in the service of men who are the members of Christ.

Indeed, we must understand this work of communion in Redemption according to all its reality, and give this work its broader meaning, that is to say, we must give the motto "Restore all things in Christ" its widest extension. We must not minimize the work of redemption; we are working toward a restoration of the universe in Christ: **Redemption** supposes and includes **Creation** and the **Incarnation.**

Sometimes we find Christians who lack perspective. They want "to save their own souls," but they do not see sufficiently that they are caught up in a community and in a drama whose only dimensions are the world and time; and that it is not a question of merely personal success, but of causing the community of which they are parts to succeed. It is by consecrating themselves wholly to this latter task that they will succeed fully themselves.

Communion in Creation

Creation is the work of the Trinity. Therefore, we Christians are as much at home in the domain of Creation as a royal child in his father's possessions. The Trinity calls upon us to collaborate in this work of creation. Such is the meaning of work. It contains something divine within it, namely, a collaboration with God in the service of his children. Whence, an enthusiasm for work, for discovery, for the meaning of creation and the world, for the unification of the world, the completion of creation, the spiritualization of matter.

"The whole world has been given into our hands; shall we not then do something with it, not only for our own personal utility, but for the glory of God. We shall gather together all those scattered words of the psalm of praise and of thanksgiving which go to make up Creation. . . .

"And just as the earth helps man, so man helps the earth to do the will of God . . . the earth and man say together: Our Father, who art in heaven." (Claudel)[11]

11 *Op. cit.,* p. 253, 268.

33

Communion in the Incarnation

The Trinity created the world only in order to render it divine in Christ. The Trinity created man only in order to communicate to him divine life in Christ. Our task is to incarnate the divine in the human, to put Christ in all things and all things in Christ. We can do this in ourselves by asceticism, in the human race through the apostolate, in creation by all human activity (work, invention, art).

For God, creation is not a final end: God created only in order to sanctify. As collaborators with God in the work of creation we must do it in the same spirit as God:

—*All is for man*... Consequently, we must subordinate all creative activity to the service of man (if not, the result is disorder).

—*But man is for Christ.* The end of all our creative activity in every domain is, therefore, collaboration in the work of incarnation, the sanctification of men and of the world. It is Christ whom we must put in all men and all things.

Communion in Redemption

But this Incarnation, because of sin, can only be brought about by way of redemption. This incarnation is redemptive. Whence the painful character of work and of the Incarnation: Incarnation—in Creation—by way of Redemption. Such are the three terms and their connection.

In face of each one of these mysteries, man is not purely passive. God in His love was not content with loading men with His gifts; He wanted to give man the possibility of "giving" in his turn, that is, of collaborating in:

—Creation: by work, invention, generation;

—the Incarnation: through the apostolate;

—the Redemption: by suffering, the painful character of creative activity and of the apostolate.

Our task on earth is, therefore, to **collaborate** in an immense work both human and divine, which began with the world and which will only reach completion at the end of the ages, in order that all may together enjoy, with God and with all men, the result acquired by the collaboration of all.

34

Humanity was *thought* of all together by the Trinity "in Filio."

It was *created* all together "in Filio."

It was *adopted* all together "in Filio."

It was *redeemed* all together "in Filio."

This gigantic work to which we must dedicate ourselves body and soul is a collaboration in Creation, in the Incarnation, in the Redemption.

In Creation, in order to incarnate in it the divine by way of redemption. Such is the full meaning of the "Restore all things in Christ,"—"all things," that is, not just the whole of humanity, but also the whole universe.

"Thus it is the whole of Creation which is in travail, striving to bring forth a supreme confession to its Creator, and we must somehow serve as its midwives. . . . Let us fly to the aid of each creature and let us supply what it lacks in order to complete this catholic work of praise which it groans and travails in pain to give birth to. . . . We must come to the aid of humanity first of all, but we must also come to the help of the forest, to the help of the thorn bush which yearns to blossom forth in roses. . . . Everywhere we must put order, measure, fecundity, law. Nature must be transfixed to its very heart by this order that we communicate to it in the name of its Creator. The Redeeming Word must be heard by all that the Creative Word gave birth to, so that nothing may be unacquainted with His revelation in glory" (Claudel).

So it is that the whole Church, and even the Universe, collaborates in this work of redeeming the world and building up the Body of Christ:

"The Universe is not just a pedestal with man for its statue; rather it should be compared to an immense stalk with humanity as its flower. So long as humanity has not blossomed forth in the glory of the children of God, creation will be in painful travail. It suffers, it groans, not like a sick man in the throes of death, but like a woman in labor." (Huby)[12]

Even in heaven the Saints continue to work for this Redemption according to their means. The Saints of heaven who are united with us in one same communion (cf. Canon of the Mass) continue the work that they began on earth and which they left for us. We pray to them not only as in-

12 *Epitre aux Romains* 8:21. (Beauchesne, *Verbum Salutis.*)

tercessors, but also as **co-workers**. Besides, final reward, full glorification, the resurrection of the body will only take place when Christ attains his perfect stature: when He is all in all.

PROJECTS

1. From Chapter 5 of the Epistle to the Romans make up two comparative tables illustrating our solidarity in Christ and our solidarity in sin (Adam), and show how this comparison is in favor of our solidarity in Christ.

2. Why, in the Confiteor, do we address not only God but also the Saints and all our brethren?

3. After reciting the formula of absolution in the Sacrament of Penance, the priest prays for the penitent saying: "May the passion of our Lord Jesus Christ, the merits of the Blessed Virgin Mary and of all the Saints, whatever good deeds you may perform and whatever sufferings you may have to bear, be for you unto the remission of sins, the increase of grace and the reward of eternal life. Amen." Explain this prayer in the light of this chapter.

4. Explain the saying of St. Paul to the Colossians 1:24: "What is lacking of the sufferings of Christ I fill up in my flesh for His body, which is the Church."

Chapter 7

THE LIFE OF CHRIST IN
EACH MEMBER OF THE CHURCH

I. United to Christ

Each member of the Church is, in Christ, a child of the Father in the fellowship of the Holy Spirit. A double and yet unique mysterious reality characterizes Christians, namely, the presence of the divine persons in them and their own divinization.

The Presence of God

If we are united to Christ, He is Himself present within us along with **the Father and the Holy Ghost.** This indwelling of God in Christians is especially emphasized in St. John. By grace God dwells in the faithful, and the faithful dwell in God.

"If anyone loves me, he will keep my word, and my Father will love him, and we will *come to him* and *make our abode* with him" (John 14:23).

"He who keeps his commandments *abides in God* and *God in him.* And in this we know that *he abides in us,* by the Spirit whom he has given us" (I Epistle of St. John 3:24).

St. Paul insists upon this presence of the Holy Spirit. He is the third person, the terminus of divine life within the Trinity. His presence within the faithful is, therefore, the proof, the *seal,* the guarantee of the presence of the Father and the Son, as well as of the divinization of the faithful.

"Because you are sons, God has sent *the Spirit of his Son* into our hearts, crying, 'Abba, Father'" (Galatians 4:6).

"The Spirit himself gives testimony to our spirit that we are sons of God" (Romans 8:16).

"... (you) were sealed with the Holy Spirit of the promise, who is the pledge of our inheritance" (Eph. 1:13).

This indwelling of God in the faithful is a *loving presence*.
God is present as a guest: He delights in the soul of the
faithful, and He communicates Himself through this presence, that is to say, He divinizes the faithful in whom He
comes to dwell.

Divinization

Indeed, if we are united to Christ, we are really divinized,
that is, we are really with Him, like Him, in Him, **children
of the Father** in the fellowship of the **Holy Spirit**. God truly
adopts us as His children. When parents adopt a child, they
consider it as their very own, yet they cannot give it life as
though it were really their own child. But our divine adoption is real: God not only recognizes us as His children, *He
really gives us His own life.*

St. John insists especially upon the reality of this adoption: "Behold what manner of love the Father has bestowed
upon us, that we should be called children of God; and such
we are" (I Epis. of St. John 3:1). This adoption is the fruit
of a communication of divine life, of a divine "seed": "Whoever is born of God does not commit sin, because *His seed*
abides in him and he cannot sin, because he is born of God"
(I Epist. of St. John 3:9). As a result we are truly "partakers
of the divine nature" (II Epist. of St. Peter 1:4). The divinization of the faithful is a true birth to divine life, and even
a new creation. "Unless a man be born again, he cannot see
the kingdom of God" (John 3:3). "If any man is in Christ,
he is a new creature" (II Cor. 5:17).

And since we are really sons, we, therefore, have a strict
right to Christ's inheritance: "If we are sons, we are heirs
also: heirs indeed of God and joint heirs with Christ" (Romans 8:17). But even now we already have the pledge of
this inheritance: "The Holy Spirit of the promise who is the
pledge of our inheritance, for a redemption of possession,
for the praise of his glory" (Eph. 1:14).

II. The Consequences of This Union

Our incorporation into Christ brings about all the following effects at once:

—an extraordinary union with Christ Himself, the incarnate Son;

—an extraordinary union with the Father and the Holy Spirit;

—an extraordinary union with the mother of Jesus and with all the members of Christ.

Union with Christ, the Incarnate Word

He is not only our Mediator, that is to say, the one through whom we receive divine life, but He is Himself **our life** and our all. "It is no longer I that live, but Christ lives in me" (Gal. 2:20). What Christ is by nature, fully and as a principle, that is, as *Son of the Father* in the fellowship of the Holy Spirit, and the *brother and redeemer of men* as son of Mary, we are through grace, in a participated way, as members, *in Him, with Him, like Him, through Him, because of Him*. He gives us a share in His divine life of sonship and introduces us into the fellowship of the Father and the Holy Spirit. He gives us His divine life and sacrifices for us His human life. He introduces us into the intimacy of His life as son of Mary. He associates us with His work of Redemption. He makes us participate, as members, in the union which He Himself has, as head, with all mankind. All things are truly held in common between Him and us: same Father, same Holy Spirit, same Mother, same care and love for the whole world.

A truly fraternal friendship is possible between Him and us. "No longer do I call you servants, but friends" (John 15:15). Friendship supposes a certain equality. ("*Amicitia pares invenit aut facit.*") His love has brought about the equality supposed by friendship: He became like to us through the Incarnation and by all His earthly life; He made us like to Him through His redeeming sacrifice, that is to say, we have become sons of God, brothers and redeemers of men. It is a friendship which is all the stronger for being not merely a reception of His life, but also a collaboration in His work of Redemption, that is, a consecration of our life to the spread of Christ's divine life. Our devotion towards Christ should, therefore, be very fraternal and friendly as well as all divine, for "the marvel of Christianity is that the same person is at once my Creator and my Brother."

Union with the Father and the Holy Spirit

"Through Him (Jesus) we both have access in one Spirit to the Father" (Eph. 2:18). We have the same fellowship with the Father and the Holy Spirit that the eternal Son in His human soul had during His earthly life. That is why in reading the New Testament we must carefully notice Jesus' attitude toward His Father and the Holy Spirit.

Toward His Father: an attitude of filial love. Jesus talks to His Father, passes His nights in prayer, speaks to Him of all His joys and sufferings. Jesus proves His love by complete, joyous obedience, even unto death. Jesus speaks of His Father. He causes us to both know and love Him. He loves His Father so much that He wanted to make us all sons of His Father.

We should likewise talk to our Father. He is present within us and awaits our love. We can truly call Him Father because we are truly His children. We should confide our joys and sorrows to Him as children do to their parents. We, too, should prove our love to Him by an obedience resembling that of Christ. Finally, we should love to speak of our Father and cause Him to be loved. We must love all men as children of the same Father. For what relates to the Father, read especially St. Matthew, chaps. 5, 6, 7 and the Gospel and Epistles of St. John.

Toward the Holy Spirit: (a) During His earthly life, an attitude of complete docility toward the Spirit. The Gospels show us Jesus as led by the Holy Spirit. It was the Holy Spirit, for example, who drove Him forth into the desert.

That is why our essential attitude in regard to the Holy Spirit must also be one of docility: "For whoever are led by the Spirit of God, they are the sons of God" (Romans 8:14). The Holy Spirit, in effect, creates in us filial piety toward the Father and fraternal love toward Jesus and our brethren. "God has sent the Spirit of His Son into our hearts crying, Abba, Father" (Gal. 4:6). He pours forth in our hearts both filial and fraternal love. "The charity of God is poured forth in our hearts by the Holy Spirit who has been given to us" (Romans 5:5).

(b) Then *the Risen Christ sent the Holy Spirit* to complete and continue His work:

—to give the initial push to the Church of the New Testament (Pentecost);

—to enlighten the Church and make it understand everything that Jesus taught;

—to strengthen it in its struggles.

Thus the Holy Spirit sent by Jesus is always at work. It is He who animates the Church from the time of Christ's departure at the Ascension until His return at the end of the world. That is why we must invoke the Holy Spirit and submit ourselves to His action, as did the Apostles in times gone by. He will make us realize our vocation as sons and our redemptive mission.

For what relates to the Holy Spirit, read:

—St. Luke (especially the first four chapters),

—The Epistle to the Romans, chap. 8,

—St. John, chaps. 14-17,

—The Acts of the Apostles (especially the beginning).

Union with the Mother of Jesus and with All Our Brethren

We have already treated of this union in the chapter concerning the Communion of Saints. Here we shall stress our union with Mary.

Mary's essential title, from which all else flows, is her divine maternity. Since in Christ there is but a single person, that of the eternal Son, by giving Christ His human nature in her capacity as a true mother, Mary is truly the Mother of God. Certainly it is God alone who is the source of this power, through the foreseen merits of Christ. Like all

41

members of the Church, Mary receives everything from Christ, even the fact of being His Mother. But it is she alone who has received this mission and this grace, and that is why she fulfills an incomparable maternal mission in the Church. Just as in times past she formed Jesus within her womb, so now she also forms Him in each one of us. She is our Mother, just as she is the Mother of Jesus. Because we are united to Jesus, she loves us with the very love with which she loves Jesus, and we love her with the same love with which Jesus loves her. It was this maternity and this filial relation that Jesus wanted to proclaim publically on the cross in the person of John:

"Woman, behold thy son. Son, behold thy mother" (John 19:27).

III. Grace, Faith, Charity

Life in God is a life of knowledge and of love. By grace we participate in this divine life, that is to say, we can know God as He knows Himself and love Him as He loves Himself.

—Grace is, therefore, our participation in divine life.

—Vision in heaven and Faith here on earth are our participation in divine knowledge.

—Charity is our participation in divine love.

But, since we are divinized as sons in Christ, we have to define this participation more precisely:

—Grace is our participation in Christ's life of divine sonship.

—Vision in heaven and Faith here on earth are our participation in Christ's divine knowledge as Son.

—Charity is our participation in Christ's divine love as Son.

Faith

Faith is the vision of Christ "grafted" onto our human vision in order to make us see with Him, through Him, like Him, with Him. In heaven, in the beatific vision, it will still be with the eyes of Christ that we shall forever contemplate all things. The object of divine faith is the "whole Christ," that is, in the mystery of the redemptive incarnation: the Trinity, humanity, Creation.

The Trinity first: we participate in its life of love in the incarnate Son. We participate in Christ's filial love and filial regard toward our adopted family.

Humanity as a whole is an object of divine faith inasmuch as it participates in the mystery of Christ, and as we see it through the eyes of Christ. We should view each man as Christ does, that is, as a living member of Christ, or as one who is at least called upon to be such, "a brother for whom Christ died." Of every man I can say: "He has been known and loved by Christ; he is called upon, as I am, to live in Christ, here below in faith and in heaven in the beatific vision."

Creation itself is in some way an object of divine faith inasmuch as it participates in the mystery of Christ and as we see it through Christ's eyes. All this can be understood by an analogy with our faith in the Eucharistic mystery: our human eyes see merely the appearances; Faith sees the reality. In a sense the whole world is like the host: appearance and reality. A person without the faith stops at the appearances of everything (man, suffering, love, etc.). Only persons of faith see the divine reality lying beyond the appearances and contained within them (man = a member of Christ in fact or by vocation; suffering and death = our participation in the sacrifice which redeems the world; etc.). Of the whole world we can say as we do of the host:

> "Faith for all defects supplying,
> Where the feeble senses fail."

When the life of grace develops, the virtue of faith develops proportionally, that is: Christ's life and Christ's view of things.

Charity

Charity is the *heart of Christ* "grafted" onto our human heart so that we can love with Him, like Him, through Him, in Him. In heaven it will still be with the heart of Christ that we shall forever love all things. The object of supernatural charity is the "whole Christ," that is, in the mystery of the redemptive incarnation: the Trinity, humanity, Creation.

The Trinity: we shall love the three divine persons with the very heart of Jesus.

Humanity as a whole is an object of supernatural love inasmuch as it participates in the mystery of Christ and as we love it with the heart of Christ.

Creation itself is in some way an object of supernatural love inasmuch as it participates in the mystery of Christ and as we love it with the heart of Christ.

PROJECTS

1. The Father and the Holy Spirit in the life of Christ and of the Christian (cf. the indications given in the foregoing chapter).

2. In reading St. John, pick out everything concerning the intimate bond uniting Christ and the man of faith: Christ gives him life, light, knowledge of the Father, the Holy Spirit, His own body and blood as food; Christ dwells in him and he in Christ, etc.

3. In St. Paul's Epistle to the Ephesians, pick out everything concerning grace such as we have studied it in this chapter: the presence of the divine persons, divinization of the Christian, fellowship with Christ, the Father, the Spirit, among ourselves.

4. With regard to Charity, compare the Sermon on the Mount (Matt. chaps. 5, 6, 7) with St. John's Gospel, chaps. 14, 15, 16, 17 and the first Epistle of St. John. Show the progress of revelation.

Chapter 8
GRACE AND THE IMITATION
OF CHRIST

I. Grace Conforms Us to Christ

"Those whom He (God) has foreknown He has also predestined to become conformed to the image of His Son, that
He should be the first-born among many brethren" (Romans
8:29).

It is therefore important for us to know *what Christ is*
and *how He lived*, for everything that He is in Himself, we
are by participation, and all that He stood for, we also must
stand for. Now Christ is essentially Son and Redeemer, and
His whole life was both filial and redemptive, being animated by a single yet double love, at once filial and fraternal. That is why the Christian will also be essentially a son
and redeemer, and his whole life, like that of Christ's, should
be animated by a single yet double love, at once filial and
fraternal.

II. Christ Is Son and Redeemer

Christ is not the Word purely and simply, but the *incarnate Word*, and by this very fact, the *Redeemer*. In consequence, our model should not be the Word as He is in the
bosom of the Trinity, but the incarnate Word as He revealed His life, His soul and His love to us during His
earthly life. Besides, how would we ever know the Word
if it were not in His incarnate state? But once again, it is
Christ as the incarnate Word in whom we participate and
not in the Word as such. Now the *incarnate Word* is at
once and inseparably the Son and the Redeemer.

III. Redeemer in His Whole Life

Christ effected our salvation by reversing the procedure of sin. Sin consists in disobedience, egoism and disordered enjoyment. To sin, Christ opposed His obedience, His love and His suffering.

Obedience—through love—in suffering.

This obedience, love and suffering made up the whole life of Christ. Calvary was but the necessary consummation of the progress of His entire life: "Consummatum est" (John 19:30). But Calvary in its turn enlightens us. It reveals to us the profound meaning of Christ's whole life, namely, the fact that His entire life was made up of redemptive obedience, suffering and love.

Redemptive Suffering

The "consummatum est" of Calvary was but the consummation of all His *redemptive suffering:*

—the suffering of the poverty-stricken *birth* in a stable;

—the blood of the *circumcision,* considered as the first blood-shedding of the Redeemer: "It was with good reason that the child who was born for us was called the Saviour at His circumcision; for it was then that He began to bring about our salvation by shedding His immaculate blood for us. Nor have Christians any reason to ask why the Lord Christ desired to be circumcised: He was circumcised for the same reason that caused Him to be born and to suffer. None of those things were done for His own sake, but all for the elect" (St. Bernard);[1]

—the *work* in the carpenter shop of Nazareth. The hymn of Matins of the Feast of the Holy Family has Jesus sing:

> "Sweat may bedew my members now," He sayeth,
> Ere yet they be with blood profusely bathed,
> Let this pain, too, be paid in satisfaction
> For sins of mankind."

—the *fatigue* and daily exhaustion of His apostolic ministry; His fasting and prayer; His agony; all the sufferings and

---

[1] Sermo 2, *De Circumcisione.* In the Roman Breviary, homily for the feast of the Holy Name of Jesus.

humiliations of His life; all the pangs of rejected love; all the sufferings of loneliness: it was not only in the garden of Gethsemane that He suffered from loneliness, but during His entire life, even in His family (cf. the Gospel), among His disciples and at times even among His apostles. All these sufferings found their completion on Calvary: "He was crucified for us" (Nicean Creed).

Redemptive Obedience

Calvary was also the consummation of *all His redemptive obedience:*
—begun in His submission to the *laws of His country;*
—in His submission to the *laws of the Mosaic covenant:* e.g., the presentation in the Temple, etc. "God sent His Son, born of a woman, born under the Law, that He might redeem those who were under the Law" (Gal. 4:4).
—in His simple and continual obedience *to His parents* (Luke 2:51). "The everyday obedience and submission of Jesus to Mary and Joseph announced, represented and anticipated the startling obedience and submission of Holy Thursday" (Peguy). This obedience ran like a thread through His entire life and led Him to complete sacrifice. "He humbled Himself, becoming obedient to death, even to death on a cross" (Philip. 2:8).

Redemptive Love

Calvary, finally, was the consummation of *His redemptive love:* "Jesus...having loved his own who were in the world, loved them to the end" (John 13:1). This love brought Him to death: "Greater love than this no one has, that one lay down his life for his friends" (John 15:13).

IV. Filial and Redemptive Love

Christ, therefore, consecrated His whole life to loving men just as He consecrated His whole life to loving His Father.

Total Consecration

Indeed, we see in the Gospel that His whole life of obedience, through love, in suffering, was *totally consecrated to the Father* and *totally consecrated to men.*

—Obedience

It was consecrated to the Father: "Behold, I come to do thy will, O God" (Hebrews 10:9). It was consecrated to men: "I came that they may have life, and have it more abundantly" (John 10:10).

—Suffering

It was consecrated to the Father: "That the world may know that I love the Father..." (John 14:31). It was consecrated to men: "The good shepherd lays down his life for his sheep" (John 10:11).

—Love

It was completely orientated toward His Father: "I abide in his love" (John 15:10). It was completely orientated toward men: "After having loved his own who were in the world, he loved them to the end" (John 13:1).

To His Father and to Men

But there was not contradiction nor choice to be made as to which tendency would outweigh the other, for filial love and redemptive love were all one in the unity of His person.

—Obedience

"My food is to do the will of him who sent me, to accomplish his work" (John 4:34). Now this will and this work is precisely our salvation. Thus Christ's obedience to His Father and His desire for our salvation were all part and parcel of the one motive power of His life.

—Love

Christ loved His Father by loving us. He loved His Father so much that He wanted to make Him loved by a multitude of brethren who would share in His own divine sonship. He loved us so much that He wanted to associate us in His own filial love. "Father, I will that where I am, they also whom thou hast given me may be with me. . . . And I have made known to them thy name, and will make it known, in order that the love with which thou hast loved me may be in them, and I in them" (John 17:24, 26).

When He was among men, He spoke to them of His Father, and we see that when Jesus addressed Himself to His Father, it was in order to speak to Him of men. For example, the whole chapter 17 of St. John: "That all may be one, even as thou, Father, in me and I in thee."

—Suffering

Christ accepted suffering, the consequence of sin, in order to transform this suffering into an instrument of Redemption and of love: love toward the Father and Redemption for men.

V. The Christian's Love

Christians, therefore, participate in this completely filial and fraternal life. Consequently, we must apply to ourselves what we said previously about Christ's sacrifice making up His whole life—obedience, through love, in suffering. Our entire life also can and must be made up of sacrifice: a life of obedience, through love, in suffering. Just as the sacrifice of Calvary was the consummation of the motive power of His whole life, so also our death constitutes the consummation of the motive power of our lives; it completes our sacrifice. We should not look upon death as a physiological accident, but as our participation in the redeeming sacrifice of the world offered by Christ. Such is the meaning of "preparation for death": we offer it in advance as a "sacrifice."

Christians must live in the same spirit as Christ. As in the case of Christ, our whole life (and its final consummation) must be governed by a single yet double love: the love of God and the love of men. We must always have before our eyes and in our heart both God and men, especially those for whom we are personally responsible. As we said of Christ, it is also in our prayer, resistance to temptation and suffering that others will find strength to pray, resist and suffer.

"In heaven, since all things are perfectly unified in the divine mystery of love, we shall love God, our brethren and all things by one unique and simple act of love. Here below, our charity still admits to a certain dualism: all of us need training, and sometimes a long one, in order not to love God without our brethren, nor our brethren without God" (P. Feret).[2]

We have to tend toward this **unity.** We should exercise our Faith and our Charity not only toward God but also toward our neighbor. We must develop within ourselves the "mind" of Christ; habituate ourselves to live in Christ, to see with the "eyes" of Christ, to love all things in Christ, with the "heart" of Christ. Then all will be unified and nothing will be profane. But to obtain this end we must habituate ourselves to seeing with the eyes of Christ by multiplying acts of Faith towards God and our neighbor.

VI. Some Aspects of This Imitation

It is not the imitation of an exterior model.

This Imitation Is a Participation

Jesus set us the example in order to permit us to participate in all His states of life and in all His mysteries. Christ is the great "sacrament" of our sanctification: He is the *symbol* of what we have to do and be; He is the *efficacious* symbol; in all His actions He merited and procured for us the grace to be able to imitate Him, and to imitate Him in such a way that our life would be a participation of what He Himself did before us and for us. We die *with* Jesus, we *rise* with Jesus, etc.

This Imitation Is a Continuation

"Our imitation is, in its deepest meaning, a continuation: we can only accomplish the Lord's will by being 'His men' in the strongest sense, that is to say, by being for Him additional humanities. It is impossible to be like Christ if we are not with Christ and in Christ" (P. Salet).[3]

"The Christian life is just the continuation and completion of the life of Christ in each one of us" (St. John Eudes). Our Christian life continues the redemptive incarnation in two different states and modes:

---

2 *Vie Spirituelle*, Oct. 1946, p. 261.
3 *Le Christ notre Vie.*

—*On earth:* in the obscurity of Faith, in hope and redemptive suffering; in the Church militant.

—*In heaven:* in light, possession, glory; in the Church Triumphant: "We suffer with him that we may also be glorified with him" (Romans 8:17).

This Imitation Is Particular to Each Person

The total incarnation of Christ is carried on in the entire body, which is the perfect image of Christ, His "pleroma." Each one of us, as a member, reproduces Christ only partially, only in one aspect of His total richness: one aspect of His filial love, of His fraternal and redemptive love. Each one of us has to reflect a particular aspect of Christ by developing the grace which we receive in conformity with our environment and the divine summons. (Whence the meaning of our imitation of the saints who have brought out one particular aspect of Christ; contemplating the saints helps us to understand Christ better.)

Sanctity for each one of us will, therefore, consist in our correspondence (in Christ) **with our own proper grace.** "To each one of us grace was given according to the measure of Christ's bestowal" (Eph. 4:7). "For his workmanship we are, created in Christ Jesus in good works, which God has made ready beforehand that we may walk in them" (Eph. 2:10). Sanctity consists in attaining that degree of conformity to Christ which the Trinity willed, and which Christ merited, for each person.

The work of redemption, the work of the love of God and the love of men, partially depends upon my fidelity to my own vocation: We are already in germ what we must become. We must, then, realize what we are in the eternal mind of God, in the thought and the love of Christ. Such is the whole meaning of life, namely, the realization of our own particular conformity to Christ which is our reason for existing and **our vocation.**

PROJECTS

1. Look for the theme of the imitation of Jesus as explained in this chapter in St. John and in the Epistles to the Ephesians and the Philippians.
2. Study the obedience of Jesus in St. John.

Chapter 9

THIS PLAN OF GOD IS A
MYSTERY OF LOVE

Gratuitous Love

In this first section we have seen that God's plan, which forms the enduring element of the Church, is to have men participate in His own divine life in Christ. We have to understand this plan as springing from pure and absolutely gratuitous love. These two traits, *love* and *gratuity*, best specify the word "grace" as it appears in Scripture, especially in the New Testament.

The whole of this loving initiative on God's part can be summed up in those phrases of St. John: "God is Love"; "There is no greater love than to give one's life." Perhaps we have become too habituated to these words! And besides we generally only apply them to Christ's death. Yet, in reality, they throw light upon God Himself and all His work.

"God Is Love"

This does not merely mean that God loves us, but that *His very nature*, that which defines Him as God, is Love.

1. **In Himself.**—God is a Trinity of persons. The life of these persons is made up of mutual knowledge and love. As for the *Father*, He has no greater love than to give life to the Son. He gives Himself wholly to the Son, and because He is God and because He is a spirit, He can give Himself wholly without losing Himself.

The *Son*, inasmuch as He receives everything from the Father, brings all back to the Father in a transport of filial love.

The Father and the Son together give themselves wholly

to the *Holy Spirit,* and He in His turn, gives Himself wholly to the Father and the Son. And thus the divine unity finds its completion in the Holy Spirit.

2. **In All His Work.**—But his circle of love, by the Incarnation of the eternal Son, was extended to include men in this life of knowledge and love. God cannot love us more than by giving us His divine life: "For God so loved the world that he gave his only-begotten Son, that those who believe in him may not perish, but may have life everlasting" (John 3:16).

3. **In Creation.**—This is the first mystery of that love which does not want to remain turned in upon itself, but which overflows in the multiple riches of creation. God created man capable of knowledge and love precisely because He planned on inviting him to share in His divine life of knowledge and love.

4. **In the Incarnation.**—Then follows the mystery of the Incarnation: the very Son of God came among us in order to reveal God's love, that love which forms the Trinity, and in order to reveal our vocation to love, in order to tell us that we are summoned to share in this life of love.

5. **In the Redemption.**—But man refused this summons; he preferred to turn in upon himself instead of opening to God's love. Then came the mystery of Redemption: God's own Son died in order to give us this life of love. Jesus has no greater love than to give His divine life; but since we are sinners, He gives us His divine life at the cost of His human life. He sacrifices His human life in order to give us His divine life.

These great mysteries of love are recalled each day in one of the prayers in preparation for Communion:

"O Lord Jesus Christ, Son of the living God, who by the will of the Father, with the co-operation of the Holy Ghost, hast by thy death (gift of human life) given life to the world (gift of His divine life) . . . ."

This opening of the Trinity to embrace humanity constitutes the very essence of the Church's mystery. Gathered together as many brethren in Christ, we enter into communion with the Father and the Holy Spirit.

6. The Church Is Love's Plan.—The Church is, therefore, basically constituted by a loving summons: gathered together in the Church in fraternal unity, we participate in the infinite love of God Himself.

It will take the entire history of the world to realize this mystery.

PROJECTS

1. Show the gratuity and love involved in salvation:
—in the Epistle to the Galatians, chaps. 3 and 4;
—in the Epistle to the Romans, chaps. 3-6.
2. Show God's loving initiative in St. John's Gospel and in his first Epistle.

Second Part

THE STAGES OF GOD'S PLAN

(What Changes in the Church)

Chapter 10

THE VARIOUS STAGES

God's plan "to gather all mankind together in Christ," which existed in Him even before the creation of the world, will only be finally realized at the end of the world, after Christ's return. Between Creation and the end of the world this plan is progressively revealed and realized in time through the means of salvation which change according to the various stages. In his treatise *On the True Religion*,[1] St. Augustine explains that the means of salvation vary in history; at present, since Christ, the Church is the organ of salvation:

"Throughout the course of the ages the ineffable mercy of God has come to man's aid by means of what are *changeable institutions*, no doubt, but ones which serve His eternal purposes, whether for the individual singly or for the human race as a whole, in order to remind them of the primitive perfection of their nature. In our times this is the Christian religion, the knowledge and practice of which provide us with full certitude and security of salvation."

But in his book of *Retractions*,[2] returning to this idea, he reminds us that in reality we have to do with the same living structure of salvation under different names: "When I said, 'In our times this is the Christian religion, the knowledge and practice of which provide us with full certitude and security of salvation,' I had in mind the name rather than the thing expressed by the name. For the thing itself, which is now called the Christian religion, existed among the ancients and goes back to the beginnings of the human race. When Christ came in the flesh, the true religion, which al-

---

[1] *De Vera Religione*, c. 10; P.L. 34, 131.
[2] *Retractationes*, lib. 1, c. 13; P.L. 32, 603.

ready existed, then began to be called Christian.... That is why I said, 'In our times this is the Christian religion,' not that it did not exist previously, but because it only received this name in the latter times."

1. For example, between the time of **Adam and Abraham,** God called men:

   (a) from *without,* by the voice of creation;
   (b) from *within,* by the voice of conscience.

"For since the creation of the world his invisible attributes are clearly seen—his everlasting power also and divinity—being understood through the things that are made" (Romans 1:20).

"By the greatness and beauty that creatures have, reason is well able to contemplate the Source from which these perfections came" (Wisdom 13:5; Knox Trans.).

"When the Gentiles who have no law do by nature what the Law prescribes, these having no law are a law unto themselves. They show the work of the Law written in their hearts. Their conscience bears witness to them, even when conflicting thoughts accuse or defend them. This will take place on the day when, according to my gospel, God will judge the hidden secrets of men through Jesus Christ" (Romans 2:14-16).

2. But at the time of **Abraham,** God spoke more clearly and revealed more of His mystery and of His plan of salvation. He chose a people, consecrated it, and confided to it the promise of the Saviour and of salvation: such was the first covenant. The means of salvation were already more numerous and accessible.

3. And yet this organ of salvation gave way before the newness of the **New Testament.**

"God, who at sundry times and in divers manners spoke in times past to the fathers by the prophets, last of all in these days has spoken to us by his Son, whom he appointed heir of all things, by whom also he made the world" (Hebrews 1:1-2).

At length the more final revelation appeared. Henceforth, men are to know God's secrets. They know that they are truly the sons of God, and they have at their disposal abundant and efficacious means of salvation. This is the Church of the New Testament.

4. But this is still not the final stage. In the **Church of the future,** this will be the vision of God face to face, the possession of God over and beyond all the means of salvation.

"Beloved, now we are the children of God, and it has not yet appeared what we shall be. We know that, when he appears, we shall be like to him, for we shall see him just as he is" (I Epistle of St. John 3:2).

Place of the New Testament Church

The stage which interests us most, and which in our eyes seems to monopolize the notion of Church, is the one lying between Christ's departure at the Ascension and His return at the end of the world. Let us call this stage the Church of the New Testament, in order to distinguish it from the preceding stage: the Church of the Old Testament, and from the final and definitive stage which is yet to come: the Heavenly Church. The Church of the New Testament is the *present expression* of God's design and *its means of realization.* We have set apart the whole third part of this work for its study.

But in order to understand this New Testament Church and its place in the over-all history of salvation, we must see clearly that it is neither a beginning nor an end, but that it lies between the Old Testament which it fulfills, and the Heavenly Church which it prepares and anticipates. We shall study this historical unfolding of God's plan in the second part of this work.

The history of the world is the story of the progressive formation of the Body of Christ, of the gathering together of humanity in God, of the "Restore all things in Christ." The Church instituted by Christ on the foundation of the Apostles is the present phase of this great mystery, of this great design of God's love. This New Testament Church was prepared, announced and prefigured by the Old Testament. It will attain its consummation in heaven, in the Church Triumphant.

The final terminus to which everything is ordered and toward which proceed the Old and New Testaments is that Jerusalem spoken of in the Apocalypse of St. John. In consequence, we have the following progression:

The **Old Testament** is a *time of preparation*, of promise, of figure. It is wholly eschatological, that is to say, turned toward its proximate end, the New Testament, and toward its final end, the Heavenly Jerusalem.

The **New Testament** is the fulfillment of the promises of the Old, but it in turn is also turned toward its consummation, the Heavenly Jerusalem.

The **Heavenly Church** is thus the consummation of the Church Militant of the New Testament and the full realization of the Old Testament. "Behold the dwelling of God with men, and he will dwell with them. And they will be his people, and God himself will be with them as their God" (Apocalypse 21:3).

The Church in the Bible

Too often Christians know the Bible only as a collection of stories. We shall see here that it recounts "a history," the History of Salvation. Let us first of all define the spirit in which we shall undertake our biblical recearch:

—The Old Testament is to be understood in the light of the New, and the New Testament can be set off to best advantage only when it is related to the Old: *"Novum Testamentum in vetere latebat, vetus in novo potet."* As St. Augustine exclaimed: "To neglect one of the two Testaments is to hobble toward Christ on one foot only."

A knowledge of the Old Testament as well as of the New is particularly indispensable for the understanding of the Church. For indeed, as St. Augustine remarked in commenting upon Psalm 30, **the prophets predicted the Church more clearly than they did Christ,** for the Church was openly prophesied, whereas Christ was never predicted except under some veil. It was the whole economy of the Old Testament, the very existence of the Jewish people which prophesied, announced and prepared the true people of God, the Church of Jesus Christ. Israel as a whole was therefore a "prophetic people."

Scripture recounts the progressive history of God's covenant with mankind and of the gift that God made of Himself to mankind. And what we call today the "spiritual sense of Scripture," or, in a still more recent way, the "plenary sense," consists precisely and very simply in reading the full unfolding of this history.

This spiritual exegesis of Scripture which concerns first of all the community, the people of God, the Church, also applies to *each member of this community*. Our personal history reproduces that of the Church, namely, a progressive passage from death to life, from sin to love. We can see exegeses of this type in St. Augustine on the Psalms, for example, in the exegesis of Psalm 3 which he applies in turn to Christ, the Church, and to the faithful.

—The **Liturgy** also provides us with a spiritual understanding of the Bible. The Church, by applying a certain text of Scripture to a given mystery of Christ or of the Church, gives us a kind of key to this text: nothing is more enlightening in this regard than the distribution of the biblical readings throughout the course of the liturgical year, as they are to be found in the breviary or the missal; the liturgies of the Easter Vigil and of the Vigil of Pentecost, with their parallelisms of prophecies from the Old Testament and prayers of the New Testament are full of suggestions in this regard. Read, for example, in the liturgy of the Vigil of Pentecost, the second prayer, which follows the account of the exodus from Egypt and the passage through the Red Sea:

"O God, who by the light of the New Testament hast made clear to us the miracles wrought in earliest times, prefiguring unto us the Red Sea as an image of the sacred font, and who in the deliverance of thy people from the bondage of Egypt, hast foreshadowed the sacraments of the Christian dispensation: grant that all nations who have merited by faith the privilege of the children of Israel, may be born again by partaking of Thy Holy Spirit, through our Lord Jesus Christ, Thy Son who livest and reignest with

Thee, in the unity of the same Holy Spirit, God, world without end. Amen."

We shall study in turn the three essential stages of the Church's history:

A. the preparatory phase (Old Testament);

B. the phase of earthly realization, extending from the Coming of Jesus until His Return (New Testament);

C. the phase of heavenly fulfillment after the Return of Christ (Apocalypse).

A. The Preparatory Phase: The Old Testament

The Gospel shows us Jesus as the Son of David, the Son of Abraham; and the Church as the Kingdom of David and the posterity of Abraham. "The Lord God will give him the throne of David his father, and he shall be king over the house of Jacob forever; and of his kingdom there shall be no end" (Luke 1:32-33). "And if you are Christ's, then you are the offspring of Abraham, heirs according to promise" (Galatians 3:29).

The Church of the New Testament, like Christ Himself, was **prepared** and **announced** by the People of God in the Old Testament. We shall distinguish some of the **essential stages** in this history of God's People of the Old Testament.[1] Such was the advice of St. Augustine in his book on the way to teach Christian doctrine,[2] and he himself often distinguished these great stages of Sacred History: for example, the six water-jars of the wedding feast of Cana represented "the six ages of the world which were not without Prophecy . . . but that the water may be turned into wine, in that entire Prophecy let Christ be discerned.[3]

The Psalms weave the principal events of this marvelous

---

1 I have freely drawn upon P. Feret, *Cahiers de la paroisse universitaire*, 1946, for the period between Abraham and Moses, and have freely quoted from him in places.

2 *De Catechizandis Rudibus*, P.L. 40, 310-348.

3 *Tract. in Joann. Evangelium*, 9, 8; P.L. 35, 1459.

history into a variety of prayer themes: e.g., of praise, thanksgiving, contrition, etc. Consequently, in order to understand the psalms we must first of all know the general outlines of this history. That is why, after each essential stage, we shall indicate those psalms which treat of the events of that period. We shall soon see how the events of the New Testament fulfill those of the Old. It will then be easy to transpose the psalms and to recite them in the light of such fulfillment, in the way Jesus Himself did and in union with Him.

The Prophets are likewise intimately bound up with the history of God's People. That is why we shall put the books of the Prophets in the periods during which they exercised their ministry.

The following table contains these essential stages and distributes the Books, Psalms and Prophets according to the various stages:[4]

1st Stage: *Abraham. The annunciation and promise of a People of God* (around 1800 B.C.).
    Book: Genesis, chaps. 12-22.
    Psalm: 104 (105), 6, 9, 42.

2nd Stage: *Moses. The Covenant and the formation of God's People* (around 1300 B.C.).
    Books: Exodus, Leviticus, Numbers, Deuteronomy.
    Psalms: 67 (68), 8-11; 76 (77), 14-21; 77 (78), 12-58; 80 (81); 104 (105), 26-45; 105 (106), 1-33; 113 (114); 134 (135), 8-12; 135 (136), 10-26.

3rd Stage: *Josue. The Entry into the Promised Land.*
    Books: Josue and Judges
    Psalm: 43 (44).

4th Stage: *David. The Kingdom* (around 1000 B.C.).
    Books: I-II Samuel (Vulgate: I-II Kings).
    Psalms: 2, 2-6; 17 (18), 51; 44 (45); 77 (78), 70-72; 88 (89), 4-5, 20-38, & 50-52; 109 (110); 131 (132), 1, 10-18.

---

4 The primary enumeration is that of the Vulgate; the number in parentheses indicates the enumeration of the Hebrew text, e.g., Psalm 89 (90), 2.

5th Stage: *The People's Sin. The Prophets* (after the schism of 972).

    Books: I-II Kings (Vulgate: III-IV Kings).

    Psalms: 105 (106), 34-43.

    Prophets: *Northern* Kingdom: Elias
                           Eliseus
                           Amos
                           Osee
        Southern Kingdom: Isaias
                           Micheas
                           Jeremias

6th Stage: *The Exile and the Purification of God's People* (587–539 B.C.).

    Psalms: 13 (14), 7; 24 (25), 22; 50 (51), 20; 73 (74); 78 (79); 79 (80); 101 (102); 105 (106), 40-47; 135 (136), 23-24; 136 (137).

    Prophets: Ezechiel
              Isaias (40-66)
              Lamentations

7th Stage: *The Restoration and Judaism.*

    Books: Persian Period (538 B.C.): I-II Paralipomenon (Chronicles), Esdras and Nehemias (Historians of the Restoration).

    Greek Period (331): I-II Machabees (around 170).

    Psalms: 119 (120) to 133 (134) (Gradual Psalms).

    Prophets: Aggeus and Zacharias (Prophets of the Restoration)
              Joel
              Malachias
              Daniel

Various books testify to the religious progress of this period:

        Judith
        Esther   (Religious refinement)
        Wisdom

        Ruth
        Tobias   (Universalism)
        Jonas

Chapter 11

THE ANNUNCIATION AND PROMISE
OF THE PEOPLE OF GOD

(Genesis, chaps. 12-22)

This is the period of Abraham, "who is the father of us all (who believe)" (Romans 4:16). Notice, first of all, **the call of Abraham** (around 1800 B.C.). "The Lord said to Abraham...." God "chose" Abraham and summoned him to come forth from his polytheistic surroundings. This theme of God's "choice" is to remain basic throughout the whole Bible. God, who chose Abraham, will continue to choose whom He will. He has chosen us also.

Then notice **Abraham's trials:** the barrenness of Sara, the conflict between Sara and Agar, the sacrifice of Isaac. Abraham continued to believe in the face of all: *"Credidit Abraham Deo et reputatum est illi ad justitiam."* "Abraham believed God and it was credited to him as justice." Whence we have the theme of **the faith of Abraham,** another basic theme which runs throughout the prophets, the Psalms and the New Testament.

Then notice carefully the **promises of the covenant;** these promises concern the future of God's People more directly than they do Abraham himself. The promise of an heir and of an inheritance, namely, Isaac and the land of Chanaan.

Notice, finally, the **universality of this promise.** Abram has his name changed to "Abraham," that is to say, "Father of a Multitude," a multitude whose God will be Yahweh; Sarai, his wife, becomes Sara, "princess." These promises will find fulfillment in the far distant future. God said to Abraham: "I will establish my covenant...I will give you and your descendants after you this land..." (Genesis 17:7). Abraham and the patriarchs were not to have the Covenant but the promises of a Covenant.

These events are of considerable import; they mark a beginning, the **historical beginning** of the relations of man with God, the true God. They stand in contrast to the polytheism which reigned before Abraham. "Your fathers served strange gods" (Josue 24:2); or as St. Paul cried: "But then indeed, not knowing God, you served those who really are not gods" (Galatians 4:8; Ephesians 2:12). From Abraham stem historically all the monotheistic religions, Jewish, Christian and Moslem. The God of Abraham was the God El or Elohim, the God who revealed Himself to Moses during the following stage, and who was later to reveal Himself as being Father, Son and Holy Spirit. The promise made to Abraham was directed toward the future: the whole future history of his posterity and, at last, of all mankind was orientated toward the realization of this promise which was to be fulfilled on two levels: first, by the possession of the land of Chanaan, and then, much later, and without any limitation as to object or beneficiaries, by the blessing of all the nations of the earth.

Abraham is rightly considered as the **Father, the Ancestor,** the real beginning of the history of God's People. As proof that they belonged to the People of God, men did not claim descent from Adam, or Noe, or Sem, but from Abraham to whom God made the promises. In the New Testament St. Matthew traces the genealogy of Jesus from Abraham down (Matt. 1:1-2). Many expressions of the New Testament must be understood in this sense, for example (Luke 19; 9), "He (Zacchaeus) too, is a son of Abraham." Likewise, the expression "to be gathered into God's people" is equivalent to "enter Abraham's bosom."

Summary:

God promised Abraham an heir, a numerous posterity and an inheritance (spiritual blessing and a land).

In return, *God asked Faith of Abraham.*

Abraham was sanctified by his Faith (Galatians 3:6). He manifested and proved his Faith *by obeying God,* that is to say:

by leaving his country and his family,
by accepting the sacrifice of his son.
(Romans 4: 3 ff.)—(Galatians 3:6 ff.)

God's promises were accomplished a first time in *the Old Testament Church:*

the heir was *Isaac*

his posterity, *the Hebrew People*

the inheritance, *the Promised Land.*

But these promises were definitively accomplished in *the New Testament Church:*

the heir is *Jesus Christ* (Galatians 3:16)

the posterity, *the Church* (Galatians 3:29)

the inheritance, the *very life of God* (the true Promised Land is heaven) (Galatians 4:6-7).

To benefit from these promises, God asks *Faith* of us as He did of Abraham (Romans 4:9).

The Church is *the true posterity* promised to Abraham, that is, *all those who believe* in God and in His promises as Abraham did. The real sons of Abraham, the heirs of the divine promises, are, therefore, those who believe (Galatians 3:7).

TEXTS

The Promise of Offspring and a Country: The Lord said to Abram: "Leave your country, your kinsfolk and your father's house, for the land which I will show you; I will make a great nation of you. I will bless you, and make your name great, so that you shall be a blessing. I will bless them that bless you, and curse them that curse you. In you shall all the nations of the earth be blessed."

Abram went away as the Lord had commanded him, and Lot went with him. Abram was seventy-five years old when he left Haran (Genesis 12:1-4).

Promise of a Son. Abraham's Faith: After these things the word of the Lord came to Abram in a vision:

"Fear not, Abram, I am your shield; your reward shall be very great." And Abram said, "O Lord God, what will you give me? I am childless, and the steward of my house, Eliezer, is my heir?" Abram also said, "To me you have given no descendants; the slave born in my house will be my heir." But the word of the Lord came to him, "He shall not be your heir; your heir shall be one of your own flesh." Then the Lord led him outside and said, "Look at the heavens and, if you can, count the stars." And he said to him, "So shall your posterity be." Abram believed the Lord, who credited the act to him as justice (Genesis 15:1-6).

Abram Becomes Abraham, and Sarai, Sara. Isaac's Birth Promised —He Is The Child of Promise. And Not Ismael: When Abram was ninety-nine years old, the Lord appeared to him and said, "I am God the Almighty. Walk in my presence and be perfect. I will make my covenant between you and me, and will multiply you exceedingly." Abram fell prostrate, and God spoke to him thus, "This is my covenant with you: You shall be the father of a multitude of nations; you shall no longer be called Abram, but your name shall be Abraham; for I will make you the father of a multitude of nations. . . . Sarai, your wife, you shall not call Sarai, but Sara. I will bless her, and will also give you a son by her; yes, I will bless her, and she shall be the mother of nations; kings of peoples shall descend from her." And as Abraham fell prostrate, he laughed and said to himself, "Shall Sara who is ninety bear a child?" Then Abraham said to God, "Oh, that Ismael may live in your favor!" God answered, "No, but Sara your wife shall bear you a son, and you shall call him Isaac. I will establish my covenant with him as a perpetual covenant for his descendants after him.

As for Ismael, I have heard you. I will bless him and make him fruitful and multiply him exceedingly. He shall become the father of twelve princes, and I will make him a great nation. But my covenant I will establish with Isaac, whom Sara shall bear to you at this time next year" (Genesis 17:1-6, 15-22).

Abraham's Faith Is Tested: After these events God put Abraham to a test. He said to him, "Abraham." He answered, "Here I am." God said, "Take your only son Isaac whom you love and go into the district of Moria, and there offer him as a holocaust on the hill which I shall point out to you."

Early in the morning Abraham harnessed his ass, took with him two of his servants and his son Isaac, and cut wood for the holocaust. Then he set out on his journey to the place which God had indicated to him.

. . . Abraham stretched out his hand, and took the knife to kill his son. But an angel of the Lord called to him from heaven, "Abraham, Abraham!" He answered, "Here I am." He said, "Do not lay a hand on the boy; do nothing to him. I know now that you fear God, since you have not withheld your only son from me." Abraham looked about and saw a ram caught by its horns in a bush. He went and took it, and offered it as a holocaust in place of his son.

". . . I swear by myself, says the Lord, since you have done this and have not withheld your only son, I will indeed bless you, and will surely multiply your descendants as the stars of the heavens, as the sands on the seashore. Your descendants shall possess the gates of their enemies. In your descendants all the nations of the earth shall be blessed, because you have obeyed me" (Genesis 22:1-3, 10-13, 16-18).

Read Psalm 104 (105), 6, 9, 42.
Read the following texts of the New Testament:

Epistle to the Romans:
  Chap. 4: Abraham's Faith.
  Chap. 9:6-8: Those who believe are the real descendants of Abraham.
Epistle to the Galatians:
  Chaps. 3, 4:1-7: The promises made to Abraham are realized in Jesus and the Church of the New Testament.
  Chap. 4:21-31: In Christ and the Church we are the children of the promise, as Isaac was (and not as Ismael).

John 8:31-58
Matt. 3:7-10
{ It does not suffice to be of the blood of Abraham in order to be the *children* of Abraham and the heirs of his promises.

PROJECTS

The Old Testament refers to Abraham more than 180 times and the New Testament more than 60. Search out these passages with their context and see why Abraham is referred to, particularly why St. Paul constantly alludes to him. Then, after having first separated these texts from their settings, draw out the common ideas to be found in these quotations, that is, bring out their roots. Finally, draw up some kind of synthesis, as for instance:

1. From the texts selected from the Old and New Testaments pick out the following themes:
  (a) Abraham is our father.
        Christ is the son of Abraham.
        The Church is Abraham's posterity.
  (b) Abraham's Faith.
  (c) The promises made to Abraham are realized in Christ and in the Church.
  (d) The real sons of Abraham are, therefore, those who believe.

2. Pick out these same themes from your Missal, particularly in the Mass of the Dead (Requiem); the Vigil of Easter (the prayers following the prophecies); the Vigil of Pentecost (the prayers following the prophecies).

3. We shall later see in the New Testament stage how a consideration of the promises made to Abraham help us to understand the Church and our Christian life in the Church. Nevertheless, you could already try to draw out some of these considerations in the light of the foregoing texts, e.g., the primacy of Faith, the gratuity of God's gifts.

69

Chapter 12

THE COVENANT AND THE
FORMATION OF GOD'S PEOPLE

(Exodus, Leviticus, Numbers, Deuteronomy)

The Events of the Exodus

The events of the Exodus are of extraordinary importance, and in reading the Bible we must pay them particular attention, since they both shape the entire exegesis of the Covenant, and because they are later transposed into the New Testament and into the Church's liturgy, particularly the going out from Egypt, the Egyptian servitude, the ten plagues of Egypt, and finally, the Passover. This last event is perhaps the most important event in the whole history of God's people. By the presentation of the first-born and the annual feast of the Passover, it is the very heart of Israel's religion, and as transposed through the Passion of Christ into baptism and the eucharistic mystery, also the very core of the Christian religion.

The Covenant. We have to insist upon the Covenant because all its details influence our understanding of the Church and the Bible, particularly of the New Testament, and above all, of St. Paul's Epistles. St. Paul stresses the absolute priority of the promises freely made to Abraham over the more contractual alliance inaugurated at the time of Moses, and whose proper instrument was the Law. It was not the Covenant which held first place at the time of Abraham, but the promises; God's plan was inaugurated through grace and Faith, not by the Law. St. Paul set in opposition Abraham and Moses; Faith and the Law; the Promise and the Covenant. For St. Paul what remained stable and enduring were Abraham, Faith, and the Promise. A **pedagogue** was necessary during the time which elapsed between this promise and the Church of the New Testament: this pedagogue was the Covenant, the Law, the Mosaic period.

Now that Christ has come, we are adults, and the pedagogue's role is finished. We have Abraham's attitude toward Christ who realizes the promises, and just as it was by faith in God's gratuitous promises that Abraham was justified, so now it is faith in the word of Jesus which justifies us. The Church is Abraham's real posterity; but because mankind progresses through history, this slow pedagogue, this slow formation, this slow purification was necessary between Abraham and the Church. But now that Christ has come, we have no more need of the law of the Covenant, of the Mosaic code; Jesus came to accomplish the promises made to Abraham, namely, that through him "all the nations of the earth shall be blessed."

In giving the Law to Moses God said: "If you hearken to my voice and keep my covenant, you shall be my special possession, dearer to me than all other people, though all the earth is mine. You shall be to me a kingdom of priests, a holy nation" (Exodus 19:5-6).

A double compact was concluded, that is, on the part of God and on the part of the people.

(a) *God's part:* God became the ally of His people to the exclusion of all others. For Israel Yahweh was truly Emmanuel: God with us.

(b) *The people's part:* Israel promised not to make any compact with other divinities; it was to have no other ally than Yahweh; it was not to seek support from neighboring peoples or their Baals. The purpose of the Covenant, namely, to sanctify the people by consecrating it exclusively to Yahweh, its God, appeared even more fully in the obligation imposed upon it by the Law, the holy law of the Covenant which regulated its internal organization. The Covenant was sealed in blood, the blood of the lamb. The final Covenant was also to be sealed in blood, but this time in the Blood of the true Lamb, in the Blood of Christ. The paschal mystery prefigured the eucharistic mystery, and this economy is recalled each day in the words of the Consecration: "This is the chalice of my blood, of the new and eternal Testament."

The Religious Meaning of These Events

Attention must be called to the religious meaning of these events of the Exodus, the Covenant and the Law.

Among all the stages of Israel's history the most important stage was that of the desert and the Covenant. This stage synthesized both what was best and what was worst in the history of God's people in the Old Testament; the best, because it was the period of the Covenant and of the Espousals of God with His people; the worst, because it saw the beginning of Israel's distrust in its God, the beginning of its great defections and infidelities.

But the Exodus is not merely a past event: *the Church continually travels along the same roads.* As long as all the families of the earth are not gathered together and blessed in Abraham's posterity, that is to say, in Christ and in the Church, God's people must continually abandon Egypt's idolatrous slavery, must continually march through the arid, desert wastes, must continually try to conquer the Promised Land. The Church dwells in the desert until Christ's return. It never ceases regretting the Egyptian pleasures it left behind, and even murmurs as a whole or sins in its leaders. But God, who is faithful, unfailingly urges it on either through chastisement or forgiveness, until it attains the new heaven and new earth that Jesus will inaugurate on the day of His parousia. And this itinerary of the Church is also that of each one of its members.

Notice that it is **a people** that the Covenant envisaged. In like manner it is the Church which is chosen. God adopts us as a family and we share in His divine favors in the measure that we become a part of this family of God.

Notice also the extraordinary and purely **gratuitous love** of God toward His people: "You are a people sacred to the Lord, your God; he has chosen you from all the nations on the face of the earth to be a people peculiarly his own. It was not because you are the largest of all nations that the Lord set his heart on you and chose you, for you are really the smallest of all nations. It was because the Lord loved you" (Deut. 7:6-7).

It is a *demanding* love because God is holy; a *jealous* love because God desires that His people keep themselves wholly for Him, and that they do not prostitute themselves to the Baals; a *merciful* love: what wretchedness was to be found in this people, the object of God's choice! Its history is as much made up of its infidelities as of the divine mercies. In Exodus, for example, we notice its continual murmurings, even and especially after the Covenant of Sinai. The present history of the members of the Church continues that of the Jewish people only too well in this regard also.

This love was directed toward *Israel first of all*. It was Israel "as a people" that was the son of God: "Israel is my son, my first born" (Exodus 4:22). "The Lord your God carried you as a man is wont to carry his little son" (Deut. 1:31). Only later do we learn that within this people each member is personally a son of God, which fact marks a great progress in revelation. The Church is also a communion of persons and each member of the Church is personally a son.

TEXTS

God Recalls His Promises to Abraham and Chooses Moses: God called out to him from the bush, "Moses! Moses!" He answered, "Here I am." God said, "Come no nearer! Remove the sandals from your feet, for the place where you stand is holy ground. I am the God of your father," he continued, "the God of Abraham, the God of Isaac, the God of Jacob." Moses hid his face, for he was afraid to look at God. But the Lord said, "I have witnessed the affliction of my people in Egypt and have heard their cry of complaint against their slave drivers, so I know well what they are suffering. Therefore, I have come down to rescue them from the hands of the Egyptians and lead them out of that land into a good and spacious land, a land flowing with milk and honey" (Exodus 3:4-8).

"But," said Moses to God, "when I go to the Israelites and say to them, 'The God of your fathers has sent me to you,' if they ask me, 'What is his name?' what am I to tell them?" God replied, "I am who am." Then he added, "This is what you shall tell the Israelites: I AM sent me to you (Exodus 3:13-14).

"So shall you say to Pharao: Thus says the Lord: Israel is my son, my first-born. Hence I tell you: Let my son go, that he may serve me. If you refuse to let him go, I warn you, I will kill your son, your first-born (Exodus 4:22-23).

The First Passover: "On the tenth of this month every one of your families must procure for itself a lamb, one apiece for each household.

73

If a family is too small for a whole lamb, it shall join the nearest household in procuring one and shall share in the lamb in proportion to the number of persons who partake of it. The lamb must be a year-old male and without blemish. You may take it from either the sheep or the goats" (Exodus 12:3-5).

"This is how you are to eat it: with your loins girt, sandals on your feet and your staff in hand, you shall eat like those who are in flight. It is the Passover of the Lord. For on this same night I will go through Egypt, striking down every first-born of the land, both man and beast, and executing judgment on all the gods of Egypt—I, the Lord. But the blood will mark the houses where you are. Seeing the blood, I will pass over you; thus, when I strike the land of Egypt, no destructive blow will come upon you. This day shall be a memorial feast for you, which all your generations shall celebrate with pilgrimage to the Lord, as a perpetual institution" (Exodus 12:11-14).

God and Moses on Sinai: On the morning of the third day there were peals of thunder and lightning, and a heavy cloud over the mountain, and a very loud trumpet blast, so that all the people in the camp trembled. But Moses led the people out of the camp to meet God, and they stationed themselves at the foot of the mountain. Mount Sinai was all wrapped in smoke, for the Lord came down upon it in fire. The smoke rose from it as though from a furnace, and the whole mountain trembled violently. The trumpet blast grew louder and louder, while Moses was speaking and God answering him with thunder. When the Lord came down to the top of Mount Sinai, he summoned Moses to the top of the mountain, and Moses went up to him (Exodus 19:16-20).

When the people witnessed the thunder and lightning, the trumpet blast and the mountain smoking, they all feared and trembled. So they took up a position much farther away and said to Moses, "You speak to us, and we will listen; but let not God speak to us, or we shall die." Moses answered the people, "Do not be afraid, for God has come to you only to test you and put his fear upon you, lest you should sin." Still the people remained at a distance, while Moses approached the cloud where God was (Exodus 20:18-21).

The Blood of the First Covenant: Taking the Book of the Covenant, he read it aloud to the people, who answered, "All that the Lord has said, we will heed and do." Then he took the blood and sprinkled it on the people, saying, "This is the blood of the covenant which the Lord has made with you in accordance with all these words of his" (Exodus 24:7-8).

God Asks Love From His People: "Hear, O Israel! The Lord is our God, the Lord alone! Therefore, you shall love the Lord, your God, with all your heart, and with all your soul, and with all your strength. Take to heart these words which I enjoin on you today. Drill them into your children. Speak of them at home and abroad, whether you are busy or at rest. Bind them at your wrist as a sign and let them be as a pendant on your forehead. Write them on the doorposts of your houses and on your gates" (Deut. 6:4-9).

"You shall not follow other Gods, such as those of the surrounding nations, lest the wrath of the Lord, your God, flare up against you and he destroy you from the face of the land; for the Lord, your God, who is in your midst, is a jealous God" (Deut. 6:14-15).

God Promises Love Toward His People: "For you are a people sacred to the Lord, your God; he has chosen you from all the nations on the face of the earth to be a people peculiarly his own. It was not because you are the largest of all nations that the Lord set his heart on you and chose you, for you are really the smallest of all nations. It was because the Lord loved you and because of his fidelity to the oath he had sworn to your fathers, that he brought you out with his strong hand from the place of slavery, and ransomed you from the hand of Pharao, king of Egypt. Understand, then, that the Lord, your God, is God indeed—the faithful God who keeps his merciful covenant down to the thousandth generation toward those who love him and keep his commandments" (Deut. 7:6-9).

—Read Psalms 67 (68), 8-11; 76 (77), 14-21; 77 (78), 12-55; 80 (81); 104 (105), 26-45; 105 (106), 1-33; 113A (114); 134 (135), 8-12; 135 (136), 10-26.

—Read the following texts in the New Testament:

Matthew, chaps. 5-7: Comparison between the Law of Moses and the Law of Jesus.

Hebrews, chaps. 1-10: Comparison between the two covenants.

St. John's Gospel: The various mentions of the Jewish Passover.

PROJECTS

1. Draw up a comparative table of the Old and New Testaments (Covenants) according to the preceding texts; for example, according to Matthew 5-7, a comparative table of the two laws; according to Hebrews 1-10, a comparative table of the two Covenants: mediator, priest, sacrifice.

2. From the office of Easter (vespers, Mass, preface) pick out all those texts which treat of Jesus as the "paschal Lamb" and say what they teach us about Jesus and the Church.

3. Explain in a few words how these considerations concerning the Passover and the Covenant help us to understand better:

(a) the Church of today (the new and final Covenant between God and mankind through and in Christ);

(b) our own Christian life within the Church (the price of our redemption; the law of Love).

75

Moses and the Religious Explanation of Creation and Sin

We must assign to this stage of the Covenant *the first eleven chapters of Genesis* as a kind of **catechism of the period,** that is to say, a religious explanation of the great problems of life. To a people who were still on a childish level, Moses explained how God created all things, and how suffering, death and sin entered into the world.

We shall outline the main characteristics of these eleven first chapters of Genesis. The three first disclose the **creation** scene under a unified and universalist aspect. Man is united to God, nature is subjected to man, man finds himself entrusted with the whole of creation by God. Unity reigns within man, with the body subjected to the soul, and men are united among themselves.

But **sin** shatters this harmony and this unity: man revolts against God; with one blow nature revolts against man, the flesh revolts against the spirit, and men become divided among themselves, and their divisions are accentuated in proportion as they drift away from God. Thus, all the evils which mankind suffer stem, not from God, but from the sin of man, from the first sin to which so many others have succeeded.

Restoration, in its turn, is presented in a universalist perspective. It will be a destruction of enmity, and, therefore, a restoration of *friendship,* a return to *harmony* and *unity* . . .

Unity of man with God.

Harmony of nature with man.

Harmony within man.

Unity among men.

We shall find this total perspective everywhere in the Bible: the messianic times shall be a time of peace and universal reconciliation, not only for humanity but also for creation. In this eschatological outlook not only humanity but creation itself will be renewed.

The first eleven chapters of Genesis also provide us with a panorama of **God's plan for the world,** for God has a plan for the world and for all mankind which will be progressively realized despite all obstacles; God will save men somehow despite themselves, that is, despite sin and malice.

The universalist perspectives of the beginning seem too narrow later on; the Bible appears to be no longer interested in any except the posterity of Abraham and even makes a choice among his heirs. But, in reality, it is in order to save the whole world that God chooses Abraham and molds the Jewish people into the people of God. This provisory economy was necessary in order to slowly educate humanity to be prepared to receive the gift of Christ and the Church.

Chapter 13

THE ENTRY INTO THE
PROMISED LAND AND THE KINGDOM

I. Entry into the Promised Land
(Josue-Judges)

The Book of Josue gives an account of the entry of God's people into the Promised Land. Note well the religious meaning of this stage: the possession of this land is presented as **the accomplishment of the Covenant;** it is God who gives it, yet the people still have to conquer it. It will always be so in the mystery of the Church: all is given by God and yet all must be conquered by men; what God gives us is precisely this power of conquest; thus all is from God and all is from us.

When the people took possession of the land of Chanaan, the first part of the promise was then accomplished. Israel was in possession of the Promised Land. But this land itself was a mere image of that true inheritance which God destined for His people—and through it for all nations—or rather it was but its first realization. Such is the reason for that continued expectation which awaited the final realization.

The Book of Judges shows us how God's People installed themselves in their conquered territories. For the direction of His people God raised up "judges" who were at first warrior chieftains and who subsequently became leaders of the people. The book's unity is assured by its religious theme, namely, Israel's lack of fidelity toward God by reason of its serving idols. By way of punishment it was delivered into the hands of its enemies, but later repented; God then took pity upon His people and raised up a judge to deliver them; then the cycle: sin, punishment, repentance, liberation, began all over again.

II. David and the Kingdom

I and II Samuel (Vulgate: I and II Book of Kings)

This is truly a characteristic stage in the history of God's people, for it marks the beginning of messianic kingship. The religious meaning of the kingdom is easy to see: God is the true king and Israel a "theocracy." Note well what is a capital passage in this regard: Nathan's prophecy to David (II Samuel, chap. 7). This prophecy concerns David's son Solomon first of all, but it is a text which will be understood in a more and more messianic sense as time passes; as is witnessed by the Book of Chronicles which in treating of these same historic events applies this prophecy, not to David's direct heir, but to his entire posterity. The two texts (II Samuel, chap. 7 and I Chronicles, chap. 17) should be read together.

This prophecy marks the beginning of messianic kingship, that is, of faith in the salvation of the world through the intermediary of the Israelite royalty and especially the royal house of David.

—The greatest king is **David**. His person and his kingdom are *the figure* and *prophecy of Christ and the Church.*

David was born in *Bethlehem* as was Jesus.

He was a *shepherd* as Jesus was to be the Shepherd.

He was a *king* as Jesus was to be the King.

He was called the "christ," which means "anointed" (consecrated by anointing with oil), as Jesus was to be the "Christ," the Anointed, consecrated by divinity itself.

He reigned at *Jerusalem,* as Jesus was to establish the Kingdom of God beginning at Jerusalem.

—God promised David that the Messias was one day to be born from among his posterity, and that his kingdom would one day become the Messianic Kingdom (II Samuel, chap. 7). Jesus, therefore, was presented as the Son of David (Matt. 1:1) and the Church as the Kingdom of David (Luke 1:31).

—David's son, Solomon, built the **Temple** of Jerusalem (I Book of Kings; Vulgate: III Book of Kings).

In the Church of the New Testament Jesus is Himself the true Temple in that He is God made present in the world (John 2:19; Apocalypse 21, 22). And in Jesus, all those who go to make up the Church, the faithful, are themselves God's Temple (Ephesians 2:21; Hebrews 3:6; I Peter 2:5).

TEXTS

The Anointing of David: And the Lord said to Samuel: How long wilt thou mourn for Saul, whom I have rejected from reigning over Israel? Fill thy horn with oil, and come, that I may send thee to Isai the Bethlehemite: for I have provided me a king among his sons (I Kings 16:1).

Isai therefore brought his seven sons before Samuel: and Samuel said to Isai: The Lord hath not chosen any one of these. And Samuel said to Isai: Are here all thy sons? He answered: There remaineth yet a young one, who keepeth the sheep. And Samuel said to Isai: Send, and fetch him, for we will not sit down till he come hither. He sent therefore and brought him. Now he was ruddy and beautiful to behold, and of a comely face. And the Lord said: Arise, and anoint him, for this is he. Then Samuel took the horn of oil, and anointed him in the midst of his brethren: and the spirit of the Lord came upon David from that day forward (I Kings 16:10-13).

The Messianic Promises to David: And the Lord foretelleth to thee, that the Lord will make thee a house. And when thy days shall be fulfilled and thou shalt sleep with thy fathers, I will raise up thy seed after thee, which shall proceed out of thy bowels, and I will establish his kingdom. He shall build a house to my name, and I will establish the throne of his kingdom for ever. I will be to him a father, and he shall be to me a son: and if he commit any iniquity, I will correct him with the rod of men, and with the stripes of the children of men. But my mercy I will not take away from him, as I took it from Saul, whom I removed from before my face. And thy house shall be faithful, and thy kingdom for ever before thy face, and thy throne shall be firm for ever (II Kings 7:11-16).

David's Prayer of Thanksgiving: And David went in, and sat before the Lord and said: Who am I, O Lord God, and what is my house, that thou hast brought me thus far?

. . . Therefore thou art magnified, O Lord God, because there is none like to thee, neither is there any God besides thee, in all the things we have heard with our ears. And what nation is there upon earth, as thy people Israel, who God went to redeem for a people to himself, and to make him a name, and to do for them great and terrible things, upon the earth, before the face of thy people, whom thou redeemedst to thyself out of Egypt, from the nations and their gods. For thou hast confirmed to thyself thy people Israel to be an everlasting people: and thou, O Lord God, art become their God.

. . . Because thou, O Lord of hosts, God of Israel, hast revealed to the ear of thy servant, I will build thee a house: therefore hath thy servant found in his heart to pray this prayer to thee. And now, O Lord God, thou art God, and thy words shall be true: for thou hast spoken to thy servant these good things. And now begin, and bless the house of thy servant, that it may endure for ever before thee: because thou, O Lord God, hast spoken it, and with thy blessing let the house of thy servant be blessed for ever (II Kings 7:18, 22-24, 27-29).

Solomon's Prayer at the Consecration of the Temple: . . . Lord God of Israel, there is no God like thee in heaven above, or on earth beneath: who keepest covenant and mercy with thy servants that have walked before thee with all their heart. Who hast kept with thy servant David my father what thou hast promised him: with thy mouth thou didst speak, and with thy hands thou hast performed, as this day proveth. Now therefore, O Lord God of Israel, keep with thy servant David my father what thou hast spoken to him, saying:

There shall not be taken away of thee a man in my sight, to sit on the throne of Israel: yet so that thy children take heed to their way, that they walk before me as thou hast walked in my sight. And now, Lord God of Israel, let thy words be established, which thou hast spoken to thy servant David my father (III Kings 8:23-26).

Read Psalms:

—for Josue, Ps. 43 (44).

—for David, the King, the Kingdom: Pss. 2, 2-6; 17 (18), 51; 44 (45); 77 (78), 70-72; 88 (89), 4, 20-38, 50-52; 109 (110); 131 (132), 1, 11-18.

Read in the New Testament:

Luke 1:26-33: Jesus is David's promised heir and the Church is His Kingdom.

Mark 11:10 ⎫ Jesus is recognized as the Son of David and
Matt. 21:9 ⎭ His Kingdom as that of David.

Matt. 22:41-46: Jesus claims to be the Son of David.

PROJECTS

1. Compare the text of II Kings 7:11-16 with the angel's words to Mary in Luke 1:26-33.

2. From one of the Gospels collect all the texts concerning Jesus as the Son of David and the Church as the Kingdom, and say what they teach us about Jesus and His Church.

3. In this spirit, study the Mass of Palm Sunday (in your missal).

4. Pick out the various passages in the Gospels which mention Solomon and his temple, and draw out the lesson of these texts.

5. Study this theme of the Temple (which is Christ and the Church) in the Mass for the Dedication of a Church (in your missal).

6. Explain in a few words how these considerations concerning the Kingdom and the Temple help us to understand better:

(a) the Church today (the realization of the Kingdom promised to David);

(b) our own Christian life within the Church (we participate in Christ's kingship).

Chapter 14

THE INFIDELITY OF THE PEOPLE AND THE PROPHETIC MINISTRY

I-II Books of Kings (Vulgate: III-IV Books of Kings) and the Various Prophets

The People and its leaders were not always faithful to the Covenant; they were prone to forget God and adore idols (III Kings 11:1-13). Idolatry began on a grand scale especially towards the end of Solomon's reign. God punished these sins by rending the Kingdom in two: the great **Schism** (III Kings 11:29-39):

—the Northern Kingdom of Israel whose capital was Samaria;

—the Southern Kingdom of Judah whose capital was Jerusalem.

This division of the Davidic Kingdom after the death of Solomon was the source of the prophets' great sorrow. The House of God was divided, and men could only look forward to messianic times for the return to unity when all would once again be one flock and one shepherd. After the schism, the history of the two Kingdoms was reduced to that of their kings (whence the title, *Books of Kings*), and seen especially in the light of whether or not the king and the nation were faithful or unfaithful to the Law of Yahweh and to the Covenant.

God reminded the Israelites of the conditions of the Covenant by sending them **Prophets,** men who spoke **in God's name.** Prophecy and the prophetic mission were justified by reason of God's choice of Israel as His People. The prophets were the authorized interpreters and the mouthpieces of Yahweh. Their essential mission consisted in proclaiming the primordial truth that "Yahweh is the God of Israel and

Israel is the chosen People of Yahweh," and in drawing out its practical consequences with regard to public and private life.

In times of ease and sin they preached repentance and prophesied punishment. In times of distress and affliction they preached confidence and encouraged faith in the promises. Only the **faithful remnant** was to share in these promises, although such promises were made to all nations in some manner as yet uncertain. The prophets foretold the messianic times which were to be the realization of the promises made to Abraham and the establishment of God's universal rule on earth.

In addition, *they foretold* in advance all that concerned *Christ and the Church* and brought about a gradual realization of the interior and universal nature of the awaited Kingdom.

1. To the Northern Kingdom God sent Elias, Eliseus, Amos and Osee.

Elias (III Kings) and **Eliseus** (IV Kings) reminded the Israelites that there is but *one God only,* the God Who had entered into a *covenant* with them (III Kings 18:17-39).

Amos reminded the Israelites that *God is just,* and that He will punish them on the *"Day of Yahweh"* if they continue to sin. Only a "remnant" will be saved (Amos 9:8-12).

Osee reminded the Israelites that *God is good* and that He will **forgive** them if they return to Him, just as a husband forgives an adulterous but repentant wife (Osee 2).

But the inhabitants of the Kingdom of Israel would not listen to the message of the Prophets and God was obliged to punish them. Their Kingdom was invaded and a large proportion of the population was exiled to Northern Assyria (Fall of Samaria in 722 B.C.) (IV Kings 17:1-23).

2. To the Southern Kingdom God sent Isaias, Micheas and Jeremias.

Isaias reminded the Israelites of God's Holiness; afflictions will purify God's People, and this purified *"remnant"* will be the *seed of the universal kingdom* of the future (Isaias 2:1-5).

Micheas predicted the messianic Kingdom and the Messias' birthplace as Bethlehem (Micheas 5:2).

Jeremias foretold God's punishments (the destruction of Jerusalem and the Temple, the Exile) and the New Covenant which was to be of an interior and universal nature, open to all men of every nation, namely, the Church of the New Testament (Jeremias 2:12-13; 2:21-22; 3:17-18; 16:10-13; 31:21-34).

But the inhabitants of the Kingdom of Judah would not listen to the message of the Prophets, so that God had to punish them. Their kingdom was invaded, Jerusalem and the Temple were destroyed and a large number were exiled to Babylonia.

TEXTS

(Douay Trans.)

The religious cause of the schism: And Ahias taking his new garment, wherewith he was clad, divided it into twelve parts, and he said to Jeroboam: Take to thee ten pieces, for thus saith the Lord the God of Israel: Behold I will rend the kingdom out of the hand of Solomon, and will give thee ten tribes. But one tribe shall remain to him for the sake of my servant David, and Jerusalem the city, which I have chosen out of all the tribes of Israel, because he hath forsaken me, and hath adored Astarthe the goddess of the Sidonians, and Chamos the god of Moab, and Moloch the god of the children of Ammon, and hath not walked in my ways, to do justice before me, and to *keep* my precepts, and judgments as *did* David his father (III Kings 11:30-33).

Elias reminds that Yahweh is the only God: And Elias coming to all the people, said: How long do you halt between two sides? If the Lord be God, follow him; but if Baal, then follow him. And the people did not answer him a word. And Elias said again to the people: I only remain a prophet of the Lord; but the prophets of Baal are four hundred and fifty men. Let two bullocks be given us, and let them choose one bullock for themselves, and cut it in pieces and lay it upon wood, but put no fire under; and I will dress the other bullock, and lay it on wood, and put no fire under it. Call ye on the names of your gods, and I will call on the name of my Lord; and the God that shall answer by fire, let him be God. And all the people answering said: A very good proposal (III Kings 18:21-24).

And when it was now noon, Elias jested at them, saying: Cry with a louder voice, for he is a god, and perhaps he is talking, or is in an inn, or on a journey, or perhaps he is asleep, and must be awaked. So they cried with a loud voice, and cut themselves after their manner with knives and lancets, till they were all covered with blood. And after midday was past, and while they were prophesying, the time was come of offering sacrifice, and there was no voice heard, nor did anyone answer, nor regard them as they prayed (III Kings 18:27-29).

And when it was now time to offer the holocaust, Elias, the prophet came near and said: O Lord God of Abraham, and Isaac, and Israel, show this day that thou art the God of Israel, and I thy servant, and that according to thy commandment I have done all these things. Hear me, O Lord, hear me, that this people may learn that thou art the Lord God, and that thou hast turned their heart again.

Then the fire of the Lord fell, and consumed the holocaust, and the wood, and the stones, and the dust, and licked up the water that was in the trench. And when all the people saw this, they fell on their faces, and they said: The Lord he is God, the Lord he is God (III Kings 18:36-39).

The Day of Yahweh, the Day of Judgment.
Woe to them that desire the day of the Lord!
To what end is it for you?
The day of the Lord *is* darkness, and not light.
As if a man should flee from the face of a lion,
and a bear should meet him;
or enter into the house, and lean with his hand upon the wall,
and a serpent should bite him.
Shall not the day of the Lord be darkness and not light,
and obscurity, and no brightness in it?
(Amos 5:18-20).

Israel is like a faithless Spouse.
Judge your mother, judge *her*,
because she is not my wife,
and I am not her husband.
Let her put away her fornications from her face . . .
(Osee 2:2).

Yahweh pardons His repentent Spouse.
And it shall be in that day, saith the Lord,
that she shall call me: My husband,
and she shall call me no more Baali.
And I will take away the names of Baalim out of her mouth,
and she shall no more remember their name.
(Osee 2:16-17).

The Universal Kingdom to come.
And in the last days
the mountain of the house of the Lord
shall be prepared on the top of mountains,
and it shall be exalted above the hills,
and all nations shall flow unto it.

And many people shall go, and say;
Come and let us go up to the mountain of the Lord,
and to the house of the God of Jacob,
and he will teach us the ways,
and we will walk in his paths,
for the law shall come forth from Sion,
and the word of the Lord from Jerusalem.
And he shall judge the Gentiles,
and rebuke many people; . . .
(Isaias 2:2-4).

God purifies His people.

Wherefore hath the Lord pronounced against us
all this great evil?
What is our iniquity and what is our sin,
that we have sinned against the Lord our God?
Thou shalt say to them:
Because your fathers forsook me,
saith the Lord,
and went after strange gods,
and served them, and adored them:
and they forsook me,
and kept not my law.
And you also have done worse than your fathers:
for behold everyone of you walketh after the perverseness of his evil
      heart,
so as not to hearken to me.
So I will cast you forth out of this land,
into a land which you know not, nor your fathers:
and there you shall serve strange gods
day and night,
which shall not give you any rest.
(Jeremias 16:10-13).

Behold the days shall come, saith the Lord,
and I will make a new covenant with the house of Israel, and with
      the house of Judah:
not according to the covenant which I made with their fathers,
in the day that I took them by the hand
to bring them out of the land of Egypt:
the covenant which they made void,
and I had dominion over them, saith the Lord.
But this shall be the covenant
that I will make with the house of Israel,
after those days, saith the Lord:
I will give my law in their bowels,
and I will write it in their heart,
and I will be their God,

and they shall be my people.
(Jeremias 31:31-33).

Read: Psalm 106:34-43.

PROJECTS

1. From one of the Evangelists or from one of St. Paul's epistles collect the texts we have just quoted from the prophets and show how they attain fulfillment in Christ and in the Church.

2. Do the same from your missal; for example, in the Advent, Christmas and Epiphany liturgies.

3. Explain in a few words how a consideration of the sins of the chosen People and of the words of the prophets help us to understand better:

(a) the Church today (the realization of the prophecies);

(b) our own Christian life within the Church (our own personal life is also a history of infidelities and of divine mercies).

Chapter 15

GOD PURIFIES HIS PEOPLE BY THE ORDEAL OF THE EXILE

(Ezechiel and Lamentations)

The exile was an essential stage in the history of God's people (587–539 B.C.). Yahweh seemed to abandon His people, but in reality it was merely the fulfillment of that purifying ordeal which had been foretold by the prophets. The exile, therefore, brought about a progress in the development of God's people, a development which was both more spiritual and more universal:

Spiritual Development:

The exiled Jews drew closer to Yahweh and to His Prophets (fusion of the two kingdoms). They began to look more towards the future, because, deprived of the Temple and its visible worship, the exiles understood more clearly that the ritual law was less important than the inner meaning of the law. In meditating upon Scripture, they understood the Covenant better, God's love and their own sin. That is why, despite their idolatrous environment, the Jews of the exile remained faithful to Yahweh.

Development Towards Universality:

Although they were geographically far distant from the Promised Land, they still remained the Chosen People, the People destined to inherit the Promises. This assurance helped the Jews to understand that the Kingdom of God is not necessarily tied up with any particular country. They began to realize that the Gentile nations, among whom they were dispersed, would also one day be able to enter God's people. Consequently, Israel became *missionary* minded, made converts, set up synagogues for the Jews of the Diaspora (this was a providential preparation for the New Testament Apostles in all the great centers of the Mediterranean world; compare Acts 2:5-12 with Tobias 13:4: "He has scattered you among the Gentiles...so that you may declare his wonderful works, and make them know that there is no other God besides him").

Religious Meaning:

It was by reason of the exile that the People of God drew nearer to God and became more missionary minded. It will always be so for God's People, which we are. This is true of the Church as a whole and of each one of its members individually. Ezechiel was the great prophet who helped the people make this kind of progress. He explained the religious meaning of the ordeal and then predicted the liberation and return of the "faithful remnant" to the Promised Land.

TEXTS

The distress of the People in the land of exile: By the rivers of Babylon, there we sat and wept, when we remembered Sion. On the willows of that land we hung up our harps. For there, they who captured us requested songs of us, and they who tormented us, mirth: "Sing to us from the canticles of Sion!" How shall we sing a canticle of the Lord in a strange land? (Ps. 136:1-4).

Israel, which had become the sterile Vine, is thrown into the fire: Thy mother is like a vine in thy blood planted by the water: her fruit and her branches have grown out of many waters. (Ezechiel 19:10)

But she was plucked up in wrath, and cast on the ground, and the burning wind dried up her fruit. Her strong rods are withered, and dried up: the fire hath devoured her (Ezechiel 19:12).

Son of man, what shall be made of the wood of the vine, out of all the trees of the woods that are among the trees of the forests? (Ezechiel 15:2).

Therefore thus saith the Lord God: As the vine tree among the trees of the forests which I have given to the fire to be consumed, so will I deliver up the inhabitants of Jerusalem (Ezechiel 15:6).

But God raises up a Good Shepherd to bring back His People: For thus saith the Lord God: Behold I myself will seek my sheep, and will visit them.

And I will bring them out from the peoples, and will gather them out of the countries, and will bring them to their own land; and I will feed them in the mountains of Israel, by the rivers, and in all the habitations of the land.

I will seek that which was lost, and that which was driven away, I will bring again. And I will bind up that which was broken, and I will strengthen that which was weak, and that which was fat and strong I will preserve; and I will feed them in judgment.

And I will set up one shepherd over them, and he shall feed them, even my servant David: he shall feed them, and he shall be their shepherd (Ezechiel 34:11, 13, 16, 23).

Read Psalms: 13 (14), 7; 24 (25), 22; 50 (51), 20-21; 73 (74); 78 (79); 79 (80); 101 (102); 105 (106), 40-47; 135 (136), 23-24; 136 (137).

PROJECTS

1. Compare the texts of Ezechiel on the Vine with John 15:1-8. Show the progress of revelation. (Jesus is the true Vine, fruitful, etc.)

2. Compare the texts of Ezechiel on the shepherd with John 10:15-21. Show the progress of revelation. (Jesus is the true Shepherd and the Church His Flock, etc.)

3. Compare Ezechiel, chap. 36 with John 4:23-24, and explain these last two verses.

Chapter 16

THE RELIGIOUS LIFE OF THE PEOPLE FROM THE EXILE UNTIL THE COMING OF JESUS

(I-II Paralipomenon or Chronicles, I-II Machabees, Daniel)

When they returned to the Promised Land, the people were invited by the prophets to rebuild Jerusalem and the Temple. **The mentality of those who were repatriated** is clearly set forth in the book of Chronicles, which sums up all previous history in a *Messianic perspective*. The great majority of the people still lived in the Diaspora, and the community of those who had returned to Palestine was far from numerous. The Chronicler wanted to embrace the whole history of his nation and even of its primitive antecedents down from the very beginning, and so began his account with the genealogies of the twelve tribes of Israel; by so doing, he pointed out the physical and religious ties which bound them together and which linked them to the first beneficiaries of the divine choice, the patriarchs.

David stands at the very center of this perspective, for David and his offspring possessed a not merely historical but doctrinal significance for the Chronicler. The point of departure was the prophecy of Nathan (II Samuel 7:12-16 and I Paralipomenon 17:11-14) with a more Messianic stress: "I will raise up thy seed after thee, which shall be of thy sons" (not just your immediate son, as in Samuel); and with a more theocratic stress: "I will settle him in my house and in my kingdom, and his throne shall be most firm forever." This perpetual character attributed to the throne of David was, therefore, a guarantee of the people's restoration. David was also a type of the Messias.

The following points characterized **this final stage** of God's kingdom:

—Israel no longer possessed political independence;

—Consequently, it tended to become more a religious community than a nation;

—Its religious life, which had been already purified in the ordeals of the exile, centered about the *Temple*, divine *worship* and the *law*.

—The religious persecution of Antiochus Epiphanes was to purify God's People still more, refine its religious feelings, intensify the desire for the Messianic times and prepare the coming of the Messias.

In a sermon on the martyrs of this religious persecution of Antiochus Epiphanes (the Machabees) St. Augustine [1] points out the religious meaning of these martyrdoms: "Don't think that the martyrs of the Old Testament were not Christians. By dying for the law of Moses, they became martyrs for Christ's sake. The Machabees did not confess Christ explicitly, but only because the mystery of Christ was as yet still veiled in the figures and shadows of the Old Law."

Several books issuing from this period bear witness to the progress of religious life on the eve of the New Testament:

—progress towards **a more interior religion,** for example, the Book of *Wisdom* (religious reflections on history); this refinement of religious sentiments can also be noticed in the prayers of *Judith* (chap. 9) and *Esther* (chaps. 13 and 14).

—progress towards a **universalism:**

Book of *Ruth:* God accepts the homage of a foreigner;

Book of *Tobias:* Religious reasons for the exile (13:3-4);

Book of *Jonas:* Conversion of the nations (4:10).

TEXTS

Joyful Gratitude for the Happy Return from Exile:
> When the Lord brought back the captives of Sion,
>   we were like men dreaming.
> Then our mouth was filled with laughter,
>   and our tongue with rejoicing.
> Then they said among the nations
>   "The Lord has done great things for them."

---

[1] *Sermo* 300; P.L. 38, 1377-80.

The Lord has done great things for us;
we are glad indeed.
(Psalm 126:1-3).

The prophecy of Nathan is interpreted in a more Messianic meaning:
And I declare to thee, that the Lord will build thee a house. And when
thou shalt have ended thy days to go to thy fathers, I will raise up
thy seed after thee, which shall be of thy sons, and I will establish his
kingdom. He shall build me a house, and I will establish his throne
forever.

I will be to him a father, and he shall be to me a son; and I will
not take my mercy away from him, as I took it from him that was
before thee.

But I will settle him in my house, and in my kingdom forever; and
his throne shall be most firm forever (I Paralipomenon 17:10-14).

**Daniel, witness of the religious depth of the People of God in its later
stages:** For thou hast executed true judgments in all the things that
thou hast brought upon us, and upon Jerusalem the holy city of our
fathers, for according to truth and judgment, thou hast brought all
these things upon us for our sins. For we have sinned and committed
iniquity, departing from thee, and we have trespassed in all things.
And we have not hearkened to thy commandments, nor have we ob-
served nor done as thou hadst commanded us, that it might go well
with us (Daniel 3:28-30).

Nevertheless in a contrite heart and humble spirit let us be accepted. As in holocausts of rams, and bullocks, and as in thousands of
fat lambs, so let our sacrifice be made in thy sight this day, that it
may please thee, for there is no confusion to them that trust in thee.
And now we follow thee with all our heart, and we fear thee, and seek
thy face (Daniel 3:39-41).

The vision of the Son of Man in the clouds of the sky: I beheld
therefore in the vision of the night, and lo, one like the son of man
came with the clouds of heaven, and he came even to the Ancient of
days, and they presented him before him. And he gave him power,
and glory, and a kingdom, and all peoples, tribes and tongues shall
serve him. His power is an everlasting power that shall not be taken
away, and his kingdom that shall not be destroyed (Daniel 7:13-14).

Read Psalms 120 to 134 (Psalms sung while ascending to Jerusalem).

PROJECTS

1. Look up in your missal in the offertory prayers the texts of
Daniel 3:39.

2. Look up in St. Matthew (particularly in Matt. 8:20; 24:30;
26:64) the application of this prophecy of Daniel 7:13-14).

B. The Stage of Fulfillment: The New Testament

Chapter 17

THE CHURCH IN THE LIGHT OF THE OLD TESTAMENT

At first sight the Gospel would seem to have but little to say about the Church. We tend to recall only isolated texts, such as Christ's words to Peter: "Thou art Peter, and upon this rock I will build my Church" (Matt. 16:18). In reality, however, the entire Gospel is filled with references to the Church, but in order to grasp them we have to see the Gospel in its relation to the Old Testament. We shall then notice that
—the entire preaching of Jesus,
—all the miracles of Jesus,
—the activities of Jesus,
all have reference to the Church. In Jesus' preaching, for example, we find mention of:
—Abraham, the Promise, Faith;
—Moses, the Covenant, the Law;
—David and the Kingdom;
—Solomon and the Temple;
—the Prophets;
—the Messias.
In the light of the Old Testament, all these themes appear as just so many new lights thrown upon the nature of the Church, the fulfillment of the promises and figures of the Old Testament. And Jesus' miracles appear as the signs of the Kingdom: Luke 7:22 (compare with Isaias 35:5-6).

But, in a still more profound sense, it must be understood that the entire **Revelation of the New Testament** (Trinity, Incarnation, Redemption) is closely correlated with the

95

Revelation of the **Church,** and in continuity with the **Old Testament.**

I. The Church's Link with the Old Testament

The entire Revelation of the New Testament is in continuity with the Old Testament. The New Testament Church is in continuity with the People of God of the Old Testament, as will appear more clearly in the following chapters.

The Trinity and the Old Testament

God's Unity is involved in the mystery of the Trinity just as much as the Trinity of Persons is, since the Trinity is not a Trinity of Gods, but a Trinity of Persons within the Unity of a single nature. Although it was the New Testament that revealed the Triune God, it was principally the Old Testament which revealed the One God. Because this notion of God's Unity had been so strongly inculcated by the long pedagogy of the Old Testament, there is no room for doubt when Jesus teaches us that God is Father, Son and Holy Spirit: He can be speaking of only the One God, the God of Abraham, Isaac and Jacob—Yahweh, the Lord God of Israel.

The Old Testament, therefore, paved the way for the revelation of the Trinity:
1. by revealing God's *unity;*
2. by revealing God as *living* (in contrast to the Baals);
3. by revealing God's *mystery;*
4. by revealing God as *Father* of His people.

Obviously, men did not understand yet the depths of this life, this mystery, this fatherhood, but these notions prepared them to receive the new revelation: the mystery of the Triune God: Father, Son and Holy Spirit, when the time came for such a revelation.

The Incarnation and the Old Testament

In order to appreciate the Incarnation, we must never lose sight of God's absolute Transcendance as it is revealed

96

by the Old Testament. God is the Creator of heaven and earth, of all beings, of Israel and of all nations. He is the transcendant God of Sinai, He Who cannot be looked upon without dying, He Who cannot be depicted. If we once lose sight of this revelation, we shall no longer appreciate the truth that God became Man. We are so accustomed to Christ's human aspect that we risk forgetting that He is God Incarnate through our very familiarity with the Gospels (cf. the Christmas and Epiphany hymns of the liturgy).

Redemption and the Old Testament

If we want to appreciate Christ's redemption, we have to develop an awareness of the sin which reigned in the world and of men's incapacity to escape it by their own unaided powers. Such is the meaning of the classical question concerning the Incarnation's delay. In this experience and history of mankind's awaiting of redemption, each one of us can understand his own history and experience. That is why the liturgy, particularly in Advent, reminds us of this long preparation for the Incarnation, this long awaiting of the Saviour, and why it puts upon the lips of the Church the appeals of the people of the Old Testament for Redemption.

II. The Church's Link with the New Testament

The entire Revelation of the New Testament is closely united to the reality of the Church.

The Trinity and the Mystery of the Church

1. God revealed the mystery of His inner life only when He also revealed the fact that all mankind is called upon to participate in it; God's revelation is not an object of speculation or of curiosity, but a mystery of love. God reveals Himself only in order to give Himself.

Throughout the whole of history there has always been a correlation between the Revelation of the Mystery of God and the Revelation of the Mystery of the Church. The first historical revelation of the true God goes back to Abraham. To him was given both a Revelation concerning the true God El, or Elohim, and a Revelation concerning the promised People of God.

Later on there was given both the Revelation of God as Yahweh and the Revelation of the covenant between Him and His Chosen People. The more God reveals Himself, the more He gives Himself.

Finally, in the New Testament we learn both the mystery of God's inner life (God is Love, God is Spirit), Father, Son and Holy Spirit, and the mystery of our participation in this life because we are sons in the Only Son and in the Spirit of the Son.

2. God revealed the mystery of His Unity first of all, so that men would not be tempted to think of "three Gods" when He revealed the distinction of **three Persons in God.** Similarly, God began by revealing the mystery of **our unity** as the People of God so that there would be no doubt possible when He insisted upon the personal value of each soul; the Mystical Body, the true People of God, is a communion of persons within the unity of Christ, just as the Trinity is a communion of Persons within the unity of a single divine life. We should not be surprised by the relatively late revelation concerning personal dignity and responsibility.

3. So long as God had merely revealed His unity, men did not know how far His love for His people extended, for they did not know to what point **God is love.** Further Revelation opened up both the Mystery of God's inner life: God is love, and the mystery of His love for us: God so loved the world....

"Greater love than this no one has, that one lay down his life...": before applying to the Mystery of Redemption and the Church this was already true of God's inner life in that the Father has no greater desire than to give His life to the Son. Because God is Spirit, He can give Himself completely; because He is Love, He can do so effectively. God's inner life, then, consists in a mystery of love: "each person exists only in order to give himself and by giving himself."

98

Through the mystery of the Incarnation and the Church the Holy Trinity extends this gift of life to us in order to have us participate in this mystery of love.

4. So long as God was not revealed as a Trinity, men did not know how far His Fatherhood extended. The people of the Old Testament could not know to what degree they were sons of God because they did not know that **God is a Father** in the strict sense and that he adopts all mankind in and through His incarnate Son: "We are sons in the Son."

The Incarnation and the Mystery of the Church

So long as men had no knowledge of the mystery of the Incarnation of the very Son of God, they did not know:

1. how far *God's covenant* with His people extended. This covenant was to be truly the marriage of His Son to humanity. The marriage allegories of the Old Testament finally received their plenary sense;

2. the exact nature of the **Messias,** the heir of the promises: He is not merely the Son of Abraham, but the very Son of God;

3. the nature of their long awaited *King:* not merely a descendant of David and the heir to his throne, but God Himself, King of the universe;

4. the *priesthood* of the Messias: true God and true man, uniting both men and God by His Incarnation;

5. the *kingdom* and the *people of God* which were identified with Christ Himself;

6. the *unity* of this kingdom, a unity within Christ Himself;

7. the *inheritance,* the Promised Land, the heavenly inheritance and divine life of which we are joint heirs in Christ.

Redemption and the Mystery of the Church

So long as men had no knowledge of the mystery of Christ Who died and rose again, they could not grasp:

1. the extent or malice of *sin.* The Old Testament depicted

99

sin as grave ingratitude and as a breaking of the Covenant, but men could not dream that sin would lead the Son of God to death on a Cross;

2. the extent of *God's love* "who has not spared even his own Son" (Romans 8:32);

3. the *Messias' love* for them: "Greater love than this no one has, that one lay down his life for his friends": it was by sacrificing His human life that He gave us His divine life;

4. their own *dignity as God's People,* purchased not with perishable silver or gold "but with the precious blood of Christ, as of a lamb without blemish and without spot" (I Peter 1:19);

5. the full meaning of the *prophecies of Isaias* (servant of Yahweh) and of the *Psalms;* their plenary sense was revealed to us only by Jesus during the course of His Passion;

6. the mysterious *identification* of the *Messias* and *Israel;* only after the Redemption was it clear that Christ included all mankind within Himself; we die with Him, we rise with Him.

After having shown how revelation is unified and brought together by the mystery of the Church, we shall now look at this mystery in itself. We shall discover the following characteristics throughout:

—the New Testament always appears as the *fulfillment* of the Old, the realization of the Old Testament promises;

—but this fulfillment is of such a *transcendant* nature compared to what men expected that it made a kind of break with the Old Testament (shadow and reality);

—although the New Testament is the fulfillment of the Old, yet it is itself *open towards the future* and awaits its consummation.

PROJECTS

Read through the Synoptic Gospels and pick out anything you find concerning the Church. You will probably end up with rather scanty results.

When you finish the second part of this work, repeat this reading of the Synoptics with the same purpose in mind.

Compare the results of your two investigations.

The Church in Jesus' Teaching

Chapter 18

THE CHURCH: THE OFFSPRING OF ABRAHAM

We shall discover the three characteristics pointed out in the preceding chapter:

(a) fulfillment of the Old Testament,
(b) transcendance in relation to the Old Testament,
(c) further perspectives.

Fulfillment

The promises made to Abraham found their realization in Jesus and in His Church. St. Matthew's gospel opens by affirming Jesus as "the Son of Abraham" (Matt. 1:1). And in the beginning of St. Luke's gospel the *Magnificat* of the Blessed Virgin and the *Benedictus* of Zachary represent the birth of Jesus as the realization of the promise made to Abraham: "He has given help to Israel, his servant, mindful of his mercy—even as he spoke to our fathers—to Abraham, and to his posterity forever" (Luke 1:55). "...To be mindful of his holy covenant, of the oath that he swore to Abraham our father" (Luke 1:73).

God had promised Abraham an heir, offspring (descendants) and inherited goods. Jesus is the heir. It is in Him that the promises made to Abraham find their realization: "In you shall all the nations of the earth be blessed" (Genesis 2:3); "that the blessing of Abraham might come to the Gentiles through Christ Jesus" (Galatians 3:14). St. Paul often reiterates this truth: "The promises were made to Abraham and to his offspring. He does not say, 'And to his offsprings,' as of many; but as of one, 'And to thy offspring,' who is Christ" (Galatians 3:16).

The offspring is, therefore, essentially Christ Himself, but all those who are united to Christ are also offspring and constitute the people promised to Abraham: "If you are Christ's, then you are the offspring of Abraham, heirs according to promise" (Galatians 3:29). The New Testament *Church* is, therefore, the **new people** in continuity with the People of the Old Testament; it inherits as a people; it is the Church as a community which acquires rights of inheritance (a common inheritance, joint heirs).

Abraham is, therefore, the Father of all believers.

The Church is Abraham's offspring.

Christians are the children of Abraham and therefore heirs of the promises.

Transcendance

The realization surpasses what went before it. The heir, Jesus, is not only the Son of Abraham according to the flesh, but also the eternal Son of God. The offspring, the true people of God, is not the offspring of Abraham according to the flesh, but *Abraham's offspring through faith*. It is this people according to the spirit which is in continuity with the "faithful remnant" of the Old Testament.

Jesus' preaching is filled with such affirmations; hence the astonishment and anger of the Jews. They believed that they were saved because they were of Abraham's stock (according to the flesh). But Jesus told them that this claim was absolutely useless to them unless they shared in Abraham's faith and good works.

"Do not think to say within yourselves, 'We have Abraham for our father'; for I say to you that God is able out of these stones to raise up children to Abraham" (Matt. 3:19).

St. John's Gospel in particular emphasizes this affirmation: "They answered and said to him, 'Abraham is our father.' Jesus said to them, 'If you are the children of Abraham, do the works of Abraham'" (John 8:39; read the whole of this Chapter 8).

Indeed, Abraham had been justified by Faith and the works of Faith and not by any fleshly advantage. Circumcision itself was merely a sign and proof of his Faith. St. Paul emphatically developed this truth in Chapter 4 of his Epistle to the Romans and in Chapter 3 of the Epistle to the Galatians. Similarly, it is by Faith and the works of Faith that we can share in the promises made to Abraham. "Abraham believed God, and it was credited to him as justice. Know therefore that the men of faith are the real sons of Abraham" (Galatians 3:7). And that is why the people of the New Testament welcome all nations, without distinction. Henceforth, circumcision and the works of the law are obsolete, and the promises pass from the Jews to the Gentiles. The Gospel expresses this passing-over in many ways:

—The *Gate* to the Kingdom is narrow: the Gentiles enter, the Jews are excluded (Luke 13:23-30).

—The *invited guests* who refused to come to the feast are the Jews; those invited in their place are the Gentiles (Luke 14:15-24).

—The *lost sheep* that Christ came to save represents the Gentiles; the ninety-nine just who have no need of repentance represent the Jews who believed themselves to be righteous because they were of Abraham's stock (Luke 15:3-7).

—The Gentiles, who were invited last to work in the *vineyard*, receive the same reward as the Jews, who were invited first (Matt. 20:1-16).

—The *murderous vine-dressers* represent the Jews; the Kingdom will be taken away from them and will be given to the Gentiles (Luke 20:9-18).

The New Testament Church, by going over and beyond the provisory economy of the Old Covenant, thus returns to the universalist outlook of the promise made to Abraham: "In you shall all the nations of the earth be blessed."

The promised **inheritance** also surpasses all that went before it. Instead of a country and earthly goods, or even divine blessings, Christ bestows a new and better inheritance: divine life. "But if we are sons, we are heirs also: heirs indeed of God and joint heirs with Christ" (Romans 8:17). This inheritance is the **Holy Spirit** (the guarantee of the presence of the Father and the Son and of our divinization): "that the blessing of Abraham might come to the

Gentiles through Christ Jesus, that through faith we might receive the promise of the Spirit" (Galatians 3:14).

Further Perspectives

The promise made to Abraham which is to be accomplished in Christ Jesus is not yet fully realized. All the nations of the world must be reunited in Christ. The mission of the New Testament Church is precisely "to preach the Gospel to every creature" and to baptize all of them in order to gather all together in Christ Jesus. Time is needed for this, and the time allotted will be that of the duration of the Church of the New Testament.

TEXTS

Read: St. John 8: Jesus and Abraham; Romans 4, 5, 6: Justification by Faith; Galatians 3, 4: Justification by Faith; Hebrews 11: Importance of Faith.

PROJECTS

1. In the light of the preceding chapter and texts show:
   (a) the importance of Faith in the Christian life and the gratuity of God's promises;
   (b) the universalism of the Church of the New Testament.
2. In the Acts of the Apostles study the various discourses of the apostles and deacons, and show how they present Jesus and the Church as the fulfillment of the promises of the Old Testament.

Chapter 19

THE CHURCH: THE NEW COVENANT

Fulfillment

Jesus respected the Mosaic Covenant and its entire religious framework, such as:

the Law (Circumcision),
the Temple (taxes),
the Feasts (Passover, Pentecost, etc.),
the religious personnel (priests, etc.).

For example, he ordered the leper he healed to conform to the Law: "Go, show thyself to the priest, and offer the gift that Moses commanded, for a witness to them" (Matt. 8:4). Jesus declared that He came **not to destroy the Law of Moses but to fulfill it.**

The Jews expected that with the coming of the Messias the Covenant and Law would be extended to all nations: Jerusalem and its Temple would then become the focal point of the whole world. And this is just what came to pass with Jesus and His Church. Philip was able to say with full truth: "We have found him of whom Moses in the Law and the Prophets wrote, Jesus the son of Joseph of Nazareth" (John 1:45). And the presence of Moses at the Transfiguration bore witness to the fact that the Covenant was fulfilled in Jesus (Matt. 17:3). In addition, Jesus Himself testified to the disciples of Emmaus that what Moses had predicted found its realization in Him (Luke 24:27).

Transcendance

But this Covenant which is extended to the whole world is an entirely *new* Covenant, and the Law, now become universal, is an entirely *new* Law. The Jews thought that the

Messias would extend the very institutions of the Mosaic covenant and the ritual obligations of the Law, as they interpreted them, to the whole world. But the Gospels show how Jesus' law fulfills the law of Moses in a transcendant manner, and the Epistle to the Hebrews shows how the new covenant fulfills the Mosaic covenant in a transcendant manner.

I. The Law

First of all, Jesus rid the Law of Moses of all the additional burdens, interpretations and deformations inflicted upon it by the Pharisees. In Chapter 23 St. Matthew recounts Jesus' terrible indictment of the Pharisees: "The Scribes and the Pharisees have sat on the chair of Moses. All things, therefore, that they command you, observe and do. But do not act according to their works; for they talk but do nothing... But woe to you, Scribes and Pharisees, hypocrites! because you shut the kingdom of heaven against men." Jesus repeated this malediction eight times: "Woe to you."

St. John also shows the opposition between Jesus and the Jews on the subject of Moses, particularly in chapters 5, 7 and 9. "Do not think that I shall accuse you to the Father. There is one who accuses you, Moses, in whom you hope" (John 5:45).

Then Jesus presents the new Law, the law of the New Testament, as an improvement over the law of Moses. The new law is both **more interior** and more demanding; it touches upon not only exterior acts, but the heart itself. For example, while Moses had forbidden merely murder (Matt. 5:21) and adultery (Matt. 5:27), Jesus forbids even feelings of hatred (Matt. 5:22) and impure thoughts (Matt. 5:28).

The new law is also more **universal**. It extended the commandment of love not merely to the members of the Jewish community, but to all men without distinction of race or religion, and even to enemies (Matt. 5:38-46). Such is the meaning of the parable of the good Samaritan (Luke 10:25-37).

But above all, the new law has Jesus Himself as its model: "A new commandment I give you, that you love one another: that as I have loved you, you also love one another" (John 13:34).

"Thus the Law had Jesus Christ in shadows and figures, as in an imperfect sketch. But it did not have the finished picture. And just as the finished painting blots out the imperfect outlines, so the perfect beauty of the Gospel blots out the imperfection of the Law by its more vivid and striking colors. That is why Jesus changes water into wine, that is to say, the Law of Moses into His Gospel...." (Bossuet)[1]

II. The Covenant

Jesus presents His passion as the sacrifice of the new covenant: "This is my blood of the new covenant, which is being shed for many unto the forgiveness of sins" (Matt. 26:28).

The Epistle to the Hebrews exalts the superiority of this new dispensation.

—Superiority of the *Mediator* of the new covenant (Hebrews 3). Jesus makes the new covenant as the Son of God, while Moses was the mediator of the former covenant merely as the servant of God.

—Superiority of the *priesthood* of the new covenant (Hebrews 5, 6 and 7). Jesus is the *perfect, sinless* and *eternal priest,* while the priests of the previous covenant were mortal men and had to offer sacrifices first of all for their own sins. The priesthood of the New Testament will then be a participation in this perfect and everlasting priesthood of Jesus.

—Superiority of the *sacrifice* of the new covenant (Hebrews 8, 9 and 10). It is offered in the true sanctuary which is Jesus Himself and no longer in a temple made with hands; it is made up of the very blood of Christ and not of animal blood; it is the final, unique and perfect sacrifice, offered once for all, for nothing can be added to it.

It is the **perfect sacrifice** which in the Church replaces the many sacrifices of the old covenant. So it is that the entire

1 Sermon of the II Sunday after Epiphany (*Oeuvres complètes,* tome 2, p. 145).

religious organization of the old covenant is replaced by the religious organization of the new covenant, namely, the Church of the New Testament in which we now live.

Further Perspectives

This covenant must ultimately embrace the entire world. Such is the very purpose of the Church's existence.

TEXTS

—Matthew 5, 6 and 7: The Law of Jesus and the Law of Moses.
—John 5, 7 and 9: The opposition of Jesus and the Jews over Moses.
—Matthew 23: Jesus' maledictions of the Pharisees.
—Hebrews: The contrast between the two covenants.

PROJECTS

With the foregoing chapter and references in mind:
1. Compare the Law of Jesus and the Law of Moses regarding the demands of purity and charity.
2. Show the superiority of Jesus' sacrifice as it is set forth in the Epistle to the Hebrews.

Chapter 20

THE CHURCH: THE NEW KINGDOM

Fulfillment

The Jews awaited the Kingdom, the object of God's promises and the Prophets' preaching. At the time of Jesus there were various Messianic currents:

1. **Royal Messianism** (from the time of the institution of royalty and of David): The Messias, the Son of David, will re-establish the Kingdom of Israel, and through it, God's reign.

Within this current, which was the most widespread, two conceptions existed:

(a) the *rabbinical* conception: the universal Kingdom would be realized without violence by the voluntary submission of all nations to the Law of Yahweh.

(b) the *popular* conception: the universal kingdom would be inaugurated to the accompaniment of great marvels, and the peoples of the earth would be subjected by force.

2. **Apocalyptic Messianism** (from the time of Daniel's prophecies): The Messias would come on the clouds of heaven to take solemn possession of His kingdom.

3. **Suffering Messianism of Isaias:** This latter was rather overshadowed by the preceding ideas.

We can then imagine the excitement aroused by the preaching of John the Baptist: "The kingdom of heaven is at hand." (Think, for example, of such emotion-charged words as "peace" and "liberation" as they were used during the last war.)

With the coming of Jesus the Kingdom was established, and all the prophecies were in the process of being accomplished. Elias—John the Baptist—had come. The theme of all of Jesus' preaching was the Kingdom of God:

—men must enter that Kingdom.
—conditions for such an entry: faith and baptism.
—the Spirit of the Kingdom: the beatitudes.
—life in the Kingdom: charity.
—the parables: "The Kingdom of Heaven is like..."

Jesus' mission was to set up this Kingdom. Until His time men awaited the Kingdom in hope, but now that the Kingdom has come, men live in and of it by faith.

Transcendance

I. Jesus rectifies the conception of the Kingdom.

Jesus accepts the title Son of David and, therefore, royal Messianism and the Messianic kingdom, but "His Kingdom is not of this world." It is not temporal monarchy.

Judaism was an ethnic and religious community. Jesus separates the cause of His Kingdom from that of the Jewish community:

(a) His Kingdom will not be bound up with a temporal power, to an ethnic and national community. Notice how new and revolutionary this is to the Jewish ideas of the time. And yet such is the true meaning of "Render unto Caesar the things that are Caesar's." The Kingdom will be universal, but in a spiritual way—in Christ. Men no longer have to issue from Abraham according to the flesh but according to faith. The Old Testament theocracy will no longer be of a temporal nature, but will be realized in the Church which is to be independent of all temporal power and governed directly by God.

(b) His Kingdom will not be tied to the Law and Jewish customs: circumcision does not render men just of itself. The Law was merely a pedagogue to lead men to Christ.

The Apostles became aware of this only gradually. Even after Pentecost, there were still hesitations: "Must one be a Jew first before becoming a Christian?" (Acts of the Apostles). It took several crises and the determined intervention of St. Paul to free the Church from Judaism: "Must one be

110

a Jew?"—spiritually, yes (faith), carnally, no (observance of the Law).

Jesus accepts the Messianism of the Son of Man coming on the clouds of heaven, but He puts it off until the time of the Second Coming.

Jesus brings out the full meaning of the Messianism of the suffering Servant and of Isaias' Son of Man: "Did not Christ have to suffer these things (Messianism of the suffering Servant) before entering into glory?" (Apocalyptic Messianism).

To enter the Kingdom we have to imitate Christ and go through what He first went through Himself: take up one's cross and follow Him. "Die with Him in order to rise with Him."

II. The Kingdom is identified with Christ.

But the real break between the Kingdom and the People of the Old Testament in relation to its realization in the New comes from its identification with Christ Himself:

(a) *Abraham's offspring* is Christ (Gal. 3:16) and Christians (Gal. 2:29).

(b) In the Old Testament *the Vine* is the people (Isaias). But Jesus said: "I am the Vine." St. Matthew applied to Jesus a prophecy which concerned the people historically: "Out of Egypt I have called my Son" (Matt. 3:15).

(c) In the synoptic Gospels a *discrimination* is made among men on the basis of their relationship to the Kingdom just as it is by their relationship with Christ: there are those who refuse and those who accept.

(d) Pentecost revealed *both* the true notion of *Christ* and the true notion of the *Kingdom.* So long as the Apostles had not understood the true notion of the Christ, they were unable to grasp the true notion of His Kingdom. It is always noticeable that a more exact understanding of the Kingdom accompanies a more exact understanding of Christ Himself. "You will know that I am in my Father, and you in me, and I in you" (John 14:20). That is why the preaching of the Apostles concerns both Christ and the Kingdom. See the

111

Acts: Christ is true God and true man. All men are summoned to enter into His Kingdom.

(e) Both Christ and the Church were revealed to *St. Paul* at the same time: Christ revealed Himself to him in His Church: "I am Jesus whom thou art persecuting." We can notice in St. Paul that as he progressed in his knowledge of Christ, he also progressed in his knowledge of the Church. Compare the great epistles (to the Romans, Galatians and Corinthians) and the epistles of the captivity (to the Ephesians, Philippians and Colossians). The *mystery of Christ* which it was his mission to preach was as much that of the Church as that of Christ.

—From the idea of the people of God and of the Kingdom we thus pass to the idea of *the Body of Christ:* "the notion of God's People remains, but it becomes more interior and spiritual. Instead of being simply His people, the Christian community is also *the Body of Christ.* Its unity stems from the life of Christ which circulates in it and in each of its members" (Cerfaux).

—Whence the extraordinary unity:

(a) between Christ and His Kingdom,
(b) between the members of this Kingdom.

Further Perspectives

The Kingdom must grow, expand, cover the face of the earth. Such is the meaning of Our Lord's parables on the grain of mustard seed (Matt. 13:31-32) and the leaven (Matt. 13:33). While awaiting its final consummation, the Kingdom contains both good and bad: parables of the net (Matt. 13:47-50) and the weeds among the wheat (Matt. 13:24-30). There is, therefore, an earthly phase to the Kingdom, and during this phase the Kingdom is in the process of growth and becoming. Because of this fact Christ must remain present in some way in His Kingdom in order to propose it to every man coming into the world, in order to extend it to the ends of the earth.

That is why Christ founded His Church upon the foundation of Peter and the other Apostles. Notice the importance

112

of this preoccupation in Christ's life; He spent the greater part of His ministry doing it: He chose His Apostles, formed them for their mission, gave them His powers, organized them with Peter at their head.

He transposed to His Apostles everything He said of Himself: "I am the light of the world"—"You are the light of the world." In reality, it is Jesus Himself Who in His Apostles and their successors remains present on earth in order to continue the establishment of the Kingdom: the Kingdom is on the march and needs to be directed; it is in the process of growth and needs to be nourished and supported; the Kingdom has not yet arrived at its goal and, therefore, must be militant, make progress, and not attach itself to present achievements nor sink into self-satisfaction.

Just as the people of the Old Testament, in going out of Egypt, had to make their way across the desert toward the promised land under the direction of Moses and Josue representing Yahweh, so now the true people of God is en route towards the true promised land under the guidance of Peter and the other Apostles, the true representatives of Christ; or, rather, Christ Himself in His Apostles leads toward the goal which is the consummation of the Kingdom in the Church Triumphant: "Behold, I am with you all days, even unto the consummation of the world" (Matt. 28:20).

Pentecost was to be the Church's real beginning: the Holy Spirit whom He sent to His Apostles was to make them understand their mission and to give them the strength to accomplish it. This coming of the Holy Spirit was also Jesus' return, but this time in His Apostles, in His Church: "You will know that I am in the Father and you in me, and I in you" (John 14:20).

It was in an **eschatological perspective** that Christ established His Church: the Kingdom needs this organization because it has not yet attained the confines of the world, and so that it can attain them. Such is the real reply to Loisy's statement: "Jesus announced the Kingdom, but there resulted only the Church." The Church is precisely this Kingdom in its earthly stage of growth: it is the Kingdom in the process of becoming. It was precisely so that the final Kingdom would be eventually realized that Jesus foresaw and founded His Church. See in this sense the parables of the steward (Matt. 24:45-51) and the servants (Mark 13:32-37); of the talents (Matt. 25:14-30) and the gold pieces (Luke 19:11-28).

The Kingdom that we know here below, the Church founded by Jesus Christ on the Apostles, is, therefore, merely *the earthly and visible phase of the Kingdom*, before its completion at Christ's return.

TEXTS

—Matthew 5: The Spirit of the Kingdom

—Matthew 13
—Matthew 24:45-51 } The parables of the Kingdom
—Matthew 25:14-30

PROJECTS

1. Using the Kingdom parables show the Kingdom in its various stages:

—the earthly stage (growth, mixture),

—at Christ's return (judgment, separation),

—the final and heavenly stage (reward).

2. In chapter 13 of St. Matthew what are we taught about the Kingdom of God by:

—the parable of the grain of mustard seed?

—the parable of the leaven?

—the parable of the net?

—the parable of the treasure?

3. Find examples in the Gospel which illustrate the beatitudes of Matthew 5:1-11, especially in the Sermon on the Mount itself (Matt. 5, 6 and 7).

Chapter 21

JESUS, THE MESSIAS, REALIZES THE PROMISES, THE COVENANT, THE KINGDOM

Fulfillment

In Him were realized the different Messianic titles:

—"*Son of Adam*" (St. Luke's genealogy, Luke 3:38). Therefore, Christ is not merely the heir of the chosen people but the new Adam who is to restore all mankind to the status of divine sonship.

—"*Son of Abraham*" (St. Matthew's genealogy, Matt. 1:1). Therefore, the heir to the promises.

—"*Son of David.*" Therefore, the heir to the throne of David His father. The King of Israel, the King of the Jews.

—"*The Messias*" (John 4:25: "I who speak with thee am he").

—"*The Saviour*" (John 4:42: "This is in truth the Saviour of the world").

—"*The Son of Man*" (who must suffer and die: Mark 8:31, who will come in glory to judge the living and the dead: Matt. 25:31).

The Messias possesses various prerogatives: He is King, Priest (Epistle to the Hebrews) and Prophet.

In Jesus are fulfilled all the prophecies of the Old Testament concerning the Messias: "We have found him of whom Moses in the Law and the Prophets wrote, Jesus the son of Joseph of Nazareth" (John 1:45). "Behold, we are going up to Jerusalem, and all the things that have been written by the prophets concerning the Son of Man will be accomplished. For he will be delivered to the Gentiles..." (Luke 18:31).

115

Transcendance

1. **His person:** He is not merely the Son of Abraham but the Son of God. The Jews expected God's representative, and it was God Himself Who came. Jesus revealed the Mystery of His Person only gradually. In the synoptic Gospels He insists perhaps more on the Kingdom than on His own person. This revelation of the mystery of the pre-existent Christ is clearer in St. Paul. It is complete in St. John: Jesus is the *Incarnate Word,* the *Son of God.*

Consequently, He realizes all the prophecies but to an unexpected degree: He is the Son of God but in the strict sense;—He is King, not merely of Israel, but of the world and all Creation (St. Paul);—He is the Son of Man coming upon the clouds of heaven to judge the world that He had received by right inheritance;—He is priest, but not in the way the high priest was (Hebrews), but priest by His very incarnation;—He is the suffering Servant, the Redeemer, not just of Israel, but of the world, that is to say, of all mankind and of creation;—the Heir, not merely of Abraham, but of God.

2. **His place in the Kingdom:** in the Old Testament the Messias is viewed in relation to the Kingdom. In the New Testament there is a progressive reversal of values: it is the person of Jesus, which becomes the focal point, and we speak of the Kingdom in its relation to Him.

Trace this progressive revelation through the Synoptics. A few indications: compare John the Baptist's and Jesus' preaching on the Kingdom. It is He that we must follow in order to enter the Kingdom;—it is in Him that we must believe;—it is our attitude towards Him which determines our entrance into the Kingdom;—what we do to any member of the Kingdom is done to Jesus Himself. See in this sense Our Lord's description of the Last Judgment: "I was hungry . . ." (Matt. 25:31 ff.).

What is merely sketched out for us in the synoptic Gospels is fully developed in St. Paul and St. John.

Further Perspectives

The Messias Himself awaits the full manifestation of His Royalty; He awaits the consummation of the Kingdom in order to return on the clouds of heaven as *conqueror* and *judge*. When He will have vanquished death and put all things under His feet, He will put all things back into His Father's hands.

PROJECTS

1. From St. Matthew show how Jesus fulfills the prophecies.
2. From the preaching of the Kingdom show how Jesus is its focal point: He it is who judges, He it is whom we must follow, etc.

The Church in Jesus' Ministry
Chapter 22
JESUS FOUNDS THE CHURCH

Jesus Chooses and Forms His Apostles

One major preoccupation sums up Jesus' life, namely, the establishment of the Kingdom of God; all His mysteries, all His preaching, all His work were aimed at this. But the earthly phase of that Kingdom, between Jesus' ascension and His final return, is realized by the Church of the New Testament. That is why Jesus dedicated His entire ministry to founding the Church, His Church.

He chose His Apostles. From the very beginning of His ministry Jesus was intent upon finding the men needed for such a work. Most of them were Galilean fishermen. Jesus was to make them "fishers of men" (Luke 5:1-11). Another was a public official (Luke 5:27-32). Jesus said to him: "Follow me."

But the choice was too important not to surround it with every precaution: after a night spent in prayer (Luke 6:12) Jesus made a solemn choice from among his first disciples. He set apart twelve of them *that they might be with him* and that he might send them forth to preach...to cure sicknesses and to cast out devils" (Mark 3:14-15). These twelve men He named apostles. Henceforth, they were to share His life, "be with him." They were the witnesses of His miracles, the auditors of His doctrine, the companions of His nights spent in prayer. Jesus dedicated the majority of His time to forming, instructing and correcting them. It was to them that He explained the meaning of His parables rather than to the crowds (Matthew 13:11). He initiated them into the ministry. He sent them forth to preach: "And as you go, preach the message, 'The kingdom of heaven is at hand'" (Matthew 10:7). At the Last Supper it was to these Apostles that He gave the power to consecrate His Body and Blood. Then after His resurrection, when He Himself had finished His earthly ministry, He commissioned them to do what He had done: "As the Father has sent me, I also send you" (John 20:21). He also transmitted to them His own power over sin: "Receive the Holy Spirit; whose sins you shall forgive, they are forgiven them; and whose sins you shall retain, they are retained" (John 20:23). And finally as a solemn commission: "All power on heaven and on earth has been given to me. Go, therefore, and make disciples of all nations, baptizing them in the name of the Father, and of the Son, and of the Holy Spirit, teaching them to observe all that I have commanded you; and behold, I am with you all days, even unto the consummation of the world" (Matt. 28:18-20).

Jesus Sends the Holy Spirit upon His Church

But the Apostles were still without the Holy Spirit. Jesus had often promised Him to them. On the morning of the Ascension He renewed this promise: "You shall receive power when the Holy Spirit comes upon you, and you shall be witnesses for me in Jerusalem and in all Judea and Samaria and even to the very ends of the earth" (Acts of the Apostles 1:8).

This promised descent of the Holy Spirit took place within the framework of the Jewish feast of Pentecost, the feast commemorating the giving of the law on Mount Sinai, as if to point out that a new era of salvation would replace the former temporary covenant of Sinai.

"When the days of Pentecost were drawing to a close, they were all together in one place. And suddenly there came a sound from heaven, as of a violent wind blowing, and it filled the whole house where they were sitting. And there appeared to them parted tongues as of fire, which settled upon each of them. And they were all filled with the Holy Spirit and began to speak in foreign tongues, even as the Holy Spirit prompted them to speak" (Acts 2:4).

After the visible mission of Jesus there now began the

visible mission of the Holy Spirit whom Jesus sent to animate His Church. And Jesus never ceases sending this Holy Spirit upon the Church to enlighten, guide and strengthen it. Christ acts in His Church *interiorly* by the Holy Spirit and *exteriorly* by the ministry of the Church.

Jesus Makes Peter the Head of His Church

Peter stood out among the Apostles almost from the beginning, and Jesus chose him in a particularly solemn fashion. There are three essential texts concerning him:

1. **Jesus makes Peter the head.**—As reported by St. Matthew 16:13-20, the scene took place at Caesarea Philippi. First of all, Jesus had Peter proclaim his faith: "Thou art the Christ, the Son of the Living God." Then Jesus solemnly declared: "And I say to thee, thou art Peter, and upon this rock I will build my Church, and the gates of hell shall not prevail against it. And I will give thee the keys of the kingdom of heaven; and whatever thou shalt bind on earth shall be bound in heaven, and whatever thou shalt loose on earth shall be loosed in heaven." Peter received the keys, that is, power to command as head and leader.

2. **Jesus gives Peter the mission of strengthening the faith of his brethren.**—It was on Holy Thursday evening; after having predicted Peter's denials, Jesus also predicted that after this momentary cowardice it would be he who would strengthen the others: "But I have prayed for thee, that thy faith may not fail; and do thou, when once thou hast turned again, strengthen thy brethren" (Luke 22:32).

3. **Jesus confers supreme power on Peter.**—After the resurrection Jesus had Peter proclaim his love three times, and He in turn three times proclaimed Peter as possessing the highest office in the Church: "Feed my lambs, feed my sheep" (John 21:15-17).

During His earthly life Jesus Himself was the shepherd (John 10:1-18), but when He was about to quit this world, it was Peter who was to assume this shepherd's role in a visible manner. It was Peter who would unite and guide the flock.

Thus Jesus saw to everything. When He departed from

this world at the Ascension, He left only His Church here below. But it was well organized around Peter and the Apostles. Animated from within by the Holy Spirit, it was this Church which was to bring about the Kingdom of God on earth. Hence, **apostolic succession** will always be the criterion of the true Church. Today, as in the time of Tertullian, we are assured of our connection with Christ by means of this apostolic succession:

"They (the Apostles) obtained the promised power of the Holy Spirit for the gift of miracles and utterance, and after first bearing witness to the faith in Jesus Christ throughout Judea and founding churches there, they next went forth into the world and preached the same doctrine of the same faith to the nations and founded churches in every city, from which all other churches, one after another, derived the tradition of faith and the seeds of doctrine, and are every day deriving them, that they may become churches. Indeed, it is on this account only that they are able to consider themselves apostolic, as being the offspring of apostolic churches.... From this, therefore, do we draw up our rule. Since the Lord Jesus Christ sent the Apostles to preach, no others ought to be received as preachers than those whom Christ appointed, for 'no one knows the Father except the Son, and he to whom the Son reveals Him.' Nor does the Son seem to have revealed Him to any other than the Apostles whom He sent forth to preach—that, of course, which He had revealed to them" (Tertullian).[1]

TEXTS

—John 1:35-51; Luke 5:1-11; 5:27-32; 6:12-16: The call of the Apostles.

—Matthew 9:35-38; 10:5-16: The first mission.

—Matthew 28:16-20; John 20:21-23: The solemn commission.

—Matthew 16:13-20; Luke 22:32; John 21:15-17: Peter, head of the Church.

—Acts 1 & 2: Pentecost and the first converts.

PROJECTS

1. Find everything concerning Peter in the Gospels. Try to reconstruct his life, his character, his role in the Church.

---

[1] *De Praescriptione Haereticorum*, 20-21; P.L. 2, 32-33.

2. Find the passages in the Gospels which indicate with what care Jesus formed His Apostles.

3. From St. John's Gospel pick out the various promises of the Holy Spirit and the effects He will produce.

C. The Phase to Come: The Apocalypse

The following is a short summary of the Apocalypse of St. John:

(a) *Aim:* a book of consolation (characteristic of every Apocalypse) for the persecuted Christian communities of Asia Minor.

(b) *Form:* a divine ecstasy (1:10) described in a special literary style. Two good reasons for not pressing its symbolism too far.

(c) *Content:* introduction, chaps. 1, 2 and 3: Christ, the master of history, examines our lives.

Chaps. 4 and 5: a celestial vision of the Father who gives meaning to all things and who acts through the Lamb Who redeems.

Chaps. 6 through 18: the work of the Lamb Who "Restores all things in Christ," even in the midst of persecutions.

Chaps. 19-22: the consummation, the marriage feast of the Lamb and the bride, the spouse of the Lamb.

But it is not only the Apocalypse of St. John which speaks of this consummation. The prophetic visions of the Old Testament mingled much eschatological material in with their descriptions of the Messianic times, and the New Testament as a whole is filled with eschatological expectancy. In the preceding pages we have seen that the Kingdom in its earthly phase both awaits and actively prepares its heavenly consummation. The New Testament frequently refers to this consummation, to the parousia, the "Day of the Lord."

The following are the principal New Testament texts having reference to this **"Day of the Lord"**:

—Mark 13; Matthew 24; Luke 21: the eschatological discourses.

122

—I Corinthians 7:29; 15:51.
—II Corinthians 4:14.
—I Thessalonians 4:13; 5:11.
—II Thessalonians 2:1-12.
—Romans 11:25 ff.;—cf. 11:11-12, 15.
—Hebrews 10:25-39.
—Titus 2:13.
—I Timothy 6:13-15; 4:1.
—II Timothy 3:1 ff.
—I Peter 1:1 ff.; 4:13; cf. I John 2:18; James 5.
—II Peter 3: The first Christians may have been mistaken as to the imminence of the parousia, but Peter has given us the solution: "Beloved, do not be ignorant of this one thing, that one day with the Lord is as a thousand years, and a thousand years as one day."

Chapter 23

THE CHURCH AWAITS CHRIST'S RETURN

Many Christians would undoubtedly be surprised to hear that the primary object of the Church's hope is Christ's return. It seems to them that Christ's life came to a close on Calvary. What follows the account of the Passion in the Gospel appears to them as a mere appendix to Christ's life, as Father de Montcheuil has remarked. Besides, is not the commonest representation of Christ that of Christ crucified? The summit of the liturgical year appears to be Good Friday, rather than the feast of Easter which follows.

The Glorious Mysteries

But we can easily widen our perspective and rectify our ideas as to the following points:

First of all, there is the **Resurrection;** it is essential to the mystery of Christ and to our Redemption. Christ died only to rise again. What saves us is not merely, nor even principally, Christ's death, but both His death and His Resurrection. "Did not Christ have to suffer these things before entering into his glory?" (Luke 24:26). And His disciples will also have to die with Christ in order to rise with Him: "We suffer with him that we may also be glorified with him" (Romans 8:17).

The summit of the liturgical year is not Good Friday, but Easter. Yet we must pass through Good Friday in order to get to Easter. "*By* His Passion and Cross *to* the glory of His Resurrection..."; we say these words three times a day when reciting the Angelus.

Then there are the **Ascension** and **Pentecost,** which are equally essential to the Mystery of Christ and our Redemption. Christ entered heaven as the firstfruits of regenerated humanity. It was only after the Ascension that the glorified Christ sent the Holy Spirit at Pentecost and so gave birth to His Church.

Now that Christ has returned to heaven and has sent the Holy Spirit, it seems that His earthly life is finished, that He has lived all His mysteries, He has completed His visible mission. The Mystery of Christ is finished: now we have the Mystery of the Holy Spirit and the Church.

The Mystery of the Return

But such is not the whole truth. Christ's life is not finished. He still has some Mysteries to live: just as He came visibly into this world a first time, so He must return visibly to this earth. Christ is like an actor who has withdrawn into the wings between two acts and prepares to return on the scene. And this return of Christ is the principal object of **the Church's hope.** This truth is written so large throughout the New Testament that it is not necessary to prove it. We have merely to open our eyes to what is so prominently taught throughout the whole New Testament, rather than make a massive collection of texts. The following are a few examples taken haphazardly to direct our attention and show under what forms this truth is presented:

"For the grace of God our Saviour has appeared to all men, instructing us, in order that. . .we may live temperately and justly and piously in this world; looking for the blessed hope and glorious coming of our great God and Saviour, Jesus Christ . . ." (Titus 2:11-13).

"You turned to God from idols, to serve the living and true God, and to await from heaven Jesus, his Son, whom he raised from the dead, who has delivered us from the wrath to come" (I Thessalonians 1:9-10).

"But our citizenship is in heaven from which also we eagerly await a Saviour, Our Lord Jesus Christ, who will refashion the body of our lowliness, conforming it to the body of his glory. . ." (Philippians 3:20-21).

Thus the whole of Scripture makes the following two af-firmations in a variety of ways:

—The Church's hope is essentially the return of Christ;

—Christ will return as **Judge**, as the **Lord** of Glory, as uni-versal **King**.

The Creed also sums up our faith in the same way:

> "And He shall come again in glory
> to judge the living and the dead:
> and of His kingdom there shall be no end."

The first time Christ did not come as Judge, but as Saviour: "I have not come to judge the world, but to save the world" (John 12:47; cf. Luke 19:10).

The first time Christ did not come in the glory which was His right as Son, but in the voluntary lowliness of the Saviour: "... Christ Jesus, who though he was by nature God, did not consider being equal to God a thing to be clung to, but emptied himself, taking the nature of a slave and being made like unto men. And appearing in the form of man, he humbled himself, becoming obedient to death, even to death on a cross" (Philippians 2:6-8).

The first time Christ did not come as a King, but as a slave (Phil. 2:7; Matt. 20:28), despite the fact that He was the King of men and of the world (Hebrews 1:2).

But one day He will return as the Judge, the Lord of Glory, the universal King: "Cum gloria, judicare, cujus regni non erit finis." Such is the essential object of the Church's hope.

St. Augustine portrays for us the dispositions with which we should await Christ's return: **like a faithful wife awaits her husband's return.**

"The chaste wife fears lest her husband depart; the adul-terous wife fears lest he return. If the husbands of both are away, the former fears that he will not arrive, the latter fears that he will arrive too soon.... He to whom we are espoused is in some way absent; He who gave us the Holy Spirit as the pledge of His fidelity is absent... Let His spouse ask herself if she be chaste... Our Spouse is absent; examine your conscience: do you want Him to come or do you want Him to delay a little longer?...

"Chaste fear, brethren, has this sign: it proceeds from love.

126

But fear which is not chaste proceeds from fear of the presence and punishments of the spouse. . . .

"In what way is this fear chaste? Let each one ask himself this question: If God made the following proposal to me, what would I answer? . . . 'Take for yourself all the earthly goods that you covet, and live in them, not merely for a time, but forever. Only remember that you will never see my face.' Chaste fear would weep and groan and would say: 'Rather, take away all these good things, and let me see your face.'" [1]

PROJECTS

1. From a Gospel or Epistle pick out texts concerning Christ's return and show what they teach us about Jesus.

Read especially:

—the parables of the Kingdom;

—the eschatological discourses; for example, Matthew 24 and 25;

—the two Epistles to the Thessalonians.

2. Compare Jesus' two comings as they are described in the New Testament and the Liturgy, following the indications given in this chapter.

See especially the liturgies of Advent, Christmas, the Ascension, and that of the Faithful Departed.

---

[1] *Enarratio in Psalmum 127*, 8-9; P.L. 37, 1681-1682.

Chapter 24
"THE WORLD TO COME"

This return of Christ will inaugurate "the world to come" which is to succeed this present world.

Judgment

At His return Christ will judge all things. When judgment is spoken of in Scripture, there is meant more this general judgment at the end of time than the particular and individual judgment at the time of our death. Here again, we shall try to clarify matters a little rather than make a collection of texts. Here are a few examples to direct our attention:

1. **In Scripture.**—Think of the great judgment scenes found in *the Synoptics:* "When the Son of Man shall come in his majesty, and all the angels with him, then will he sit on the throne of his glory, and before him will be gathered all the nations, and he will separate them one from another, as the shepherd separates the sheep from the goats" (Matt. 25:31; cf. Matt. 19:28). It is on that day that the weeds will be separated from the wheat: "The harvest is the end of the world" (Matt. 13:39).

Think of *St. Paul:* "He who judges me is the Lord. Therefore, pass no judgment before the time, until the Lord comes, who will both bring to light the things hidden in darkness and make manifest the counsels of hearts; and then everyone will have his praise from God" (I Cor. 4:5).

"I charge thee, in the sight of God and Christ Jesus, who will judge the living and the dead by his coming and by his kingdom... I have fought the good fight, I have finished the course, I have kept the faith. For the rest, there is laid up for me a crown of justice, which the Lord, the just Judge, will give to me in that day; yet not to me only, but also to those who love his coming" (II Timothy 4:1 and 8).

2. **In the Liturgy.**—Likewise, in the liturgy of the faithful departed, there is question more of the general judgment at the last day than of the particular judgment.

Think of the *Dies Irae:*

> Day of wrath! O day of mourning!
> Heaven and earth in ashes burning . . .
> When from heaven the Judge descendeth . . .
> When the Judge his seat shall gain . . .
> With thy favored sheep O place me. . . .
> (cf. Matt. 25:32).

Think of the *Libera:*

> Deliver me, O Lord, from eternal death on that awful day,
> When the heavens and the earth shall be moved,
> When thou shalt come to judge the world by fire.

The real judgment is, therefore, this general judgment on the last day; the particular judgment which awaits each one of us in particular when we quit the body is only a partial anticipation of it, as we shall see later.

The Resurrection of the Body

The resurrection of the body will come to pass at Christ's glorious return. We have put so much stress on the life of the soul that we must rediscover the importance of this resurrection of the body in the New Testament and the Liturgy.

Here are a few indications for directing our attention in reading these sources:

1. **In the New Testament.**—Think of the discussions of St. Paul with the Sadducees in Chapters 23 and 24 of the *Acts of the Apostles:* "It is about the hope and the resurrection of the dead that I am on trial."

Think of his great argument in I Corinthians 15: "If there is no resurrection from the dead, neither has Christ risen . . . But as it is, Christ has risen from the dead, the firstfruits of those who have fallen asleep."

To die is to sow a glorious body—a definition to which we are not accustomed: "What is sown in corruption rises in incorruption; what is sown in dishonor rises in glory..." (I Cor. 15:43). He affirms this everywhere: "...we eagerly await a Saviour, our Lord Jesus Christ, who will refashion the body of our lowliness, conforming it to the body of his glory by exerting the power by which he is able also to subject all things to himself" (Phil. 3:21).

Through grace the Holy Spirit is given to us as the pledge of our resurrection: "If the Spirit of him who raised Jesus from the dead dwells in you, then he who raised Jesus Christ from the dead will also bring to life your mortal bodies because of his Spirit who dwells in you" (Romans 8:11). "We who have the firstfruits of the Spirit—we ourselves groan within ourselves, waiting for the adoption of sons, the redemption of our body" (Romans 8:23).

Think of the Discourse on the Bread of Life in Chapter 6 of St. John: "He who eats my flesh and drinks my blood has life everlasting and I will raise him up on the last day." Only too often we consider the Eucharist as merely food for the soul, but Jesus gives it to us also as a pledge of our bodily resurrection. We must rediscover this aspect of the Eucharist in the Liturgy: "O sacred banquet...wherein the pledge of future glory is given unto us."

Similar ideas are expressed in patristic literature. Here, for example, is how St. Cyril of Alexandria puts it: "Not only the soul had to be renewed in newness of life through the Holy Spirit, but this gross and earthly body of ours also had to be sanctified through a corporeal communion in conformity with its nature, and so also receive incorruption... For it is impossible that He who is Life by nature does not triumph over corruption and destroy death. Consequently, although death condemns the human body to corruption, because Christ is in us through His flesh, we shall necessarily rise again." [1]

2. **In the Liturgy.**—*The Apostles' Creed:* "I believe...in

---

[1] *In Joan. Evangel.,* lib. 4; P.G. 73, 580-581.

the resurrection of the body." In the *Nicean Creed:* "I look for the resurrection of the dead."

In the Epistle of the *Burial Mass:* "If we believe that Jesus died and rose again, so with him God will bring those also who have fallen asleep in Jesus...for the Lord himself will descend from heaven; and the dead in Christ will rise up first" (I Thess. 4:13-18). The Gospel: "I know that he will rise at the resurrection, on the last day" (John 11:21-27).

The Everlasting Kingdom

At His return Christ will begin His everlasting Kingdom, the New World. Notice this connection in the *Creed.* It is only after the second coming of Christ, His manifestation in glory and the judgment, that His complete and final reign will begin: "He shall come again in glory to judge; and of His Kingdom there shall be no end." The life of the world to come begins after the resurrection of the body. "I look for the resurrection of the dead and the life of the world to come." Similarly in the *Apostles' Creed:* "I believe...in the resurrection of the body and life everlasting."

This connection is equally conspicuous in *St. Paul:* "Then comes the end, when he delivers the kingdom to God the Father.... And when all things are made subject to him, then the Son himself will also be made subject to him who subjected all things to him, that God may be all in all" (I Cor. 15:24 and 28).

The close relation of everlasting life and the life of the world to come in the two Creeds shows us that the everlasting life of which Scripture and the liturgy speak is properly that life of the world to come which will begin with the return of Christ, the general judgment and the resurrection of the body. It is easy to fall into the mistake of imagining eternal life to be a kind of spatial reality, a nebula of souls, into which the elect enter after death. In this way we conceive of it as a survival of the soul: "Man does not die completely; his soul survives."

But Scripture puts things differently. Life everlasting is

131

not primarily a timeless reality; it is the life of the world to come succeeding this present one. It is **not a survival of the soul,** but its **true life,** which we prepare here below, which we await, which we can anticipate in some manner here below by grace and in heaven by vision. Here are a few New Testament examples which may serve to focus our attention on this point:

"Those who shall be accounted worthy of that world and of the resurrection from the dead..." (Luke 20:35).

The two passages, Mark 10:30 and Luke 18:30: "... and in the age to come life everlasting" throw light on a parallel passage in Matthew 19:29: "...shall possess life everlasting."

"...those who were once enlightened, who have both tasted the heavenly gift and become partakers of the Holy Spirit, who have moreover tasted the good word of God and the powers of the world to come..." (Hebrews 6:4).

This life of the world to come is presented as the realization of the "Restore all things in Christ" which is being prepared in this present world through the labor of the Church Militant (cf. I Cor. 15:28). Then the Church will participate in the life of the Trinity, in the Glorified Christ, in risen bodies and in a renewed creation.

Let us come back to some of these points:

1. **In the Glorified Christ.**

The Church will participate in the life of the Trinity in the Glorified Christ. Eternal happiness will be made up of *knowledge* and *love:* when gathered together in the Church Triumphant, we shall know the mystery of love which constitutes the Holy Trinity (I Cor. 13:2; John 17:3; I John 3:2), and we shall share in it together as sons in the glorified Son (Eph. 1:5; 2:6; Romans 8:29).

The Trinity is Unity and Love. Its work is a work of unity and love. The Trinity is a Communion of Persons within the unity of a single life, and It acts according as It is. In Christ we are like the Trinity a Communion of Persons within the Unity of Christ's Life. This life is not only an image of the Trinity, but in Christ a participation in the very life of the Trinity. God does not adopt us one by one, but as family, as a "Church." Thus eternal happiness will consist not only in communicating in the divine life, but in communicating in it *together*. Eternal happiness will be made up of this double life: love of God in love of neighbor. This mutual love of one another will be all the greater for our having worked together to establish this communion of persons and to prepare this eternal happiness.

2. In Risen Bodies.

Scripture never presents the life of the world to come without corporeal perspectives. We should recall here the importance of the resurrection of the body which was pointed out above, and what will be said later about the condition of the elect before the resurrection of the body.

3. In a Renewed Creation.

In Scripture the material universe is always associated with the fate of mankind:

In Creation (Genesis 1:28; 2:15; 2:20): "Fill the earth and subdue it."

In the Fall (Genesis 3:17): "Cursed be the ground because of you." (Cf. Romans 8:20): "For creation was made subject to vanity not by its own will but by reason of him who made it subject...."

In the promise of Redemption: in the prophets, particularly, the Messianic and eschatological future is always presented in a creation which is renewed, at peace and reconciled with man: "The wolf shall dwell with the lamb..." (Isaias 11:6).

In Redemption (Colossians 1:20): "It has pleased God the Father...that through him he should reconcile to himself all things, whether on the earth or in the heavens, making peace through the blood of his cross."

In the glorification of the last day (Romans 8:19 and 21): "For the eager longing of **creation awaits** the revelation of the sons of God...because creation itself also will be delivered from its slavery to corruption into the freedom of the glory of the sons of God." (Cf. Apocalypse 21:1): "I saw a new heaven and a new earth."

This new heaven and new earth indicate the renewal and glorification of our universe. These texts throw light on others:

133

The return of Christ is called a "regeneration": *Palin-Genesia:* a new birth (Matt. 19:28).

The last times are called "the times of the restoration of all things": *"apo-catastasis panton":* the restoration of all things to their former state (Acts 3:21).

There are some fine texts of St. Thomas in this regard: for example, he asks if on the last day the world itself will be renewed and spiritualized for all eternity, as our bodies will be. He puts the objection: "Where there is no freedom, there is no merit; and where there is no merit, there is no glorification; and, therefore, since the material world is not free, it will not be glorified." He escapes this difficulty in the following manner: "Although insensible bodies do not merit this glory, yet man merits this glory for the whole universe...." [2]

Thus "everlasting life" is not the life of the soul alone, nor a mere survival, but a true, complete, eternal life with all its human dimensions, corporeal, social and cosmic.

PROJECTS

From a Gospel or Epistle, and from the Liturgy of the Dead, All Saints and the Dedication of Churches, pick out texts concerning:
1. the Judgment;
2. the Resurrection;
3. life everlasting;
and show what they teach us on each one of these subjects.

Do not be content with the references given in this chapter, but examine their whole context.

---

[2] 4 *Sent.* d. 48, qu. 2.

Chapter 25

THE HOPE OF THE MEMBERS
OF THE CHURCH

As a living member of Christ and the Church everything that happens to me, either as one of the faithful here below, or as one of the elect in heaven, is only a participation in the Mystery of Christ and the Church.

I. The Faithful

We already anticipate *life everlasting*, the life of the world to come, in a real although limited manner. *Grace* is, properly speaking, this anticipation. To clarify these notions let us see how they are presented in St. Paul and St. John.

In St. John

The faithful already possess life everlasting: "He who believes in the Son has everlasting life" (John 3:36). The Holy Spirit guarantees it to us: "And in this we know that he abides in us by the Spirit whom he has given us" (I John 3:24). But this life is very imperfect in comparison to its full manifestation: "Beloved, now we are the children of God and it has not yet appeared what we shall be. We know that, when he appears, we shall be like to him, for we shall see him just as he is (I John 3:2).

In St. Paul

We await the life to come, but already we have within us a pledge, an earnest, a guarantee, the firstfruits, in the Holy Spirit whom Christ sends us:

"And not only it (creation), but we ourselves also who have the firstfruits of the Spirit—we ourselves groan within ourselves, waiting for the adoption as sons, the redemption of our body" (Romans 8:23).

This Spirit is, therefore, a pledge of our resurrection: "...he who raised Jesus Christ from the dead will also bring to life your mortal bodies because of his Spirit who dwells in you" (Romans 8:11).

"Now it is God who is warrant for us and for you in Christ, who has anointed us, who has also stamped us with his seal and has given us the Spirit as a pledge in our hearts" (II Cor. 1:22).

"Now he who made us for this very thing (immortality) is God, who has given us the Spirit as its pledge" (II Cor. 5:5).

"And in him (Christ) you, too, when you had heard the word of truth, the good news of your salvation, and believed in it, were sealed with the Holy Spirit of the promise, who is the pledge of our inheritance, for a redemption of possession, for the praise of his glory" (Eph. 1:13-14).

Through grace, the life to come is, therefore, already made present in some manner, by anticipation, for the faithful in the Church Militant, that is to say: in the faith, in the struggles for redemption, in a mortal body, in an as yet still unrenewed creation.

II. The Elect

We might be tempted to believe that at death the history of the faithful Christian who has become one of the elect would be finished. But such is not the case, since the history of Christ is not finished.

Christ's History Is Not Finished

He has not yet returned; He has not yet appeared as Judge, as the Lord of glory, as universal King. Consequently, in a way which is very mysterious to us He continues to await His Return and His Manifestation. Although Christ is visibly absent from this world in which redemption is at work, nevertheless, it is He who invisibly directs this work of redemption in the Church through the Holy Spirit. And He Himself continues to exercise His priesthood in heaven in the way described to us by the Epistle to the Hebrews:

"Thou art a priest forever..." (Heb. 7:17).

"He became to all who obey him the cause of eternal salvation, called by God a high priest according to the order of Melchisedech" (Heb. 5:9-10).

"For Jesus has not entered into a Holies made by hands, a mere copy of the true, but into heaven itself, to appear now before the face of God on our behalf" (Heb. 9:24).

So long as the work of redemption goes on, Christ is our intercessor:

"He is able at all times to save those who come to God through him, since he lives always to make intercession for them" (Heb. 7:25).

"It is Christ Jesus who died; yes, and rose again, he who is at the right hand of God, who also intercedes for us!" (Romans 8:34).

Nor Is That of the Elect

Scripture, which is so rich in references in regard to the life to come which will be inaugurated by Christ's Return, Judgment, the Resurrection and Glorification, is a great deal more reticent regarding the lot of the elect between the time of their particular judgment and the general judgment. It is perhaps this fact which explains the long hesitation of Christian theology in this regard.

"In the fourteenth century Benedict XII had to condemn the opinion that the souls of the elect would have to await the final resurrection before obtaining the beatific vision. Now this opinion was not just professed by a certain number of theologians. Benedict XII's own predecessor on the throne of Peter, John XXII, had warmly defended such an opinion in a series of sermons to the people of Avignon in 1331 and 1332, and had maintained it again during the last years of his life, especially in a Consistory of January 3, 1334. This opinion, which was discussed with great passion at the time, had in its favor a lengthy roll of witnesses, some of whom were among the greatest names of tradition, both Latin and Greek. These future elect, whose period of trial was now over, were often represented as 'held in a kind of sweet sleep,' or of tranquil joy full of hope, while they awaited at 'the gates of heaven' in an 'atrium,' in a 'place of repose . . .' all figurative expressions indicating with different nuances the delay that was believed to be imposed upon the souls of the just until the end of time" (H. de Lubac).[1]

We have to keep hold of both ends of the stick: on the one hand, Christ has not yet returned, nor have the Resurrection or the general Judgment taken place; and, therefore, the "New World" has yet to be inaugurated. But, on the other hand, the elect already possess **the vision of God in** heaven. Consequently, we have to say that just as grace is a real but limited anticipation here below of the life to come, lived out in faith and amidst the struggle for redemption; so, while awaiting Christ's return, heavenly glory is a real but *limited anticipation* of the life to come in a state of vision and intercession.

We shall develop these two words: "limited" and "intercession."

1. **Anticipation limited to the soul alone.**

(a) Life everlasting is *not yet lived in the glorified body.* "...at his death, man will receive in proportion to his works, although not fully, since only according to his soul and not yet according to his body" (St. Thomas).[2] God did not create us as pure souls, and the eternal happiness that He wants to procure for us is not a happiness of the soul simply. God created us as men, and the happiness that He offers us is one belonging to the "whole man."

The separation of soul and body at death produces a violent and scandalous state which is the result of sin (Genesis 2:17 and 3:19). "...sin entered into the world and through sin death..." (Rom. 5:12). "The wages of sin is death..." (Rom. 6:23). In this sense sin still leaves its mark in even the elect, since they are separated from their bodies, and death will not be finally vanquished until Christ's return:

---

1 *Catholicism*, pp. 82-83.
2 4 *Sent.* d. 47, qu. 1, quaest. 3, ad. 1.

"Then comes the end...the last enemy to be destroyed will be death..." (I Cor. 15:24-25).

"For in subjecting all things to man, he left nothing that is not subject to him. But now we do not see as yet all things subject to him" (Heb. 2:8).

Only then will Christ's victory be complete for the elect themselves:

"For the trumpet shall sound, and the dead shall rise incorruptible. . . . When this mortal body puts on immortality, then shall come to pass the word that is written: 'Death is swallowed up in victory! O death, where is thy victory? O death, where is thy sting?'" (I Cor. 15:52-55).

"For so the Psalmist sings: 'For thee my soul hath thirsted, for thee my flesh, oh, how many ways!' Thus did the soul of the Royal Prophet yearn for the first advent, whereby he knew that he was to be redeemed; and with much greater eagerness did his flesh look forward to the final coming, at which shall be accomplished its glorification. For then all our desires shall be satisfied, and the whole earth shall be filled with the majesty of the Lord" (St. Bernard).[3]

(b) Everlasting life is *not yet lived in a renewed creation.*

If the state of the separated soul is a violent and scandalous one, it is not only because the soul should live in the body, but also because man should live in the world. God made them together: one with the other, *one for the other.*

"The Lord God formed man out of the dust of the ground..." (Gen. 2:7). "The Lord God took the man and placed him in the garden of Eden to till it and to keep it" (Gen. 2:15). Let us recall the texts cited above concerning the renewal of creation.

St. Thomas speaks of a natural love of man for the universe: "Every animal loves its like, whence we see that likeness or resemblance is the basis of love. Now man has some likeness to the whole universe, and so is called a small world. Therefore, man naturally loves the whole world and desires its welfare." [4]

---

3 Sixth Sermon for Advent (*St. Bernard's Sermons,* Westminster, Md.: Carroll Press, 1950. Vol. I, p. 50.
4 4 *Sent.* d. 48, qu. 2, a. 1.

(c) Everlasting life is *not yet lived in the finally victorious Church*.

Redemption is not complete, and so long as mankind as a whole has not attained its heavenly Home, the happiness of the individual elect cannot be complete. For, indeed, man is a "part" of the human race as a whole: "Every man is both a single person and a part of the human race as a whole; for which reason he must undergo two judgments: one, the particular judgment, which will take place at his death, when he will receive in proportion to what he accomplished while in the body, although not fully, since only according to his soul and not yet according to his body; another, the general judgment, when he will be judged as a part of the human race as a whole" (St. Thomas).[5]

"The resurrection of the body is put off until the end of the world so that all may rise together...and so that the joy of each one may be greater because of the general joy of all" (St. Thomas).[6]

The elect, therefore, await Christ's return, the general judgment, the resurrection of the body, the glorification of the universe, the final and complete victory of the Church.

2. In Intercession.

By their intercession the elect collaborate in hastening the success of redemption. Although they can no longer merit, they can intercede. Christ is always interceding (Epistle to the Hebrews). Consequently, there is no reason why it should be otherwise for the elect. This is the traditional doctrine of the Communion of Saints (cf. Part I, chap. VI). The elect can no longer either merit nor make satisfaction, but they can intercede by reason of the merits which they acquired while on earth: *"Precibus et meritis."*

"The saints cooperate with us in obtaining salvation" (St. Thomas).[7]

Thus the psychological state of mind of the saints in dying resembles that of St. Therese of Lisieux: "I shall spend my time in heaven doing good upon earth."

---

5 4 *Sent.* d. 47, qu. 1, quaest. 3, ad. 1.

6 4 *Sent.* d. 43, qu. 1, a. 3.

7 4 *Sent.* d. 15, qu. 4.

"So long as God's work is not completed, so long as there are still some petitions of the Lord's Prayer which are not accomplished, can we admit that there is no place for hope in heaven and that its proper object is missing? The happiness of the individual does not replace that of the whole. One same aspiration, one same desire, one same pulsation unites the life of the Church Triumphant and that of the Church Militant, until the day when Christ will be 'complete' that is to say, until the day of His second coming in glory" (Fr. Charles).[8]

The Three States of the Christian

The Christian, therefore, knows three states:
—one on earth as a soul in a mortal body;
—one between death and the resurrection as a soul separated from the body;
—one at Christ's return as a soul in a glorified body.
"Let us consider the three different states through which the children of God must pass:

There is that of *the present life;* then that of *heavenly bliss;* and finally that of the *general resurrection;* and these three different states are in some manner three different ages through which the children of God grow into the complete perfection of the fulness of Jesus Christ:

"The present life is like childhood, youthful vigor will follow in heaven, and the prime of life will be realized in the final resurrection . . ." (Bossuet)[9]

We have a natural symbol in the case of the **butterfly:** it passes through two stages before achieving its final state: it is first a caterpillar, then a pupa, and finally a butterfly.

PROJECTS

1. From St. John's Gospel or one of the Epistles of St. Paul (Romans, chap. 8; Ephesians) pick out all the texts concerning grace, and show what they teach us about the relation between grace and the life to come.

2. In the Epistle to the Hebrews study everything concerning the actual priesthood of Christ.

3. Study Chapter 15 of the first Epistle to the Corinthians, and draw out St. Paul's teaching on death and the resurrection.

4. Study the collect prayers of the Mass of various saints, and show how the Church relies upon their merits and prayers.

---

8 *Spes Christi* (N.R.T., 1934, pp. 1020-1021; 1937, pp. 1057-1075).
9 *Cloture du Jubilé* (Oeuvres complètes, Louis Guérin, tome 1, p. 744).

Chapter 26

OUR TASK HERE BELOW

We have to prepare ourselves together for the world to come. Together, that is, with all mankind, with all creation, in the Church Militant. The Church has to transfigure the whole world and lead it as a whole towards its final consummation. Our hope is, therefore, not of an egotistical nature. There is no way for it to be such, for it is at once *personal* and *communitarian,* just as is the whole mystery of the Church which is a communion of persons in Christ. Nor is our hope a kind of escapism or an opium; for, on the contrary, it calls upon us to work with all our energies, both human and Christian, to prepare the whole of mankind and all creation for the life to come; to dispose, in the best possible way and with all the love in our power, this present world, which will be the body of the world to come.

Prepare Mankind for the Life to Come

1. The Apostolate.

We are in the Church Militant whose essential mission is "to restore all things in Christ." Because the Church is Catholic, it is essentially missionary. As members of this missionary Church we are also essentially missionary. We have to give the Christian life to all men and to every human community: this is the essential apostolate of the Church and the mission of Catholic Action.

St. Paul's Epistles are filled with exhortations to put to good use this present time given to us for the apostolate:

"I charge thee, in the sight of God and Christ Jesus, who will judge the living and the dead by his coming and by his kingdom, preach the word, be urgent in season, out of season; . . . work as a preacher of the gospel, fulfill thy ministry" (II Timothy 4:1-8).

We must "present every man perfect in Christ Jesus" (Colossians 1:28).

All personal advantages must be sacrificed to this one, unique task:

"This is why I bear all things for the sake of the elect, that they also may obtain the salvation that is in Christ Jesus, with heavenly glory" (II Timothy 2:10).

"And in doing good let us not grow tired; for in due time we shall reap if we do not relax. Therefore, while we have time, let us do good to all men . . ." (Galatians 6:9).

Besides, "the sufferings of the present time are not worthy to be compared with the glory to come that will be revealed in us" (Romans 8:18).

2. Temporal Activity.

If we want Christian life to be possible, we must concern ourselves also, and first of all, with making human life possible: such is the proper object of what is commonly called temporal activity. The Church recognizes that a minimum of well-being is necessary for the practice of virtue: those who lack indispensable earthly goods cannot aspire after heavenly goods. The misery of the poor and the luxury of the rich are equally obstacles to Christian hope. It is precisely because we want to prepare for the life to come that we have the duty to order this present world in a both human and Christian manner.

3. Scope of Our Activity.

All this indicates the extraordinary scope of our activity: our life is of eternal import not only for ourselves, but also for others.

But we are not to judge the real result from immediate facts: St. Thomas [1] explains that we have to await the end of the world in order to know the complete influence of a man in the work of redemption: every man continues to do either good or evil after his death: in the memory of men in whom he leaves a good or bad impression, in his children

---

[1] *Sum. Theol.* III, qu. 59, a. 5.

who retain something of their father, in the consequences of his acts. It is therefore necessary that all this should find its evaluation in the last judgment. Only to take some recent examples, think of the influence that was exercised by Charles de Foucauld, St. Therese of Lisieux and Pius X only, practically speaking, after their deaths.

Such notions should make those who enjoy immediate success in their apostolate more humble and give courage to those who sow apparently without results:

"He who reaps receives a wage, and gathers fruit unto life everlasting, so that the sower and the reaper may rejoice together. For herein is the proverb true, 'One sows, another reaps.' I have sent you to reap that on which you have not labored. Others have labored, and you have entered into their labors" (John 4:36-38).

Prepare Creation for the World to Come

Such is the meaning of work, of scientific discovery, of artistic activity. Creation is the work of God. He invites us to collaborate in this work of creation: in itself, therefore, work has something of the divine, *in itself*, by its very nature (collaboration with God in the service of His children), and not merely because it can be "offered up" or acquire value by virtue of a good intention.

The world is not merely a temporary companion of our stay on earth, but something which will accompany us forever in the world to come, as will our bodies. Consequently, we must respect it and love it now as **our companion for all eternity,** "because creation itself will also be delivered from its slavery to corruption into the freedom of the glory of the sons of God" (Romans 8:21).

Our task here below is, therefore, to collaborate personally in an immense work, at once divine and human, which began with the Creation and which will be completed only at Christ's return, so that we may all enjoy together, with God and with all men, the result achieved by the collaboration of all. Let us have a firm grasp on the meaning of this immense action unfolding itself throughout history and in

144

which we are engaged. Think of the dimensions, not just of Christendom, but of mankind, of the world, which is all one whole in the divine plan. We are members of Christ, that is to say, members of mankind, citizens of the world. "Each man is both a sending and receiving station, bound by innumerable waves to all the rest of the world" (Fr. Huby).[2]

PROJECTS

In the two Epistles to Timothy study the counsels which St. Paul gives to Timothy, and show how you can draw profit from them.

---

[2] *Epître aux Romains,* p. 298.

Chapter 27

SOME CONSEQUENCES

The Object of Hope

The object of our hope is, therefore, not just our own personal beatitude, but the **kingdom which is to come,** the Church in its everlasting consummation. We walk together towards a goal which is not death, but, over and beyond death, and by its means, the general glorification of the Church and of creation: "Through the passion and cross to the glory of the resurrection."

This eschatological tension is the very soul of the Church, the motive power of the apostolate. We must restore all things in the glorified Christ: all human values, all created values. This general tension of the Church must also be the soul of our personal life in the Church.

We can point out here the importance of eschatology in every undertaking; for example, the Communist eschatology: history marches towards a goal, towards a victory.

There will be the same difference and the same opposition between the earthly and heavenly phases of the Church as there is between our earthly body and our glorified one. We often think of the eternal Kingdom in terms of ourselves personally, but exactly the opposite view should be entertained, that is, we should think of *ourselves as bound up with the Kingdom,* as a unit of the greater whole. Here below we remain in the earthly phase of this Kingdom; and, therefore, in a mortal body, and in a creation which is not yet glorified: we are members of Christ in the Church Militant. One day we shall pass over into the Kingdom's heavenly phase, and then we shall exist in glorified bodies and in a glorified creation: we shall be members of Christ in the victorious Church. But to attain this end we have to share in

Christ's death (individual eschatology) and in His resurrection (general eschatology).

The Price of Hope

In this Christ is truly the "firstfruits": He is the first to accomplish what all are to accomplish in their turn. But He is the pledge that all the rest will follow. Now Christ entered into His glory only by passing through death and the resurrection. Redemption will only be fully accomplished when the entire Church passes through death and the resurrection. Christ's sacrifice has as its aim the rendering possible of mankind's sacrifice, as a sharing in His own sacrifice: such is the full meaning of "We suffer with Him in order to be glorified with Him."

The Church Militant will only pass over into the fulfillment of the Church Triumphant, creation will only be finally set free of its slavery to corruption on the last day, at Christ's return, at the general judgment, when all is completely purified and brought to its consummation.

It is not, therefore, in their present state that the earthly Kingdom, our bodies and creation as a whole will pass over into the world to come: all must undergo the **dissolution** of death and the **renewal** of the resurrection.

"Now this I say, brethren, that flesh and blood can obtain no part in the kingdom of God, neither shall corruption have any part in incorruption... For this corruptible body must put on incorruption, and this mortal body must put on immortality" (I Cor. 15:50-53).

Truly "the shape of this world will pass away"; we must "lose ourselves" before "finding ourselves." In its present state the world is not such as it issued forth from the hands of God. It is a world troubled by sin, a world whose redemption is not yet fully accomplished. Consequently, it is not the world, as we now know it (mankind, our bodies, creation), which will pass over into eternity. Or, if you wish, the everlasting Kingdom will not come to pass in the world as it now stands. Such is the meaning of Jesus' statement: "My kingdom is not of this world." Whence the **illusion** of

147

seeking final happiness here below, in the present state of things. Such is the error of Communism, for example, or that of all those who "settle down" in this life, satisfied with carnal and earthly goods, like power, money, the flesh.

This passing over into a new world will not be made without shock and suffering: whence our mixed reactions when confronted with death. There is the longing for heaven: "I desire to die in order to be with Christ"; but there is also apprehension about being torn away from this earthly life and from our own body:

"For we who are in this tent sigh under our burden, because we do not wish to be unclothed, but rather clothed over, that what is mortal may be swallowed up by life" (II Cor. 5:2).

Love with Hope

We must not despise the realities of this world under the pretext that this world will pass away. Rather, we must love them correctly: "If you have risen with Christ, seek the things that are above." This shows us how we should love; even now we should love with a heavenly love in the risen Christ. Even now we are to deal with what is eternal; and, in a sense, what is not eternal nor capable of becoming so is bad. What is eternal is Faith's view of all human and earthly realities, and the charity and hope which correspond to this general outlook of Faith. What Christ asks of us is to live in all things by Faith, Hope and Charity, and so to transfigure even now this present world.

This brings up the problem of humanism and renunciation. Since we are not in our final state, there is no question of just loving everything that is actually good and beautiful; rather, we should love only what we can transform into eternal values through Faith, Hope and Charity. This rule is relative to each individual. "Do not lay up for yourselves treasures on earth, where rust and moth consume, and where thieves break in and steal; but lay up for yourselves treasures in heaven, where neither rust nor moth consumes..." (Matt. 6:19). "What does it profit a man to gain the whole world if he suffers the loss of his own soul?" (Matt.

16:26). Present sacrifices are not final sacrifices: we give up a partial and passing good, a participated beauty, for a total and everlasting good, for perfect beauty. When we pass from a limited and egotistical love of a creature to the correct love of this creature, we pass from a creature who is loved temporarily in time to a creature who is loved forever in eternity.

Such is the meaning of the formula used so often in the liturgy: *Terrena despicere*[1] *et amare caelestia. Terrena,* things earthly, that is, everything which in this present world is loved in an illegitimate manner, and which, in consequence, will not pass over into eternity. *Caelestia,* things heavenly, that is, everything which in this present world is loved legitimately and which will, therefore, pass over into eternity.

"Esteem and praise creatures in such a way that you love their Creator. Suppose that a husband were to present his wife with a ring, and that his wife were to love this ring more than her husband, who gave it to her. Would not such affection in a wife be blamed as a kind of adultery in regard to her husband's gift, although she would be loving what her husband gave her?" (St. Augustine).[2]

"The Blessed Hope" (Titus 2:13)

"We have made the end of the world so terrifying that the thought of it conjures up nothing but catastrophes. But we should also and especially see in it Christ's return in glory to accomplish the final judgment, to consummate the work of human history, to inaugurate the new heaven and the new earth" (De Montcheuil).

It is of this heavenly Jerusalem, of this final state of the Kingdom and of the Church of which the Apocalypse speaks.

"I saw a new heaven and a new earth... And I saw the holy city, New Jerusalem, coming down out of heaven from God, made ready as a bride adorned for her husband. And I heard a loud voice from the throne saying, 'Behold the dwelling of God with men, and he will dwell with them.

---

[1] The primary meaning of "despicere" is not "to despise," but "to look at from above," that is "to situate in its true place." It is only the secondary meaning which is pejorative, namely, "to look down upon."

[2] *Tract. in Joan. Epist.,* 2, 11; P.L. 35, 1995.

And they will be his people, and God Himself will be with them as their God. And God will wipe away every tear from their eyes. And death shall be no more; neither shall there be mourning, nor crying, nor pain any more, for the former things have passed away'" (Apocalypse 21:1-4).

Let us rectify in the same sense the Liturgy of the Faithful Departed: it is a liturgy of joy, light and peace.

"Through Christ our Lord. In whom the hope of a blessed resurrection has shone upon us, that those who are afflicted by the certainty of dying, may be consoled by the promise of future immortality" (Preface for Masses of the Dead).

A Glimpse of Heaven

But already here below, as a religious society, the Church manifests something of the perfect community to be found in heaven. Temporal society of necessity has as its objective only the earthly good of all, and it possesses means of earthly activity which split up mankind into numberless rival groups. The Church, however, proposes an objective which is both eternal and common to all men; it bears visible witness to a brotherly community of men over and beyond earthly and rival interests.

Without awaiting the economic, social or political transformations which are to resolve these human contradictions into a harmonious synthesis, the Church presents the visible witness of a religious society in which men are linked together in a common purpose: union with God through Christ's sacraments, brotherly union through worship and mutual service.

It is especially the parish, the liturgical, brotherly and missionary community, which must show forth this unity of all the faithful of all states of life, gathered together here below in Faith, Hope and Charity, while awaiting the final gathering together in heaven in the vision, the possession and the love of God.

PROJECTS

1. Study the Liturgy of the Faithful Departed, and show how it is one of joy and hope.

2. Study the Anointing of the Sick (Extreme Unction):
   (a) Do you find any mention of death?
   (b) What are the essential ideas dominating these texts?

Conclusion

By reviewing the whole of revelation, from the creation of the world in Genesis down to the consummation of this world in the Apocalypse, we have learned that the Church truly stands at the beginning and the end of all things.

1. It is not one object of revelation among many others; there is, so to speak, **but one single object of revelation:** "the mystery of God giving himself," and this is basically the mystery of the Church. The sole object of our faith is the love which constitutes God's intimate life, in the mystery of the Trinity, the love which is expressed and which gives itself in the mystery of the redemptive Incarnation so as to associate mankind with this intimate life of love in the unity of Christ, in the mystery of the Church. "We have come to know and have believed the love that God has in our behalf" (I John 4:16).

2. But we have also seen that there is a **progress in this revelation.** It is *hope* which is characteristic of the Old Testament; *faith* of the New Testament; the *vision*, Heaven. And love remains—it is the common measure.

3. There is also a **progress in the means of Salvation.**

God progressively draws nearer to His creatures:

—First of all He communicates himself by means of created signs and the law of conscience.

—Then by means of the prophets and the religious structure of the old covenant.

—Then the Son of God Himself comes to His own, and the Church of the New Testament visibly continues His presence and his activity until His return.

—And finally, God will give Himself without any intermediary, face to face: "I saw no temple therein. For the Lord God almighty and the Lamb are the temple thereof" (Apocalypse 21:22).

Third Part

THE CHURCH OF THE NEW
TESTAMENT

Chapter 28

A GENERAL SURVEY

The Church of the New Testament is the **present expression** of God's eternal plan and the **means of its realization.** It both *expresses* and *brings about* the gathering together of all mankind in Christ. It is in it and through it that this encounter of love between God and man is realized. This provides us with the two great divisions of this third part of our work.

The Church's Nature

The Church of the New Testament is the People of God as it now exists. Consequently, it is truly the "**Body of Christ,**" that is, Christ as He is made manifest and rendered sensible to us. All religious literature since the beginning of the Church has taken pleasure in casting light upon the harmony which exists between the mystery of the Incarnation and the mystery of the Church. The encyclical of Pius XII, *Mystici Corporis Christi* (On the Mystical Body of Christ), clearly recalled this doctrine. Just as Christ is the Incarnation of the Word in a human nature, so the Church is the incarnation of Christ in an institution of human appearance. The Church participates in the mystery of the Incarnation and prolongs it in some manner.

The Incarnation of Christ knew two "states," or better, two phases: 1. one of *humiliation* (kenosis) before the Resurrection; 2. one of *glory* after the Resurrection.

Thus the Church also knows two states, or two phases:

1. The earthly phase until Christ's return, in which it participates in the mystery of Christ in His redemption and in some way prolongs His incarnation as it was before His resurrection. It is thus the "**Body of Christ the Redeemer.**"

155

2. The final phase after Christ's return, in which it will participate in the mystery of the risen and glorified Christ. It will then be the "**Body of the Glorified Christ.**"

Because it is the "Body of Christ," the Church is One and Holy: "Credo in Ecclesiam, Unam, Sanctam. . . ."

We are going to group our study of the nature of the Church around these three points:

1. The Church as the **Body** of Christ.
2. The **Unity** of the Church.
3. The **Holiness** of the Church.

The Church's Mission

The whole organization of the Church of the New Testament has as its aim to construct this "Body of Christ," to make mankind God's family. It is here that we rediscover all that is generally said in the religious literature, since the beginning of the Church, concerning the Church's role, its saving mission and the means at its disposal. We should be reminded, in particular, of the great traditional image of the Church as Spouse and Mother.

1. As regards Christ, the Church is a **Spouse** whom He uses to reach and sanctify mankind.

2. As regards His members, the Church is, therefore, a **Mother** who *engenders* unto Faith and divine Life and who *educates* in this Faith and Life. As Christ's only Spouse she is the **universal** Mother of salvation.

—This function as Spouse and Mother gives the Church its *apostolic* character.

—This universal function gives the Church its *catholic* character.

We are, therefore, going to group our study of the mission of the Church around these three points:

1. The Church as **Spouse** and **Mother.**
2. The **Catholicity** of the Church.
3. The **Apostolicity** of the Church.

"Credo in Ecclesiam, Catholicam, Apostolicam. . . ."

156

For the sake of clarity of exposition we are going to study the second point first: namely, the Church's Mission. It was in His Mission of salvation that Jesus revealed to us the mystery of His divine person. Similarly, it is the Mission of the Church that will enlighten us as to its nature.

But this whole study of the Church is really a reflection on a **Mystery.** The Mystery of Christ is already complex, and we must react against any tendency to lose sight of one of its constituent parts: He is true God and true Man within the unity of a single person. The Mystery of the Church is still greater because it is the meeting place of the other mysteries, namely: the Trinity in Christ, the redemptive Incarnation, Christ in a society of human appearance. We have to grasp the meaning of this mystery in order to carry on this study in a religious manner. It is a mystery which can only be grasped by praying, contemplating and living it.

Because it is a mystery we cannot express it in a few clear and distinct ideas: we must view it from many angles, from various points of view. This is what we shall try to do by considering the Church in its Mission (Spouse, Mother, Catholic, Apostolic) and in its Nature (Body of Christ, One, Holy).

In each one of these aspects we shall discover the mystery as a whole, but under various lights.

A. The Mission of the Church

Chapter 29

THE CHURCH AS SPOUSE
AND MOTHER

The Church as Spouse

This image of the Church as Spouse has two chief meanings:
—the Church is loved as a spouse
—the Church plays the role of a spouse.

Loved as Spouse.—Already in the Old Testament, since the time of the prophet Osee, the love of God for His People was compared to the love of a husband for his wife. The covenant of God with His People was presented under the aspect of a conjugal union between Yahweh and Israel.

"Husband now thou hast, and the name of him is the Lord of hosts, thy Creator" (Isaias 54:5). (Knox)

In this sense the image is used again in the New Testament and applied to Christ as the Bridegroom and to the Church as His Bride (Mark 2:19-20; Matthew 9:15; 22:1-12; John 3:29; Apocalypse 21:9-10; 22:17; 19:7; II Corinthians 11:2; and especially, Ephesians 5:21-33):

"Husbands, love your wives, just as Christ also loved the Church, and delivered himself up for her...."

To this union between Christ and the Church St. Paul applies the very words used by God to the first married couple, Adam and Eve: "For this cause a man shall leave his father and mother, and cleave to his wife; and the two shall become one flesh. This is a great mystery—I mean in reference to Christ and to the Church" (Eph. 5:31-32).

Christian writers, the Fathers of the Church, in commenting upon this passage of Genesis, have, like St. Paul, all alike thought of the union of Christ and the Church: "Christ left His Father by descending on earth in the Incarnation; He left His Mother by abandoning the Synagogue in order to unite Himself with the Church." They generally pursue the comparison with Adam and Eve: "The Church is the spouse of Christ: she was formed while Christ slept the sleep of death; she issued forth from the side of her Spouse when His side was pierced by the blow of a lance, when from that wound flowed forth the sacraments" (St. Augustine).[1]

The Church is, therefore, the New Eve, born from the pierced Heart of Christ, the mother of redeemed mankind.

This image, therefore, emphasizes the following aspects:

1. *The close union between Christ and us:* one existing between spouses. In this image there is also the idea of election, of choice: the disciples of Christ are called "electi," chosen (Eph. 1:4; Col. 3:12). They are also called "genus electum," the chosen race.

2. *Mutual love.* Here we have to stress the distinction of persons. Union with Christ does not suppress our personality, but develops and strengthens it. Marriage supposes a distinction of persons, that is why the Incarnation is considered a marriage, not between the two natures of Christ, but between Christ and the Church.[2] This image, therefore, successfully completes that of the Mystical Body: our union with Christ is one between persons (not inanimate members).

3. *Transcendance of Christ.* The initiative and the choice stem from Christ. Christ's role consists in His giving life to His spouse through sacrifice, in bestowing a dowry upon her, in introducing her into the intimacy of His own divine family.

4. *Dependence of the Church.* Its attitude is one of receptivity towards Christ. Whence an attitude of humility, dependence and gratitude. We are God's heirs with Christ and because of Christ. We participate in His privileges: what He is by nature, we are through alliance.

---

1 *Enarratio in Psalm.* 138, 2; P.L. 37, 1785.
2 St. Gregory, homily already quoted, of the 19th Sunday after Pentecost.

But this image also shows the Church's role in relation to Christ.

Her Function as Spouse.—Christ wants to reach us through the visible mediation of His Church. When He Himself was on earth, He reached His disciples directly, without any intermediary.

—He gave them Faith by His Word,

—He gave them Life by His sanctifying actions.

—He educated them in Faith and divine Life by all His pastoral activity. He was Himself their Shepherd.

But between His departure at the Ascension and His return at the end of the world, He reaches us through the intermediary of the living instrument of salvation which He left here below, and which he uses as a spouse in order to sanctify us:

1. He gives us Faith through the *Word of the Church;*

2. He gives us Life through the *Sacraments;*

3. He educates us in Faith and divine Life through all *the pastoral activity of the Church.*

"The Church can remit nothing without Christ; but Christ does not want to remit anything without the Church. Assuredly the Almighty can do anything by Himself: He can baptize, consecrate the Eucharist, ordain, forgive sins. But as a humble and faithful Spouse He does not want to do anything without His partner: 'what God has joined together, let no man put asunder'" (Isaac of Stella).

The encyclical *Mystici Corporis* comments upon this idea in several places:

"It was possible for Him (Christ) personally, immediately to impart these graces to men; but He wished to do so only through a visible Church that would be formed by the union of men...

"This is not because He is indigent and weak, but rather because He has so willed it for the greater glory of His unspotted Spouse" (Nos. 13 and 46). (Paulist Press Trans.)

The Church as Mother

Christ, therefore, associates the Church as a spouse in all His work of salvation; He renders her fruitful by entrusting

160

her with His own powers; consequently, she becomes a Mother and begets us to divine life. "In regard to herself the Church is both mother and children; for, taken as a whole, all those who go to make up the Church bear the name of mother; but, taken singly, they are called children" (St. Augustine).[3]

1. The Church is a mother because she **engenders us:**
—unto Faith, by preaching or Evangelization,
—unto divine Life, by the Sacraments.

2. The Church is a mother because she **nourishes** her children. She gives them as their food the Body of Christ in the Eucharist and the Word of God in the Holy Scriptures. The Fathers of the Church employed very realistic images in this regard. "The Church is a nursing mother whose breasts are the Old and New Testaments."[4]

3. The Church is a mother because she **educates** her children. She educates them in Faith and divine Life by her ministry, which is often called her "pastoral" activity in reference to the image of the Good Shepherd.

In these maternal tasks we can see the realization of the different orders of Christ to His Church:

"Preach the Gospel"—in order to engender unto Faith.

"Baptize them"—(Sacraments) in order to engender unto Life.

"Teach them to observe all that I have commanded you"— in order to educate in this Faith and Life.

We can also see the three standard powers:
—the power of teaching, that is, her maternal mission of **evangelization** (Faith);
—the power of order, that is, her maternal mission of **sanctification** (Life);
—the power of jurisdiction, that is, her maternal mission of **education.**

This maternal mission of the Church is as vast as the work of Christ Himself: she is His only Spouse and, therefore, the Mother of the whole human race. She has to beget all mankind unto divine life and carry it at her breast in order

---

3 *Quaestionum Evangeliorum,* lib. 1, qu. 18; P.L. 35, 1327.
4 St. Augustine, *Tract. in Joan. Epist.,* 3, cap. 2; P.L. 35, 1998.

to unite it to Christ. This is the whole problem of the apostolate, as we shall see in studying the Church's catholicity.

The men that the Church must sanctify and unite to Christ are, first of all, outside her. She gives them life by taking them to herself, by incorporating them within herself. This differs from human maternity in which being born consists in issuing forth from the maternal womb.

"The Church begets men for Jesus Christ, not like other mothers, by bringing them forth from her womb, but by drawing them into her womb from the outside, by incorporating them into herself, and by means of this incorporation into the Holy Spirit who animates her, and through the Holy Spirit into the Son who bestowed Him upon us by the breath of His mouth, and through the Son into the Father who sent Him; so that we attain fellowship in and with God, Father, Son and Holy Spirit" (Bossuet).[5]

Image of the Sun and the Moon

The Church in her functions as spouse and mother is a kind of intermediary between Christ and men. It is through her that men receive the Light and Life of Christ. But in her turn she receives from Christ everything that she is. The Fathers of the Church took pleasure in comparing the Church in this function of spouse to the Moon in its relation to the Sun and the Earth (see the patristic commentaries on Genesis 1:16: "God made the two great lights, the greater light to rule the day and the smaller one to rule the night").

The fundamental theme, into which many other secondary ones are woven, is the following:

At night, during the absence of the sun, the earth lies in darkness. It receives light and warmth only through the moon. But the moon itself receives from the sun the light and warmth which it communicates to the earth. Similarly, mankind now lies in darkness, because its Sun, Christ, is absent from this world. (In this sense the Fathers consider the Church as a *widow*, because Christ, her spouse is absent.) This night lies over the earth from the time of His departure

5 *Lettres à une demoiselle de Metz*, lettre 4 (*Oeuvres complètes*, tome 8, p. 298).

at the Ascension until His return at the end of the world. Fortunately, however, there is a "light to rule the night," the Church. The Church **transmits to us the life and light of Christ.** And just as the Moon itself receives everything that it communicates to us from the Sun, so the Church receives everything that it communicates to us. "The moon draws her light from the sun, and the Church is beautiful like the moon because she takes her light from Christ her Spouse, and shines with His grace" (St. Thomas).[6]

Here is how Origen treats the same theme:

"Just as God ordered that there be in this firmament already called heaven two great lights to divide the day from the night, so also can it be in us, if we strive to be called and to be 'heaven': we have lights in us which enlighten us, Christ namely and His Church. For He is the light of the world, and He enlightens the Church with His light.

"And just as the moon is said to receive her light from the sun, so as to enlighten the night, so the Church, which receives her light from Christ, enlightens all those who are in darkness, as Christ told His disciples saying: 'You are the light of the world'" (Matt. 5:14).[7]

The Church Is Truly Our Mother

To understand this, think, for example, of what the Church is for Protestants: adherence to the Church for a Protestant is a consequence, but a necessary consequence of the faith which justifies:

"For all those who confess their faith in God, belonging, submission and devotion to the Church, the visible body of Christ, are an unavoidable necessity . . . All those to whom the Holy Spirit gives the certitude of justification cannot persist in their solitude: they are summoned to join themselves with their brothers in the faith, to make up this visible body of which the glorified Christ is the heavenly and invisible Head" (Pastor Casalis).[8]

For us Catholics adherence to the Church is not a consequence of a salvation which is already acquired, but this very salvation itself is a consequence of our adherence to the Church. It is not our gathering together into one which constitutes the Church; the Church is our mother, not only

---

6 *Commentary on the Canticle of Canticles* 6, 9.
7 *In Genesim Homilia* 1, 5-6; P.G. 12, 150-151.
8 *Positions Protestantes* (Le Cerf, *Recontres*), pp. 15-50.

because she educates her already formed children, but because she really brings them into the world.

Even when Protestants call their Church "Mother," it is not in the same sense that we do. Protestants say: "The Church is the mother of those whom God is (already) the Father" (*Positions Protestantes*); Catholics say: "No one can have God for Father if he has not the Church for Mother"; the Church is "the mother who engenders God's children."

1. It is in the Church that *Catholics:*

—*receive the life of Christ* through the sacraments: "To beget for the Church is to receive her children within her womb. They die when they leave it" (Bossuet). We can fully agree with Calvin when he says: "There can be no entrance into eternal life except by being conceived, brought into the world and nourished at the breasts of this mother." [9]

—*receive the mind of Christ,* His word: "I myself would not believe in the Gospel if the authority of the Church did not lead me to do so." This thought of St. Augustine does not represent a personal opinion, but the very essence of the Catholic position. It was to the Church and not to a Book that Christ entrusted His revelation. The Gospels are merely a summary of the Church's primitive catechesis. In addition, it is the Church that gives us the exact meaning of Scripture. The Church is truly the mother of our faith.

—*receive the will of Christ:* the Church is the mistress of perfection. It is she who transmits and interprets the will of Christ for us. All Christians can say with Claudel: "Blessed be this Mother at whose knees I have learned all things."

2. This presence of the Church is lasting.

This presence and activity of the Church in the life of the Christian is not a temporary pedagogical necessity. The Church is not a mother whom her children need only for a time, and whom one day they will be able to do without in order to enter into relation with Christ and God alone. She is not even a mother of whom we have less need as we advance; on the contrary, it may be said that the more we penetrate into God, the more we unite ourselves with Christ, and the more we remain close to her, the more we shall act under her direction, the more we shall surrender to her

9 *Institution Chrétienne.*

164

spirit. No one, no matter how advanced he may be, can get teaching and life from God without going through the Church.[10]

3. This presence of the Church is **visible**, and not purely spiritual. Entrance into the Church comes about by means of a visible rite, Baptism. Faith is adherence to apostolic preaching set forth in a definite Creed. Obedience to the Church is obedience to visible persons, etc.

4. This presence of the visible and lasting Church is, nevertheless, the means of an **immediate communication of the soul with God:** "The problem and paradox of the Church can be seen in the fact that she must both be constantly and actively present in the dialogue between the soul and God, and yet not hinder such intimacy, not harm in any way the character of immediate communication between the soul and God" (De Montcheuil).

As we explained in the case of Christ, the Church does not mediate according to a human mode; it is not just a question of passing through the Church, but it is in the Church and in it alone that we enter into communion with Christ, and in Christ with the Trinity. In short, we Catholics are truly "the children of our Holy Mother the Church." Such is the origin of our love and respect for the Church. Even her imperfections, which stem from what is human in her, render her in some manner closer to us:

"We need a redemptress mother, one who, however celestial she be in the deepest recesses of her being, never turns coldly away from her children, when their soiled fingers touch her, and when folly and wickedness rend her marriage robe. We need a poor mother, for we ourselves are poor" (Karl Adam).[11]

Filial Attitude towards the Church

If the Church is our Mother, we must love and respect her as loving sons respect their mother. In practice, how-

---

10 In this third part I shall often quote, sometimes rather freely, from notes taken during courses which Fr. de Montcheuil delivered in Paris. These courses have since been published, e.g.: *Leçons sur le Christ; Aspects du Mysté de l'Eglise; Mélanges théologiques.*

11 *The Spirit of Catholicism,* New York: Macmillan, 1930. Chap. XIII, p. 228.

ever, it often happens that at the "wild age" children stray away from their mother, forget everything they have received from her, criticize her and are sometimes even ashamed of her. Certain Catholics also experience this type of "wild age." They find that their mother is old-fashioned. They sometimes blush to admit that they are her children, or even openly make fun of her. Now supposing that a good mother were, in one way or another, not quite up to date, would not a loving son, by way of proving his real affection for her, help to make her so without wounding her feelings in any way? On the other hand, similar remarks coming from a son who does not really prove his love, could easily hurt her deeply. So it is in the Church: those who want to help keep the Church perpetually young and up-to-date must begin by proving the sincerity of their filial affection for the Church in all spheres of their life.

Mary, the Image of the Church

Traditionally, there is often a comparison drawn between Mary and the Church. Mary is the Mother of Jesus, but who remains a Virgin since she gives birth without the intervention of a man. Similarly, the Church is both Mother and Virgin because she too bears children by divine intervention. In Mary, as in the Church, it is the Holy Spirit sent by Jesus who insures fruitfulness. And Mary, like the Church, brings forth Christ.

"Like Mary the Church is at once a Mother and a Virgin. . . . Mary bore the Head of this Body in a corporeal manner; the Church bears the members of this Head in a spiritual manner. In neither does virginity impede fecundity, nor does fecundity harm virginity" (St. Augustine).[12]

PROJECTS

1. Collect the texts which point out Christ as Spouse or the Church as Spouse, and show what they teach us in regard to the relations of Christ and the Church:
    (a) in the Gospels;
    (b) in St. Paul's Epistles;

---

12 *De Sancta Virginitate*, cap. 2; P.L. 40, 397.

(c) in the Apocalypse;
(d) in the liturgy of the Dedication of Churches;
(e) in the marriage liturgy.

2. Pick out the theme of the Church as Spouse and Mother in the various texts of the Easter Vigil (particularly in the collects and in the blessing of the font) or in the Vigil of Pentecost, and show what they teach us about the Church.

PRACTICAL ATTITUDES

Do we have a filial attitude towards our Holy Mother the Church? (Respect, thankfulness, love, active collaboration?)

Chapter 30

CATHOLICITY OF THE CHURCH

I. The True Notion of Catholicity

What is meant is not primarily the *de facto* universality of the Church, that is to say, its actual establishment on various continents and among a variety of different civilizations. That is but one manifestation of its Catholicism, its visible expression. Indeed, the Church was already Catholic on Pentecost morning. In order to understand this fact, we have to recall the universality of the mission Christ bestowed upon His Church.

The Universality of the Church's Mission

1. The Church **received** a universal mission **from Christ:** Notice the universality of Christ's instructions to the Church:

"Preach the Gospel to every creature" (Mark 16:15).

"Make disciples of all nations" (Matthew 28:18).

"You shall be witnesses for me...even to the very ends of the earth" (Acts 1:8).

"This gospel of the kingdom shall be preached in the whole world, for a witness to all nations" (Matthew 24:14).

We also discover this note of universality in the various images of Matthew, chaps. 5 and 13: "salt of the earth," "light of the world," "leaven."

2. This mission is as universal as the **work of Christ Himself:** Redemption is universal; all humanity has to be redeemed and incorporated into Christ. The Church, therefore, has to attain all humanity and everything in humanity; it has to put Christ in all things and all things in Christ.

3. But if Christ entrusts this universal mission to the

Church, He also gives it the strength and the **powers** to accomplish it. Christ, Who is the source of life for all mankind and the principle of Redemption and universal reconciliation, is incarnate in the Church and continues through it, with it and in it, the work which He began on earth. Accordingly, the Church is, as Bossuet puts it, "Jesus spread abroad and communicated," [1] Jesus spreading Himself and communicating Himself to all men.

The Catholicity of the Church is this universal vocation and the efficacious power for accomplishing it. The Church can and must gather within itself all mankind of whatever civilization or state of life; it must reach every man and everything in every man, in order to incorporate it fully in to Christ: not only his religious life, but his intellectual life, his cares, his joys, the work of transforming the world. There is nothing for which it has not the mission and power of incorporating within itself in order to incorporate it in Christ.

4. It is also **creation as a whole** that it has the mission and power of sanctifying and consecrating to God. This universal mission of the Church in regard to creation shows up in the various blessings to be found in one of the Church's official books called the **Ritual.** In it are to be found blessings for the various *foods* (butter, cheese); for the different *fruits of the earth,* and the harvests; for the various *animals* (birds, bees, etc.); for the various *dwellings* of men and animals; for a variety of *inventions* (radio, airplanes, etc.).

We have to understand the religious meaning of these blessings: through them the Church consecrates all creation and all human work to God. Such is also the meaning of the *Ember Days:* they are the Church's consecration of the four seasons.

In the ancient churches and cathedrals were represented all creation, the fauna and flora, the seasons, human activities, the arts and crafts, the ages, etc.—in a word, the whole universe. The cathedral of stone is a symbol of the Church's universal mission.

Finally, in the sacraments: **created objects,** the fruits of

1 *Lettres a une demoiselle de Metz,* lettre 4 (*Oeuvres complètes,* t. 8, p. 297).

169

nature and man's work, become signs of grace, e.g., bread, wine, oil.

Consequently, the Catholic Church is nothing other than the *realization* and *expression*, in time and space, of the "Restore all things in Christ."

"The Church is a great deal more than the means for saving souls; it is the world in its divine form, the sole meeting place through which the whole of the Creator's work returns to the Redeemer" (Fr. Charles).[2]

The Work of the Whole Church

This universal mission is the work of the whole Church. It is well to emphasize this point before showing the proper role of the hierarchy. It is the entire Church which is charged with this universal mission, but in an organized, hierarchical and apostolic manner, as we shall show in treating of the Church's apostolicity. It is in the light of this universal mission of the Church that we should understand the powers and responsibilities of the hierarchy.

1. The encyclical, *Mystici Corporis*, gives us a timely reminder of this truth:

"The salvation of many depends upon the prayers and voluntary penances which the members of the Mystical Body of Jesus Christ offer for this intention, and on the assistance of pastors of souls and of the faithful, especially of fathers and mothers of families, which they must offer to our divine Saviour as though they were His associates" (No. 46). "We desire that all who claim the Church as their mother should seriously consider that not only the sacred ministers . . . but the other members as well of the Mystical Body of Jesus Christ have the obligation of working hard and constantly for the upbuilding and increase of this Body. We wish this to be remembered especially by members of Catholic Action who assist the bishops and priests in their apostolic labors" (No. 112). (Paulist Press Trans.)

Since Christians participate in the life of Christ, who is not only the Son of God, but also the Brother and Redeemer of men, they must participate in this filial love. "To us it has been granted to collaborate with Christ in this work of salvation, 'from one and through one saved and saving'" (No.

---

2 *Missiologie*, pp. 85-86.

65). Like Christ the love of Christians must embrace the whole human race.

Now "Christ proved His love for His spotless Bride not only by His tireless labors and constant prayers, but by His sorrows and sufferings, gladly, lovingly endured for her sake.... It was only with His blood that He purchased the Church" (No. 122).

Consequently, Christians have to participate in this redemption of the world in the same way, through a constant apostolate, especially through Catholic Action; through prayer, especially "the Apostolate of Prayer"; through suffering, in union with that of the Redeemer.

2. This encyclical echoes the Gospel: Matthew 5. It was to the crowd that Jesus said: "You are the salt of the earth... You are the light of the world, like a city set on a mountain, like a light which gives light to the whole house."

3. Such is also *the teaching of St. Paul:* each member of the Church, in union with all the others, contributes to the growth of the Church.

II. How the Church Realizes Her Mission of Catholicity

The Church must enter into human life in all its various manifestations. Since all things have to be restored in Christ, and since this comes about through and in the Church, it must, therefore, incorporate within itself all human diversity in order to incorporate it in Christ Himself. This is the Church's maternal mission, namely, to receive within her womb that humanity which previously lay outside her. Consequently, she must **adapt herself** to all the diversity which she has to incorporate within herself in order to bring it to life in Christ, she must enter into human life in all its various manifestations. Whence the *problem of adaptation:* The Church must be present everywhere there is a human value to be incorporated. As we shall see, this brings up the problem of the missions and of a native clergy, as well as the problem of the apostolate and of Catholic Action.

Adaptation and Catholicism

This adaptation of the Church is not a stratagem to facilitate the assimilation and incorporation of all human values. Rather it is necessary for the very realization of its Catholicism. In fact, if there is a fundamental likeness among men in that they are all created in the image of the Trinity, there are also profound differences among them, differences which are the work of God Himself. These differences of civilization, mentality, and character represent real values in that they are so many reflections of God. All this wealth and variety must be incorporated in Christ since grace crowns and transfigures nature. Incorporation into the Church will not, therefore, be a levelling but an **improvement** of whatever authentic riches are to be found in each man and in each human group. If the Church adapts herself to civilization, as well as to individuals, it is precisely in order to permit them to "realize" whatever they contain of real value. The Church has as its mission the assimilation of all human values in order to lead them to their completion.

Assimilation and Purification

In assuming such values the Church purifies whatever is incomplete or imperfect in them. The life which the Church brings about is not any kind of life whatsoever, but a life of charity, a life of communion within the unity of Christ. Incorporation in the Church conserves and transfigures whatever good there is, but rejects whatever is spoiled or limited. This is true both as regards individuals and civilization. Here we rediscover once more the great law pointed out previously, namely, that the Incarnation comes about only by way of Redemption; it is a redemptive Incarnation.

St. Augustine interprets St. Peter's dream at Joppa (Acts 10:9-16) in a curious and interesting manner. He explains that in order to give life the Church has to "eat" men and "kill" their sins. St. Peter represented the Church when he saw a certain vessel coming down towards him like a great sheet, containing all sorts of animals, four-footed beasts, reptiles and birds, which were symbols of all the nations of the earth. In this vision the Lord gave us a figure of the Church, which is to absorb all peoples and transform them into its own body; and he said to Peter: "Kill and eat" (Acts 10:13). "Kill and eat, O Church, kill first, and then eat; kill them as they are, and cause them to become what you are." [3]

Only the Church, therefore, can carry to its perfection that religious impulse which God inserted in the hearts of men and civilizations. There may be real religious values outside the Catholic Church, but they can find fulfillment only by being incorporated into the Church. But it is also true that the Church's Catholicism finds its actuality through this assimilation of new values, which will benefit the religious life of all its children. This poses the problem of the Missions and of the whole apostolate, especially of Catholic Action.

III. The Problem of the Missions

When Pius XII opened St. Peter's College (Rome) for priests coming from mission lands, he declared:

"The proper end of missions is to *plant* the Church in new lands in such a way that after having become deeply rooted they can prosper and grow without the help of foreign missionaries."

Since the Church is to assimilate all the true values of men and civilizations, it must be present everywhere and at home everywhere. We shall see that missions are needed for the *growth of the Church;* for *charity;* for *Catholicism.*

Necessary for the Growth of the Church

"Today the Church has not yet reached adulthood; certainly it does not lack any of its organs, but it has not spread to the ends of the earth; the visible Church does not yet coincide with man's planet.... The Church is in a stage of growth; it must grow or else see its vitality atrophy.

[3] *Enarratio in Psalm,* 30, Sermo 2, 5; P.L. 36, 242. (Cf. *Enarr. in Ps. 123,* 5; P.L. 37, 1642; Sermo 4; P.L. 38, 33-52.)

By our baptism we are members of a Church which is still in a period of growth. When the work of the missions is accomplished, there will still be *millions of sinners* to convert, there will still be even *millions of pagans;* there will still be the *souls of all the living to save,* but it will be the Church as established everywhere which will continue this labor until the trumpets sound on the last day. It is not the Japanese Mission which has to convert all the Japanese; its role is to plant the visible Church in Japan, and it will be the Japanese Church which will convert the archipelago" (Fr. Charles).[4]

Necessity for Charity

Charity only exists when it desires to spread itself; indeed, it consists in this very effort of universal giving. The Church, therefore, exists truly only when it is universally missionary. Its very existence implies the **will to be in all places. One** does not possess the life of charity unless one seeks to communicate it. Consequently, both in the case of the individual apostle and in the case of the Church, the impulse comes from within. Humility is safeguarded because charity is not an attitude of someone who possesses it towards someone who does not; rather, Christians possess in the spiritual order only because they give, and in the very act of giving, in the **will to give.** It is only through the efforts they expend to enrich others, that they acquire something for themselves. And if they do not continue to give, not only will they cease to acquire, but they will lose all (Fr. de Montcheuil).

Necessity for Catholicity

When the Church goes towards a people who have not yet received the faith, it encounters a grace of God at work which is peculiar to each human group, and within this group, peculiar to each man. Now this grace can only find fulfillment in and through the Church. The Church does not go to fill a simple vacuum, rather it is drawn by a divine

---

4 *Missiologie,* p. 87.

summons. Those towards whom it goes are not aware of summoning its aid; but it hears the summons because it is more clear-sighted about man than man himself. A divine grace has to be "delivered" and brought to fulfillment (cf. Romans 8: All creation groans and travails...). It is not only they who will benefit by this deliverance, but the whole Church into which they enter and which will help them in a new way to make the most of the treasure it has received from God.

In this way the missions are the actualization of the Church's Catholicism, not only by numerical increase in its membership, nor even by a qualitative increase, but by causing all the variety of the divine gift to blossom forth.

Catholicity is not something that we possess and give; we possess it only through the very will **to give,** and it comes into being through these different contributions. We should not consider ourselves as those who give to those from whom they have nothing **to receive:** but as those who give to those from whom they may very well get more than they will have ever given.[5] There is no real love among us unless we, in our turn, want to receive from those to whom we are now giving. If the Church goes to all peoples, it is because there is a particular grace at work in each people, and because the Church must guide it towards its fulfillment and take it to itself—which are but two aspects of the same thing. This missionary activity of the Church, therefore, opens a circuit of graces.

Some Consequences

1. Since it is a question of guiding towards its fulfillment the particular grace which is at work in any human group so that the entire Church may be enriched by it, we should not think merely in terms of individual conversions. The Church has to establish itself in this group, in this people, in order to permit this particular form of grace, this particular religious temperament, to expand and express itself within the unity of the Church. Consequently, the Church must be

---

5 See some examples in Fr. Daniélou's *The Salvation of the Nations.*

so implanted and organized there that it can live off its own resources, and so that there will appear a religious life bearing its own proper traits. Whence the **necessity of a native clergy**: the Church must be really implanted and grafted onto the wild stock for it to bear new fruit. In this way fruitful exchanges will be established between all parts of the Catholic Church.

2. Since it is a question of bringing a particular grace to completion, we have to see it at work, see where it leads. Whence the necessity of a **religious study of a people**.

3. Respect for what is authentically religious, for what bears marks of religious promise, must carry with it respect for all the human and cultural heritage bound up with it. It is irreligious to destroy or upset the praiseworthy elements of a human culture, for by so doing we diminish some rich aspect of the Church's future heritage.

4. We have to avoid tying down Catholicism to our ways of thinking and living, even in regard to the legitimate aspects of such involvement; within the Church we all need to develop our **own way of being Christians**, but we must avoid the temptation of imposing it upon others. We must not make others think that they have to give up their own values in order to enter the Church. They have not only the right, but even the duty of conserving them for the good of the Church itself. *A fortiori*, should we never present Catholicism as bound up with what is still un-Christian in us (Fr. de Montcheuil).

In this context we can see the necessity for the study of the various religions and civilizations of mankind.[6]

"There are aspects of Christianity which we have not yet discovered, and we shall discover them only when it will have been refracted through all the facets of the prism. Up until now it has been refracted only through the Greek and Roman worlds; it still remains to be refracted through the Chinese and Hindu facets in order to find fulfillment at the end of time, when not only every individual, but every civilization will have been Christianized" (Fr. Daniélou, *op. cit.*).

---

6 Cf. Huby, *Christus,* a manual of the history of religions.

IV. The Problem of the Apostolate

This problem can be posed and solved in just about the same terms as the missionary one.

The Apostolate, a Missionary Problem

1. In order to Christianize all activities we have to enter into human life in all its various manifestations. There have to be as many native apostles and particular forms of religious life as there are environments.

"...This activity is consonant with the principle willed and adopted by the Pope and sanctioned by his predecessors in regard to the missions, namely, a native clergy for each people; for each different environment apostles of these environments from these environments. Such is the method to follow, and a vital point in all Catholic Action" (Pius XI, 1934).

From this point of view every apostolate is a missionary one: the Church has to be **planted everywhere**, but it must be planted concretely, **really**, that is, where real problems exist, where real influences are at work. It may very well happen that the Church is considered as officially established in an area where in fact it is not really present and at home. (This differs from the Mission properly speaking, in which the Church is not established in any way.) But we must not delude ourselves: the Church is never fully established; it must continually make progress; must continually deepen its penetration of all the realities of human existence.

2. The problem must be constantly rethought: Is the Church really at the disposal of all? Is it really present in all departments of life?

The Church must fulfill its mission and forget no aspect of its universality. It has to attain all creatures, all nations, the whole world. There are riches peculiar to each person and each community which it has to bring out, which it has "to restore in Christ." This mission is unlimited. As commissioned by Christ to extend the mystery of Redemption throughout space and time, the Church must be filled with

177

some all-embracing love that Christ bears towards all creatures, all nations, the whole world. So long as the Church is not present and at home everywhere, it must continue to exist in a missionary state.

What is the present status of this mission of Christ and the Church after twenty centuries of redemption? Are the riches of Christ and His Church known by all, in reach of all, in such a way that the Christian way of life is accessible to all men in every place? The Church continually runs the risk of believing itself to be established in a country or a given environment just because a hierarchy, a clergy, churches and good works are set up there. We freely admit that the Church is established in the dioceses of Christendom. But we must not delude ourselves. Is the Church really and concretely present where the real problems exist, where the real influences are at work, where real human communities live?

To put the question that way is already to answer it. Sometimes the Church is simply not present in areas where real problems exist, and consequently cannot bring Christian solutions to bear upon them. There are influences at work without the presence of the Church to Christianize them. There are areas of leisure, work, finance, commerce and transportation in which the Church is more or less absent. Yet it is up to the Church to enter into human life in all its various ramifications so as to Christianize all its activities. As human life develops and becomes differentiated, the Church has to adapt itself and take up new positions. The difficulty comes when human life undergoes radical transformations and the Church fails to keep pace with them.

Formerly, before the era of great inventions, rapid transportation and heavy industry, human life was organized on a territorial basis; men worked and exchanged the fruits of their work on the spot. Most human problems were thus forcibly enclosed within a limited territory. Under such conditions the presence of the Church was also of a territorial nature: the parish corresponded to the commune or the manor. There was no chasm separating human life and the Church. This does not mean that everyone was Christian, but that everyone had at their real and immediate disposal the Church in its parochial form.

Since then human life has almost ceased existing on a territorial basis. Today's real problems—particularly in great industrial cultures—no longer lie within the narrow limits of a commune, but at the crossroads of regional, national and international influences. New human communities have grown up on bases other than territorial ones, e.g., on the basis of transportation, leisure activities, finances, etc. But the presence of the Church has, on the whole, remained a narrowly territorial one—the parish, which in many cases no longer corresponds with a real, human dimension, and which, in any case, no longer suffices for contacting and resolving all the problems of a world awaiting the Gospel.

The essential task today is one of building up the Church within the dimensions of the real environmental world. The same impulse, which in times past forced the Church to found parishes so as to be present within human life organized territorially, must now force the Church to adapt these parishes to the real needs of today and to try in every way possible to be present in environments resulting from the factory system, new modes of transportation, leisure activities, intellectual movements, and all their resultant institutions.

3. As in the case of mission lands the Church has to **respect** the authentic values contained within each man and particular to each of life's environments. Incorporation within the Church will bring such values to fulfillment by **purifying them** of their limitations.

The Church will be revealed in all its fullness only when it once again becomes the People's Church.

The Apostolate in the Modern World.

In place of petty apologetical preoccupations of "defense and condemnation" we shall be occupied in discovering all the values contained in other religions, in other Churches, in contemporary movements, so as to integrate these values

179

through a process of purification if necessary. We shall baptize them.

Consequently, we have to acquaint ourselves with contemporary aspirations, with the great modern currents of thought so as:

—to see what they contain of truth and error,

—to penetrate more deeply into our own teaching as a result,

—and so as to present it in such a way that it appears to our contemporaries as the real answer to their aspirations in so far as they are right and positive.

"What you worship in ignorance, that I proclaim to you" (Acts 17:23).

> "What characterizes the modern world is that it is being built up outside the Church and even in opposition to the Church, when all the while it is the Church alone which can provide the solution to its antinomies (person and community, present and future) and the answer to its aspirations (for an integrated human community, for one world, for progress realized through cooperation)." [7]

The problem is more serious today than ever, for history is made up of periods and epochs (cf. Peguy), and we are now in the midst of an "epoch." We are at a moment of "qualitative change," as the Marxists put it.

Two discoveries characterize the modern world:

—*A world view*—men think in terms of the world. Henceforth, problems will be posed in terms of continents and the world (The European Problem, etc.).

—*An historical approach*—men think in terms of history. They envisage the possibility of unlimited evolution and progress.

Moreover, the Catholic Church today finds itself faced with another "church," another "religion": for Communism is not only a party and a social doctrine, but a spirit and a way of life. *Communism* offers a panoramic view of the world in all domains and furnishes an answer to all problems. In short, it presents all the characteristics of a church or religion, namely: an explanation for man and history; a *mystique;* a faith; a hope; a reason for living; a task to which one can dedicate oneself; a system of morality; a community;

---

[7] Beirnaert, *Fidélite à l'Eglise* (Etudes, Oct. 1946).

a hierarchy. It is a leaven, a yeast, tending to arouse and transform the entire world (catholicity).

On each one of these points it stands in opposition to the Catholic Church. The world today is torn between these two forces, fashioned by these two leavens. The Socialists themselves admit this fact: "It is an heroic faith and vision which will carry the day; that of Rome or that of Moscow, the Christian faith or the Bolshevik one" (Daniel Mayer in the *Populaire*, 12/6/46).

This situation invites us to study Communism under its different aspects. It is **on the doctrinal plane** that the problem is posed and not just on the personal one. In fact we must compare the two systems point for point: one final end in comparison to the other, one code of morality in comparison to the other. It is only too easy to oppose the principles of one side (Catholic or Communist) to the persons of the other. But this is not an honest way of playing the game and backfires on those who engage in it; for every bad Communist held up to scorn a bad Catholic can always be found.

We must also present the Church's teaching, not just as a pure and simple condemnation of Communism, but as the answer to everything just and positive contained in its aspirations. If our outlook is more comprehensive than that of Communism, it is because it begins by embracing the good to be found within its opponent's position. Communism possesses values we should do well to accept and make our own, e.g.: a world vision, a feeling for community, for the meaning of labor, the idealism of a great project to be realized co-operatively, the importance of economic conditions for the spiritual liberation of mankind.

The only way to combat Communism effectively is to solve the problems it poses, those problems which explain its success.

V. Catholicism and the Catholic

Catholicism is diversity in unity. The Church's Catholicism must live in each member of the Church.

181

1. To be a Catholic is **to be concerned for the whole Church,** for the whole world. We have to develop Catholic minds and Catholic hearts. We must be Catholic first and foremost, and this means that we must not lock ourselves up in any chapel but rather measure all things in the light of the whole Church. Any spirituality must be Catholic first of all; and so must any apostolate (this may mean the sacrifice of the particular good of a Congregation, of a good work, or of a parish, in favor of the general good of the Church).

2. To be a Catholic is **to accept the differences of others,** and to understand them; to accept and love others as other, except in regard to their sins or inadequacies. This demands a great deal of humility and broadness of outlook.

3. To be a Catholic is **to enrich oneself with the differences of others.** We have to give to others, but we also have to take from them. Every man is our superior in some way, and it is up to us to discover this wealth and profit by it.

4. To be a Catholic, finally, is **to be fully personal,** is to develop fully our gifts of nature and grace, so as to love, serve and develop the Church's Catholicism. We must utilize the example of others, not in order to imitate them directly, but in order to develop ourselves along our own personal lines. There are no limits to such development.

PROJECTS

1. Study some of the blessings found in the Ritual (for example, those of water and salt), and show how they reveal the Church's role in regard to created things (exorcisms, blessings, consecrations) (the great themes recalled in these texts: the mysteries, the facts of Sacred History, etc.).

2. Show the universality of the Church's prayer in the various collects of the Good Friday Mass.

PRACTICAL ATTITUDES

Do we have a Catholic attitude:
—towards the persons around us?
—towards the missions?
—towards the great problems facing the world today (wars, unemployment, misery, persecutions)?
What shall we do in a practical way in regard to each one of these points?

182

Chapter 31

THE CHURCH AND CIVIL SOCIETY

The Church is Catholic, it has a universal mission. Does this mean that it must answer all man's needs and itself organize the City of Man? It is clear enough that it is civil society which takes care of the railroads and not the Church. But what is the Church's place in the organization of society? Too frequently only a juridical reply is provided for this problem. First of all we *limit* Civil Society to the State, that is, Society's form of government; then we study the *rights* of the Church, the *rights* of the State, and the *relation between these rights*. We then conclude that the State is subordinate to the Church, and that the Church has a kind of "indirect" power over the State.

Here we shall try to stand back from such problems a little, to enlarge our perspectives and to situate the role of Civil Society in God's plan.

We shall study the following three points in succession:

1. We can distinguish *two aspects* in the one plan of God.
2. To realize this plan there are *two societies* connected with these two aspects.
3. The Church's task is *not to organize the earthly city but to animate it*.

Two Aspects of God's Plan

In the one plan of God we can somehow distinguish two aspects. God's final purpose in creating men was to make them His children in Christ. God creates in order to divinize. These then are the two aspects of God's one plan: **Creation—Divinization.** For example, God, with the co-operation of parents, creates a child (birth) in order to make this child His own son (baptism).

The question may be asked as to why God does not create us as sons from the very first. We see that as a matter of fact God always tests His creatures before establishing them in their final state. For example, God put Adam to the test in the earthly paradise before confirming him and his descendants in the state of happiness. God also subjected the angels to a test. Similarly, we have to prove our love here on earth before being conducted into eternal blessedness.

Confronted by this fact we can discover the following justification of it: God wants us to choose Him *freely;* He does not want to impose upon us; He is freedom and love. Those who are not "God" by nature can only be divinized by an act of free love. God makes creatures in His own image, that is, capable of knowledge and love, so that they can participate in His own life of Knowledge and Love. He creates free beings and invites them to participate freely in His life of love. He does no violence to our freedom, even and especially when He floods us with His grace. This test, therefore, reveals to what degree God respects the freedom He has conferred upon us, and what price He attaches to having our free, personal love. Hell is the stupefying proof of the price God attaches to our free, personal love. This is a traditional theme: "God has not created us without us, and will not save us without us."

Now creatures have nearly always *succumbed* in the face of this test. Adam fell. A great number of the angels fell. These are the *demons* who appear so prominently in the life of Jesus. And like Adam each one of us succumbs. Sin consists in preferring oneself to God, in retiring within oneself instead of laying oneself open to God, in seeking happiness in oneself rather than finding it in God.

That is why the process of divinization is at the same time a process of **redemption,** of restoration. Grace is not only *"elevans,"* but also *"sanans,"* that is, not only raises creatures to the state of grace, but it also cures sin; it raises up sinful creatures and makes of them children of God, freed from sin.

184

Two Societies

There are two societies established to realize God's one plan: "God has divided the care of the human race between two powers, ecclesiastical and civil, the one charged with the care of divine things and the other with that of human things. Each of them is supreme in its own order" (Leo XIII, Immortale Dei; Denzinger 1866).

Civil Society organizes the **temporal well-being** of mankind.

The Church organizes the **eternal happiness** of mankind.

We may ask why there is this division into two societies. Some theologians think that this division results from sin: If Adam had not sinned, they say, he would have engendered sons of God. Creation and divinization would have coincided perfectly. Man would have been created a son of God. Likewise, there would have been but a single society with the father of the family as its priest and the head of the City as its High Priest.

But such a hypothesis is put forward only to try to justify a fact situation. We should do better to pause over the facts themselves.

1. The first fact to be considered is that **Christ willed** to dissociate His Kingdom from that of Caesar.

"Render to Caesar the things that are Caesar's..." (Matthew 22:21).

"My kingdom is not of this world" (John 18:36).
But the world did not immediately become aware of this distinction between the two societies.

(a) *Before Jesus* there was the Jewish theocracy. A single society saw both to things human and to things divine. Certainly the powers of king, priest and prophet were differentiated, but the king governed and summoned his people to war in the name of God. And the Jews expected Jesus Himself to be a political liberator who would expel the foreign occupation forces and re-establish the Jewish dynasty.

(b) *Jesus* did not meet with a great deal of enthusiasm when He affirmed that His Kingdom was of another order,

185

and that men should obey Caesar (Matt. 22:21). Similarly St. Paul (Romans 13:1-7) and St. Peter (I Peter 2:13-17).

(c) *After Jesus,* the new Society founded by Him, the Church, was persecuted by the empire for three centuries. But with the Conversion of Constantine in 313 the situation changed, and before the end of that century, Theodosius even considered making Catholicism the official religion of the empire. In any case, the Church appeared openly in civil society, built churches, and Catholics exercised official functions in the empire.

Then appeared the conflicts over the frontiers separating the two societies; for example, the emperor intervened in Church Councils and in theological discussions.

With the collapse of the Empire and the barbarian invasions, the Church soon found itself exercising functions which would be properly those of civil society; bishops became defenders of the city, and monks clearers of the forest. Soon the pope found himself the political arbiter of the new secular rulers.

But such rulers progressively freed themselves from this political wardship of the Church (cf. the quarrels between Boniface VIII and Philip the Fair of France). This movement ended in arrangements called *Concordats* by which the two societies treated each other as equals. And at the end of the 19th century Pope Leo XIII consecrated the principle of the "supreme power" of civil society *in its own order*. By the Lateran Treaty under Pius XI and the creation of Vatican City, the Church finally appears as a purely spiritual power supported by a tiny temporal body. Like Christ the Church can now truly say: "My Kingdom is not of this world."

2. To this fact that Christ willed such a separation of the two societies we have to add that **any infringement** of Christ's will in these matters **harms both Societies.**

—either Civil Society absorbs the Church (cf. the Russian Orthodox Church).

—or the Church infringes upon the rights of Civil Society (Clericalism).

We can discover a justification for this desire of Christ, for we can relate the two Societies to the two aspects of God's plan, namely, creation and divinization.

1. The movement of *creation* is a *going out* (*exitus*) from God: God gives men *carnal life*. Creation, therefore, goes from unity (divine) to multiplicity (of creatures).

2. The movement of *divinization* is, conversely, a *return* (*reditus*) towards God. God offers the opportunity of an intimate sharing of His own divine life to the men He creates; this is grace. God takes back within Himself, so to speak, the men He placed in existence outside Himself. Divinization, therefore, goes from multiplicity (of creatures) to unity (divine).

Civil Society corresponds to the first movement: it organizes everything on the properly human level; its task is to make good use of the riches of creation for the sake of the temporal well-being of mankind.

The Church corresponds to the second movement: it organizes everything concerning divine life. Its purpose is to draw all men—and even all creation—back to God. Consequently, the Church is not composed of all mankind, but only of that part of mankind which returns to God through the testing process we mentioned above. The Church is **divinized mankind, redeemed creation.**

For creation is equivocal. A man can become one of the elect or one of the damned. An invention like atomic energy can serve life or destroy it. Creation must be "signed," "sealed," given its "value": it must be saved, redeemed, divinized by the Church and in the Church.

These considerations concerning the respective missions of the two Societies also explain what is called the "indirect power" of the Church over the State. *Creation is not an end in itself,* but must return to God: its end is its divinization. In consequence, the earthly city must be organized in such a way as to permit man to realize his true vocation, which is divine and eternal. To accomplish this the **Church must provide Society with the correct notion of the final end of**

man and of personal freedom. And by the presence and activity of its members it must guide the construction of the world into channels in conformity with man's true vocation. Civil society itself does not have the mission of assuring this final end: it is the Church's mission. But it must remain open and receptive to man's eternal vocation.

Both Societies are indispensable. One assures man's temporal welfare. The other assures man's eternal welfare. The Church receives the "matter" it has to divinize from Society. Society receives from the Church that profound inspiration which must animate it in its task of organizing the world.

The Church's Mission in Regard to Civil Society

We are forcibly aware that contemporary men sometimes harbor a certain distrust for the Church and its role in Society. Even lately the Church appeared to those influenced by Marxist Communism as the ally of Capitalism. But such distrust has shifted ground by reason of recent international events. With the world divided into two camps the Church appears as a diplomatic power, and the press is quick to find a political interpretation in any of the papal discourses or principal religious acts. This distrust for the Church has deep-rooted causes. It is a case of civil society coming of age and confronting the former child-parent relationship between itself and the Church.

What is going on between Society and the Church is a little like what happens within families when children start showing independence in regard to their parents. When the child is still little, it is entirely dependent upon its parents. But as the process of growth and education proceeds, the child soon strikes out on its own, develops its own personality, gives signs of independence: "A man shall leave father and mother..." Often enough during this stage adolescents pass through a real crisis. They systematically mistrust everything which reminds them of their former dependence and which seems to hinder the full development of their personality. Then comes the day when they quit father and mother for good in order "to cling to their wife" and found a home of their own.

Once this break has been made and parents no longer appear as a "danger" to personal independence, the child frequently regains confidence in them, and the stage is set for true "friendship" and "collaboration" between the grown-up child and its parents.

What is now going on between Civil Society and the Church is undoubtedly analogous to this type of adolescent crisis. Everything in this drive for independence is not necessarily bad. Indeed, this dissociation of powers and competences is willed by Christ and beneficial in its results. For, in fact, the Church has a different role in relation to mankind's eternal life and in relation to the temporal organization of mankind. She plays a properly maternal role in regard to the first, but only that of a leaven in regard to the second.

The Church, the Leaven of the World

The image of **the Church as "the leaven of the world"** indicates the Church's mission with regard to the earthly, temporal life of mankind.

—It recalls once again the *universality* of this mission; for the whole world, the whole of Civil Society awaits its leavening influence. This universalism is also to be found in such associated images as "the light of the world, the salt of the earth."

—It also defines its *mode of action;* the Church must be a leaven at work in the earthly City, it must **animate** all things, but not organize all things. The organization of the earthly city belongs to Civil Society, not the Church, except in extraordinary and temporary cases. The Church is neither a ghetto nor a brand of Fascism. It is not a ghetto because it animates all things. It is not a kind of Fascism because it does not organize all things; it organizes only what pertains to salvation.

—This image of leaven of the world also recalls the duty of being *missionary minded.* The Church is a leaven which must be taken and kneaded into the dough so that the whole mass will rise. Consequently, we can't just sit back and wait for the world to come looking for this leaven in our activities, in our parishes; we have to take the initiative.

—Finally, this image indicates what is a *constant danger* for the Church and Catholic Action. The Church is a leaven and its dough is the whole world, Civil Society in its entirety. It does not have to go looking for the dough it is called upon to leaven; it is given it. The danger lies in the fact that the Church may be tempted to leaven only its own dough. For example, the Church should be a leaven in all hospital life, that is, in all hospitals, in all maternity homes, in all sanitariums. But it may be tempted to leaven only its own institutions: Catholic hospitals, Catholic maternity homes, Catholic sanitariums.

There is obviously no question of refusing the Church the right to have and to keep its own institutions, but it must never forget that it also has the mission to be present as a leaven in all hospitals, all maternity homes, all sanitariums and all schools. Its mission is to animate hospital life or school life wherever it may be found.

The situation is the same as regards leisure activities, work, and in general the entire organization of the earthly City. The earthly City needs the leaven of the Gospel, not for its organization, but for its inspiration. Only the Church can provide the world with the true notion of person, of freedom, of the family, of the final end. The drama of the present time lies in the fact that the Gospel leaven is only too often absent from the new world which is in the process of being constructed. Rather, another leaven is at work in the world with entirely different ends in view, namely, Marxian Communism.

—Furthermore, the very presence of the Church as a visible society in the world places it like a city set on a mountain, like a standard set up among the nations. Civil Society has a temporal role, and consequently it does not exhaust man's aspirations towards divine life. By its very existence the Church reminds Civil Society that temporal things are precarious and that there is more in man; that all civilizations and all Civil Societies are limited to this present world, that a deeper, nobler and more durable bond than that of earthly attachment to one's country unites men. By its presence alone the Church untiringly repeats to Civil Society that mankind as a whole is called to share in the divine life, and thus it invites Civil Society to look beyond its proper boundaries and its earthly interests.

Supplementary Mission

Sometimes, however, the Church, for example, through its Catholic Action movements, is required to organize certain temporal services by way of substitution or education. To what point is this in conformity with the Church's mission and how far can it extend such substitution?

Let us try to lay down some criteria for the solution of such delicate questions:

1. *Material Criterion.* This limit is relative to **the degree of evolution of Civil Society.** The less Civil Society is capable of organizing correctly, that is to say, according to a just conception of man, the various services of the earthly city, the more the Church will be required to play a supplementary role. We can see immediately what is stable and what is relative in this material criterion. As regards *the stable element:* the Church is not called upon to organize such services if Civil Society possesses fitting means to organize them correctly, that is, in conformity with man's true vocation. But we also see that such activity is *relative according to place and time.* According to time: it has become a commonplace to remark that in times past under the Barbarians or even in medieval Christendom, the Church had to do with a society that was still under age, and that, consequently, it had to make up various deficiencies which would normally be cared for by Civil Society. Such a state of affairs still exists today in certain missionary lands where the missionary is both priest and doctor, and where the Church may build roads, etc. But this criterion also reminds us that we cannot base present attitudes on past examples. Civil

191

Society today is now more evolved, more aware of its rights and better fitted to realize its vocation.

And yet this is also relative to place, for Civil Society has not developed in a uniform manner in all parts of the world, as, for example, in Spain, Belgium and in France. In France, for a variety of reasons, Civil Society has developed self-awareness more rapidly and more strongly, and this has purified the Church and Catholic Action proportionately.

Similarly, with one and the same country this evolution can vary according to localities. Consequently, the activities of Catholic Action cannot be transposed in a purely material manner from one country to another. What is still legitimate in Spain or in Belgium may no longer be so in France, and what is legitimate in the west of France would not necessarily be so in the Paris area.

But this first criterion is not sufficient; it must be completed by a second. Still it does throw some light on our problem. For Catholic Action movements it may be summed up in the following practical motto: "Provided it is done in the right spirit, do not do anything which is best done by someone else."

2. *Spiritual Criterion.* Such a supplementary role may be very extensive, yet must never abolish the distinction between the Church and Civil Society by any kind of general substitution of services. To what degree can a Catholic Action movement be burdened with temporal activities and supplementary roles and still remain a Church Movement? On condition that it keeps as its primary end an **apostolic motive,** and provided that it keeps evangelical and educational characteristics in its methods. In other words, on condition that the Movement takes care to see to the purity of the end and the **purity of the means.**

This purity supposes that the services of the Movement are destined primarily to educate its members and the environment in which they live, rather than organize the earthly city. For example, the establishment of vacation camps may depend upon a Catholic Action movement to the degree in which they serve as a means of education.

This purity also supposes that *supplementary services* be

just that; the Movement must be ready to turn them over to the competent organs of Civil Society as soon as this becomes feasible. What is more, the Movement takes pleasure in this progress of Civil Society and facilitates such progress.

This idea of a "leaven," therefore, shows both the Church's role and its limits. We have to beware of two extremes:

1. The first is that of *refusing to allow Civil Society to take over tasks which it becomes capable of assuming* for the common good, and continuing to claim them for the Church, or for the Church alone. This is "clericalism."

2. The second is that of *becoming uninterested in the organization of the earthly city* to the degree in which it is no longer assured by the Church, and of occupying ourselves exclusively with that area which the Church continues to organize (angelism).

It is in the measure in which the Church sincerely recognizes the competency of Civil Society and assumes its essential role of divine maternity and earthly leaven in its regard, that there will be established friendly relations, and even collaboration, between Society and the Church, like those which exist between grown-up children who have established their own homes and their parents.

PROJECTS

Study the Scriptural passages cited in this chapter and show Christ's and the Christian's attitude toward Civil Society.

Chapter 32

THE APOSTOLICITY OF THE CHURCH

This Catholic mission is to be the work of the entire Church. As a whole it works towards "the restoration of all things in Christ." But it works in an organized, hierarchical fashion, for the Church is "apostolic," organized, hierarchical. The Church is both Catholic and Apostolic. It is to Peter, the Apostles, and therefore to their successors that Christ has entrusted the responsibility for the Mission, the pastoral charge, "during the time of His absence."

I. The Meaning of the Hierarchy

We have to understand this hierarchical and apostolic structure of the Church:
  —in regard to the very essence of the Church,
  —in regard to Christ,
  —in regard to the Church's Mission.

In Regard to the Very Essence of the Church

The Church is hierarchical in its very essence because **everything in the Church comes from God through Christ:**
—The Father sent the Son: see how this refrain runs through St. John. And the "mission" He received from the Father, Jesus passes on in His turn: (John 20:21; cf. Matt. 28:18-19; Mark 16:14-18) "As the Father has sent me, I also send you."
—Christ received life from the Father, and in turn passed it on to us (John 10:28; 17:2).
—The *word* in which we must believe comes from the Father through Christ (John 12:49), and in His turn Christ

194

transmits this word (John 15:15), "Go and make disciples of all nations" (Matt. 27:18); "Go into the whole world and preach the gospel" (Mark 16:15).

—All power is given to Christ by the Father (John 17:2 and 18), and Jesus transmits the powers He received: (Matt. 28:18), "Feed my lambs, feed my sheep" (John 21:15).

Thus everything comes from God: the Incarnation calls our attention to the fact that it is God Who comes to us, and not we who go to God. The Church draws our attention to the fact that it is Christ Who comes to us, and not we who go to Christ; we do not raise ourselves to Christ's level by our own efforts.

In Regard to Christ

In the Church all initiative necessarily comes from Christ, since it is His mission, word, life and power that the Church has received and which it must transmit.

Christ builds His Church from within, through the Spirit, but also through the hierarchy. And these are not two separate means which would, as it were, come into play alternately; rather, they are conjoined means; He offers us life in the sacraments, light in apostolic preaching, direction in the members of the hierarchy. The hierarchy, therefore, is what represents Christ and His activity here on earth; it is a means of communicating with Christ, and was established by Christ Himself. It is in some manner the "sacrament" of Christ: it "represents" Him. It is this special bond with Christ which gives meaning to the Catholic hierarchy; Christ's activity in the Church through the Spirit is bound up with the activity of the hierarchy. It is this, too, which explains the Catholic's attitude towards the hierarchy: he submits to the hierarchy in order to submit to Christ and His activity.

The fact of having to draw life from the sacraments instituted by Christ and not by us, of having to receive His word from the preaching of Apostles chosen by Christ and not by us, of having to come to know Christ's will in the same manner, all this puts concretely the fundamental truth that the members of the Church cannot sanctify themselves by their own efforts, but that **all initiative comes from Christ,** and that Christ desires to attain us only in His Church.

In Regard to the Church's Mission

—The hierarchy receives from Christ the responsibility for the Church's mission: the pastoral charge. At the origin of the apostolate there is always a call: **it is Christ Who chooses,** who takes the initiative. Remember the calling of the Apostles: "Come, follow me." It will always be so in the Church, and from the top to the bottom; one must be called in order to share in the Church's mission.

—But the fact of the hierarchy does not divide the Church into two blocks, one of which—the hierarchical Church—would alone be active; the other of which—the Church of the faithful—would be entirely passive. On the contrary, it was so that the whole Church would be hierarchical and apostolic that Christ established the hierarchy and entrusted it with His powers. The hierarchy is not the whole Church, but the **whole Church is hierarchical;** the Apostles are not the whole Church, but the whole Church is **apostolic,** which means that as a whole and on every level it participates in the hierarchical apostolate, in the apostolic mission.

—The Church is not a democracy (as Protestant liberals conceive it). It is not the mass of the faithful who delegate their powers to the bishops and priests; rather the latter hold their mission and powers directly from Christ.

—Nevertheless, they have received these powers from Christ in order to serve the faithful: it was to organize the entire people in its march, the kingdom in its growth, the whole Church in its militant phase, that Christ gave them His powers.

II. The Mission and Powers of the Hierarchy

Canon law and theological manuals present us with the classic distinction of three powers:

—power of teaching (guard the deposit of faith),

—power of order,
—power of jurisdiction.

This way of presenting things stems from a situation in which the Church is established and the only problem is one of administration; the function of the hierarchy is then defined by its powers. However, we no longer live in such situations. Now it is not so much a question of administering an established Christianity, but of founding a Christian community, first of all, and even of establishing the Church. We must, therefore, grasp the missionary nature of the hierarchy: the hierarchy is "missionary" in the strongest sense of the term; it has received Christ's mission, *His pastoral charge*.

This Mission, this pastoral charge, includes:

—the mission of *evangelizing in the name of Christ,* of bearing witness in word. Let us recall here once and for all that the teaching mission properly signifies the ministry of the word, that is, of the deposit of revelation and not just any teaching (cf. St. Paul: the mystery of Christ);

However, it is in these Christian schools and on every level of education from the primary grades to the university that the Church shows the world that human culture must be in conformity with the Gospel. Christian education realizes a union between the Gospel and all concrete existence.

—the mission of *sanctifying in the name of Christ:* the ministry of the sacraments;

—the mission of *directing the Church in the name of Christ:* the ministry of jurisdiction.

Because it has the mission, it has power: the power of teaching (with the guarantee of infallibility); the power of order; the power of jurisdiction. The powers are limited to the mission.

It has been remarked sometimes that these three powers correspond to the three different aspects of Christ Himself:

—He is a prophet: power of teaching
—He is a priest: power of order
—He is a King; power of jurisdiction.

197

This corresponds to the more classic presentation of the power of teaching, and recalls Jesus' words: "I am the truth."

St. Hilary calls the Church: "the mouth of Christ, because it is to it and through it that the mysteries are revealed." [1]

In his catechism Bossuet asks the pertinent question: "Why is Scripture not mentioned in the Creed?" Answer: "Because it suffices for it to show us the Holy Catholic Church through which we receive both Scripture and the understanding of what it contains."

This ministry of the word was officially entrusted by Jesus to Peter, the Apostles, and to their successors, that is, **to the episcopate as a whole in union with the Pope.** Their obligation is not only to keep the deposit of faith intact, but **to** transmit it, preach it, and draw out all the consequences which the Church needs in its present circumstances: they have to constantly draw from it light for the solution of contemporary problems.

They are the judges and doctors of the faith. In the exercise of this mission of teaching and evangelization they have the guarantee of the privilege of infallibility.

1. **Importance of this mission:**

Scripture shows us the importance of this mission of evangelization:

—Faith is necessary for justification; now faith is at the basis of apostolic preaching: "Faith depends on hearing" (cf. Romans 10:14-18).

—The importance of the ministry of the word, of verbal testimony, shows up in the life of Jesus; the mission He entrusts to His Apostles; in the life of the Apostles: Acts 6:4; I Cor. 9:16.

—The ministry of preaching is always associated with the ministry of the sacraments, but it precedes the latter ministry: "Go and teach all nations, baptizing them... (Matt. 28:19); "Preach the gospel to every creature. He who believes and is baptized shall be saved." But those who will

---

[1] *Tract. in Psalm.* 138, 29; P.L. 9, 807-808.

not believe will not be baptized: "He who does not believe shall be condemned" (Mark 16:15-16).

—When there was question of a choice, the Apostles reserved for themselves the ministry of the word. St. Paul: "Christ did not send me to baptize, but to preach the gospel" (I Cor. 1:17); St. Peter: "It is not desirable that we should forsake the word of God and serve at tables" (Acts 6:2). They put deacons in charge of this latter work: the Apostles were to be entirely devoted "to prayer and to the ministry of the word."

The sacraments are "signs for the faithful," signs of Christ at work in His Church. And this raises a **pastoral problem:** sometimes the sacraments are administered to people who are not prepared for faith through the ministry of the word (baptisms, mass, marriages, etc.).

2. **Some clarifications as to Infallibility:**

Infallibility bears only upon the proper object of the ministry of the word.

—The Church as a whole is infallible, that is, the whole Church will never accept a doctrine contrary to the faith.[2]

—the Ecumenical Councils are infallible.

—The Pope, speaking *ex Cathedra*, is infallible. "The Roman Pontiff, when he speaks *ex Cathedra*, that is, when in discharge of the office of Pastor and Teacher of all Christians, by virtue of his supreme Apostolic authority he defines a doctrine regarding faith or morals to be held by the Universal Church, by the divine assistance promised to him in the person of St. Peter, is possessed of that infallibility with which the divine Redeemer willed that His Church should be endowed for defining doctrine regarding faith or morals; and, therefore, such definitions of the Roman Pontiff are irreformable of themselves and not from the consent of the Church.[3]

—Doctrinal decisions involving the infallibility of the Church are rather rare, and the mission of teaching is normally accomplished in more ordinary ways; teaching given by the whole hierarchy, that is to say by the whole Church,

---

2 Vatican Council, session 3; Denzinger 1800.
3 Vatican Council, session 4; Denzinger 1832-40.

through the *ordinary magisterium,* cannot be false. Infallibility is the assurance given by Christ to the Church so that it will never be mistaken in the transmission and interpretation of Revelation.

Mission of Sanctification: the Ministry of the Sacraments

This corresponds to the more classic presentation of the power of order, and recalls Jesus' words: "I am the life."

The hierarchy has the mission of transmitting the life of Christ: Christ entrusted the sacraments to the hierarchy.

It is in Scripture that we must discover the importance of the Sacraments, not only for the personal life of Christians, but for the **building up of the Body of Christ,** for the organization of the Church.

Baptism builds up the Body of Christ (I Cor. 12:13; Gal. 3:26-27; Romans 6:1-11; Col. 2:9-12; Titus 3:5-7; Mark 16:16; Matt. 28:19); "He who believes and is baptized shall be saved" (Mark 16:16); "Unless a man be born again of water and the Spirit, he cannot enter into the kingdom of heaven" (John 3:5).

But it is especially St. Paul who emphasizes the importance of baptism in the building up of Christ's Body: "For in *one Spirit* we were all baptized into one Body..." (I Cor. 12:13). "For all you have been baptized...you are all one in Christ Jesus" (Gal. 3:26-28).

The *Eucharist* builds up the Body of Christ and assures its unity. "The bread that we break, is it not the partaking of the body of the Lord? Because the bread is one, we though many, are one body, all of us who partake of the *one bread*" (I Cor. 10:16-17).

Mission of Governing and Educating in Christ's Name

This corresponds to the more classic presentation of the power of jurisdiction, and recalls Jesus' words: "I am the way."

The hierarchy has received from Christ the mission of governing the Church during the time of His absence, during the time the Church spends on earth. Christ gave the power of jurisdiction to the Apostles, but only in dependence upon Peter. Consequently, a bishop possesses legitimate jurisdiction only when it is conferred upon him by the Pope, who can also deprive him of it; and the Pope can always intervene directly in a diocese. But the Pope cannot govern without the bishops: they exist by divine right since they were instituted by Christ.

When the hierarchy commands in its proper field and in conformity with the mission it receives from Christ, it expresses Christ's will, and Christ wants us to obey it. Christ did not promise that His representatives would always make the best decisions. But when they command us in Christ's name and under the conditions laid down by Him, Christ wants us to obey them. Our submission to the hierarchy manifests our will to be subject to Christ.

Our faith in the Church is really tested in this power of jurisdiction, for what is human in the members of the hierarchy shows up more clearly in their government in Christ's name than in their power of order and teaching. Christ is more veiled.

We shall come back to the role of the Pope when treating of the Church's unity. Here we shall insist only on the bishop's function.

III. The Bishop's Pastoral Charge

The Bishop Has the Pastoral Charge of His Diocese

In a country, responsibility for the Church rests on the body of its bishops in union with the Pope; and in a diocese on the bishop. He has the pastoral charge of the diocese.

He is responsible for the apostolate. He is neither an administrator nor an ecclesiastical prefect, but a missionary.

At his consecration the pontifical reminds him that he is responsible for his Church. Canon law reminds him that he has charge of all those who live in his diocese. He is the Spouse of his Church; such is the meaning of the episcopal ring: "Receive this ring, the pledge of fidelity, so that you guard God's Spouse, Holy Church, without stain."

1. He is charged with the ministry of the word, he has the mission to evangelize. He is *judge and doctor of the faith;* no one can exercise the ministry of the word in his diocese, except by his delegation.

2. He is charged with the ministry of sanctification. He possesses the fullness of the priesthood; he is filled with the Holy Spirit. He can transmit the priesthood in whole or in part. Just as he is father of the faith by his preaching, so, too, he is father of the priesthood and of all life communicated by this priesthood which he shares with his priests.

3. He is responsible for the government of his Church: he governs it in Christ's name. Consequently, obedience must be rendered to the Bishop *as to Christ Himself:* "Do nothing apart from the bishop." "Be obedient to your bishop, as Jesus Christ in His human nature was subject to the Father." "One with your bishop, as the Church is one with Jesus Christ and as Jesus Christ is one with the Father" (Letters of St. Ignatius of Antioch).

He Shares It with His Priests

This question has been thrown into relief in a recent book by Fr. Masure, *Prêtre diocésain:* "Our priesthood does not primarily nor chiefly consist in the individual power of consecrating the body of Christ and of validly administering the sacraments, but rather in our subordinate participation in the religious and apostolic functions of our bishop. He has ordained us as his collaborators because he himself cannot fulfill all his obligations alone.... Historically and theologically the priesthood issued from the episcopate or rather from the Apostolate, in the primitive sense of this word, meaning the powers and functions of the Twelve."

In varying degrees priests participate in the bishop's pastoral charge, in the mission of the Apostolate; they share with the bishop the responsibility for this mission.

1. Priests *participate in the priesthood of the bishop;*
2. Priests participate in the *mission of evangelization,* in

the ministry of the word. They have to be delegated by the bishop. It is in this sense that the authorization to preach should be understood. When a priest preaches in the presence of a bishop, he kneels first before him to ask his blessing.

3. The bishop also shares the government of his diocese with his priests; for example, he entrusts the government of parishes to pastors. Notice, then, the pastor's responsibility: he represents the bishop in his parish; he has charge of souls. Such is the meaning of the ceremonies of installation. He possesses the ordinary jurisdiction; he has the duty to administer the sacraments, in certain cases, even in peril of his life.

Assistant priests in the parish have merely delegated jurisdiction.

These questions of jurisdiction are important: they show that only the bishop has the mission of government and that others can participate in his task only when he **delegates it**. (It is in this sense that we should understand the conditions of liceity for the sacraments. They are always actions of the Church, and, consequently, it has the right to lay down the precise conditions of their administration.) Certain activities of individual priests are invalid without jurisdiction, for example: confessions without faculties; marriage without jurisdiction. Others are illicit, for example: baptisms of children without the pastor's authorization. In short, the priest only participates in the power of his bishop and, therefore, must remain in close union with him.

"Priests share in the bishop's power of consecrating in a participated way, which is clear from the fact that they consecrate on an altar consecrated by a bishop, in sacred vessels consecrated by a bishop, and in that they themselves are consecrated by a bishop" (St. Thomas).[3]

Therefore, we see both:

1. How the priest is associated in the pastoral charge of the bishop, in his spiritual fatherhood, in his responsibility for the Mission;

2. How he should be united to his bishop since he performs everything only in participation with him. "The priest

3 *IV Sent.*, d. 13, qu. 1, a. 1, quaest. 5.

is seated like the bishop, but on a lower seat; he baptizes, he consecrates the Eucharist, but in the absence of the bishop or by his delegation; sometimes he imposes hands for penance and even for confirmation in virtue of an episcopal delegation" (St. Epiphanes).

He Shares It with His Faithful: Catholic Action

We can distinguish the duty of the apostolate which stems from baptism and confirmation, and the closer participation in the apostolate of the hierarchy given to laymen in Catholic Action.

1. The apostolate of Christians **as members of the Church.**
Baptism makes us members of Christ and the Church. It makes us participate not only in Christ's life of divine sonship, but also in His redemptive life, and consequently, in His desire for the redemption of the world. As members of Christ in the Church we participate in the life and cares of this Church as it grows and expands.

Every Christian has, therefore, a right to and a mission for the apostolate, given to him by his baptism and confirmation. This is what Piux XI recalled when he said: "It is the sacraments of Baptism and Confirmation which impose, amongst other obligations, that of the apostolate, that is, the duty of spiritual help to our neighbor. By Confirmation we are made soldiers of Christ. Now this implies that the soldier would strive and fight, not so much for himself as for others. But even Baptism imposes the duty of the apostolate, because through it we become members of the Church, which is the Mystical Body of Christ.... Now every Christian receives the supernatural life...and in consequence must transmit it to others who do not possess it or who possess it but sparingly or only in appearance." [4]

Let us add that marriage gives a "care of souls," those of one's partner and of one's children. The encyclical *Mystici Corporis* insists upon the special role of fathers and mothers in the building up of the Mystical Body.

---

[4] Letter to Cardinal Cerejeira, Patriarch of Lisbon, January, 1934.

This participation of the faithful in the apostolate and life of the Church is what we call the "Priesthood of the faithful."

2. The laymen's apostolate in **Catholic Action.**

Catholic Action causes this apostolate to rise to a participation in the Apostolate of the hierarchy, that is, in the apostolate which is properly speaking the mission of the Apostles.

"Catholic Action is a participation of the laity in the apostolate of the hierarchy" (Pius XI).[5]

"It does not differ from the divine mission entrusted to the Church and to its hierarchical aposolate" (Pius XI).[6]

"It is the cooperation of the laity in apostolic work, in the work of the apostolate properly so-called, since the bishops are the successors of the Apostles" (Pius XI).[7]

"A participation in the apostolate of the hierarchy, but not in the hierarchy itself." [8]

"The mandate is given to the movement as a whole, not to individuals." [9]

Catholic Action poses problems that we shall study in the following chapter.

PROJECTS

1. From a Gospel (particularly St. John's) or an Epistle select all the texts concerning Baptism and the Eucharist;
   Show the place of these sacraments in the life of a Christian:
   —union with Christ,
   —participation in the death and resurrection of Christ,
   —union with the Church, the Body of Christ, etc.,
   —relationship to sacrament and faith.
2. Study the shepherd theme in the New Testament (St. John, I Epistle of St. Peter) and show what it teaches us:
   —about Jesus Himself,
   —about the mission of the Apostles.
3. Study the texts of the Sacrament of Holy Orders and show how the mission of the priest is conceived in them:
   —co-operation with the bishop,
   —his responsibilities,
   —his powers,

---

5 Encyclical *Ubi Arcano Dei*, Dec. 23, 1922.
6 Letter *Quae Nobis*.
7 Discourse to the Federation Nationale Catholique, 1929.
8 Directives of the German Bishops, 1933.
9 Assembly of the Cardinals and Archbishops of France, 1946.

—his role in the Church, etc.

4. Make a study of the character of St. Paul as it is found in the Acts of the Apostles:

—his life,

—his apostolate,

—his spirit.

PRACTICAL ATTITUDES

Are our relations with the hierarchy in line with what we have studied in the above chapter? (faith, respect, obedience, active collaboration).

Chapter 33

PROBLEMS OF CATHOLIC ACTION

I. Catholic Action: Twofold Mission

Catholic Action is the way the Church's apostolate is exercised today in a world which has become unified and mature. As in the case of the Church, Catholic Action has a diverse mission:

—as regards mankind's *eternal life,*
—and as regards mankind's *temporal organization.*

In the first case it has a mission of *divinization* (a maternal one like that of the Church). In the second case it has a mission of *animation* (a leavening role like that of the Church).

Apostolic Mission

Catholic Action has to awaken the faithful to the apostolate, associate them in the apostolate, organize the apostolate.

1. **Awaken the apostolic spirit** of the faithful. It has to remind them of their divine vocation and of their eternal destiny. It has to arouse the desire of passing on this Christian life to others, of making it known (evangelization), of rendering it possible and desirable (authentic witness).

2. **Associate the faithful in the Church's essential apostolate** which is a missionary one: this means making the Church really present and at home in all places, that is, where the real problems exist, where the real influences meet, where the real human communities are to be found. The first step is to develop an awareness of the absence of the Church in the given environment which the Catholic Action movement has the mission to evangelize. We must

first of all make an inventory of the persons, professions, institutions and environments from which the Church is, in fact, absent. We must also draw up a list of these groups which do not, in fact, participate in the common life of the Church.

A development of this kind of awareness is absolutely essential: it stands at the origin of a great many specific *vocations*. Each Catholic Action group must foster this awareness in one way or another. The members of the various kinds of Catholic Action must feel that they themselves are *responsible* for the coming of the Kingdom of God in their particular environment. As missionaries of the Church they must seek appropriate means to advance the Church, to organize their Christian witness so that it will really influence all men, all the centers of influence, all human communities. In addition they must invite all the faithful to participate actively in the Church's life in which both clergy and laity have their respective roles to play.

3. **Organize this apostolate.**

It is the Church which must be advanced in a specific environment. It is not, therefore, a question of simply raising up individual apostolates. We have to organize the evangelization of a given environment. The various movements of Catholic Action are specifically adapted instruments which enable the Church to evangelize different areas of human life. For example: The Christian Family Movement, family life; the Young Christian Students, student life.

That is why the members of the varous Catholic Action movements, after they have developed an awareness of the absence of the Church in the area entrusted to them, must say to themselves: "We are responsible for the Church in these various domains. How are we going to make the Church really and actively present in the lives of these people, in these problems, in these centers of influence, in these human communities?" "We are also responsible for the interior life of the community of the Church so that it may be more purely Christian, more unhesitatingly Catholic."

The movements of general Catholic Action contribute the

active collaboration of laymen to the life and organization of the Church, in so far as it is a religious society, and especially to the advancement of the parish. These laymen bring to the parish and the different ranks of the hierarchy problems with which society as a whole confronts the Church: spiritual problems of evangelization or charity which the hierarchy and the organized laity can adequately answer. The positive role of General Catholic Action is to render the members of the Church more active in the very life of the Church, to render the community of worship more religious, the community of teaching more missionary, the community of the faithful more universally brotherly.

Animating Mission

Catholic Action has to invite the faithful to become involved in temporal activities and to animate them.

1. Invite involvement.

Catholic Action has to remind Christians of their primordial duty of becoming involved in this task of bringing a just, fraternal and human state of affairs into the world in collaboration with all men.

Christians are invited to do so for two essential reasons:

(a) First of all, because virtue requires certain human conditions; heroic sanctity cannot be demanded of all men in a continuous fashion. Certain basic human needs as regards housing, work and dignity are normally required for the practice of virtue. Such a point is not hard to understand. We can't just preach Christian morality to the working masses; we have to bring about conditions in which such morality is practicable.

(b) Moreover, the Christian faith demands it. If we believe in Creation, in the dignity of the human person, in the vocation of all mankind, in universal Redemption through Christ, this faith must first of all be translated into the respect and service of man and the building of a human order, otherwise faith is merely hypocrisy and our religion Pharisaism. "For I was hungry and you did not give me to eat" (Matt. 25:42).

Because our faith surpasses the human outlook of men of good will, it necessarily includes it. Here are a few examples:

—Faith in Christian dignity called for and demanded the *freeing* of slaves.

—We want *industrial enterprises* to correspond to the exigencies of Christianity; this means that they must be human first of all, that is to say, they must respect and serve the human person in all domains.

—Our *Christian hope* goes beyond this world; it is really transcendant: its object is the world to come which will be inaugurated by Christ's return. But because of this very transcendance Christian hope demands the building of a better world here below as a kind of anticipation of the world to come and as a preparation for this new world.

This duty of involvement is so much the more necessary in the case of adults than in the case of young people. And for married people it will normally mean the involvement of the home as a unit.

2. **Animate this temporal activity.**

It must animate the Christians involved in their various temporal activities. That means:

—helping them to view their various problems from a Christian standpoint;

—giving them the required strength through the friendly and spiritual support of team work and the spiritual help of the Church.

Christians, thus involved and animated by Catholic Action, have to influence the building of a new world *in a Christian spirit,* not by some kind of noisy manifestation of zeal, but by providing the true notion of the human person, of the family, of freedom, all the real bases of a completely human order. The most efficacious apostolate will not always be one of explicit and direct evangelization, but will often consist in this adapted and progressive educational approach, which really makes its way towards God, and which prepares the revelation of His true name.

Although Catholic Action, through its members, must thus animate the organization of the world, its job, as an institution, is not to organize the world itself, nor to administer the structural set-up of the world. As an institution, Catholic Action must act in and upon the world in the same way the Church does, namely, like a leaven.

Unity within the Person

These two tasks are unified on the level of the human person. Catholic Action is a Church movement and not something organized by Civil Society. On the level of the movements themselves, then, there is a certain dualism, as we pointed out in the chapter on the Church and Civil Society.

But on the level of persons, these tasks are unified: one and the same person has to organize the apostolate under the authority of the Church and organize the earthly city under the authority of Civil Society.

Moreover, it is generally *by the same acts* that persons bear witness to Christ and work towards building up the earthly city.

1. These acts bear witness to Christ habitually, that is, by their very qualities of unselfishness, purity, perseverance in generosity, universality of this generosity, exclusion of all hatred and distinction of persons.

2. And *occasionally*, by their explicit reference to Christ and to the Church. For example: on occasions when one must dissent as to the use of certain means (refusal of violence towards persons) or during extraordinary events (strikes, layoffs, etc.). By the fact that all these acts are seen to stem from their true source and cause, Christ and the Church, they become an explicit testimony in favor of Christ and the Church.

II. The Respective Mission of Priests and Laymen

Generally

We have to react against the common tendency of conceiving the layman in terms of the priest and as at the service of the priest. On the contrary, it is by seeing the priest at the disposal of the layman that we shall preserve the dignity and the apostolate both of the layman and of the priest. It is well to begin with what is the normal state of affairs and to judge exceptions only under this light: "The primary and natural state of the Christian is that of being a layman; the priest is a layman who has become a priest" (Cardinal Suhard).[1]

1. The Layman's Vocation.

Let us try to look at matters very simply. The normal state is that of the layman, that is, the state which the Creator foresaw in Genesis: "It is not good that man is alone; I will make him a helper like himself. . . . Be fruitful and multiply; fill the earth and subdue it." Man was to return to God by bringing all creation to completion. We may sum this up in the following way:

God's plan is to restore the whole domain of creation in Christ at the cost of Redemption. In face of these three mysteries, man is not purely receptive; on the contrary, the Holy Trinity goes so far as to invite him to collaborate in each of these three mysteries: God enables him to make a real contribution in his turn:

1. *by collaborating in the mystery of the Creation:*
—of persons: love, procreation, education,
—of things; work, art, skill,
—of the whole human order: economic and political activities.

2. *by collaborating in the mystery of Christianization,* meaning: the divinization of creation brought about by the Church and in the Church (the Apostolate).

3. *by collaborating in the mystery of Redemption* through the painful elements contained in work and the apostolate.

In short, man must build a human world as the prolongation of creation under the authority and organization of civil society; and he must Christianize it under the authority and organization of the Church. Man is, therefore, necessarily caught up in what we have agreed to call, perhaps wrongly, "the secular domain, temporal society":

---

[1] *Priests Among Men.*

—home life with all its family problems;

—professional life with all its technical problems;

—earthly citizenship with all its economic and political problems.

It is in this context that man must normally realize his divine and apostolic vocation. Such is the layman's task.

2. The Priest's Vocation.

Let us now consider the vocation of the priest. His domain is not the secular and the temporal, but the sacred and eternal. The priest is committed to neither a family nor a profession nor to the construction of the earthly city. He is freed from family, technical and political problems strictly speaking. He belongs immediately, totally, exclusively to Christ and to the Church, and it is this fact which gives him his special characteristics. He is a *man of God,* a living sacrament of Christ, that is to say, an efficacious sign of Christ; by his entire ministry he signifies and produces Christ. He is a *man of the Church;* he is in the strongest sense of the term an ecclesiastic, a churchman.

But why is the priest thus freed from the layman's way of life? Is it because the latter's way of life is evil? Certainly not, since it is a collaboration in the divine mysteries. However, because of sin, the layman's way of life is so burdened with earthly and carnal necessities that he is constantly in danger of being engulfed by them completely; the organization of the earthly city demands so much of his time and energy that he continually runs the risk of setting them up as the final end of his activity.

Christ and the Church free the priest so that he can help the layman to realize the normal vocation of man. It is in this light that we are to understand the saying of the Cure of Ars: "Leave a parish without a priest for a while and men will begin worshiping beasts." Such is also the tragic dilemma of Graham Greene's priest in *The Power and the Glory:* if he stays in his persecuted land, he endangers the life of those Christians who give him shelter; but if he leaves, there will no longer be anyone to bear witness for God in that country.

For the love of both God and man, the priest thus freely

213

sacrifices his own personal rights so that other men may find in his sacrifice the indispensable help they need for making over their homes and the world. The example of his sacrifice is an abiding testimony to supernatural values for other men, and, as it were, a living prophecy of the world to come, for "the appearance of this present world shall pass away." At the same time, the priest's sacrifice draws down God's grace on the world.

The priest's self-renunciation is based neither on ignorance nor upon a kind of contempt for the human values of the layman's way of life, but upon the **conscious and voluntary sacrifice** of these real values. As Pere de Grandmaison said: "The true religious are not those who are ignorant of the great natural attachments, but those who sacrifice them."

The mission of the priesthood is, therefore, orientated towards that of the layman. The priest's job is not to replace that of the layman nor to put the layman at the priest's disposal; rather he has to help the layman to discover his own vocation and bring it to realization.

It is my belief that these considerations show sufficiently how indispensable the priesthood is to the world, how great it is, and what love it supposes and constantly demands on the part of the priest towards the Lord to whom he sacrifices everything, and towards his brethren for whom he sacrifices everything.

In Catholic Action

Catholic Action is a missionary problem. It has to raise up a living, radiating, native presence of the Church in a given environment so as to allow for the blossoming forth of all the religious aspirations lying dormant in this given environment. In this missionary work the immediate and primary apostles are the laymen themselves. Through Catholic Action the faithful are thus called upon to participate directly in the fundamental apostolate of the bishops, namely, the extension of the Church in the world. The priest has at his disposal all the riches of his priesthood, the Word of God and the Sacraments, with which to help the laity to fulfill

214

this missionary task. Without the priesthood, no laity—without the laity, no re-Christianization.

All is therefore finally ordained to the re-Christianization of the world, to the concrete establishment of the Church as a leaven in all the mass of human dough. The various preoccupations of both priesthood and laity find their unity in this common purpose: both must share the same anxieties and the same hopes, but both do not work in the same way. There is neither separation nor confusion.

1. **The Laymen's Mission.** Laymen have as their mission the work of spreading the Church in those environments in which they are concretely engaged and which are entrusted to them by the Church:

> "Just as the Pope who is responsible for the whole of Christendom really distributes various territorial portions of his immense burden among his brother bishops, so likewise does he distribute certain categories of souls among the laity so that they may be won over and christianized. He entrusts the apostolic duty of converting the working masses to Christian workers. It is up to them to feel responsible for this class of men and to take the initiatives they see fit. This is a true participation of the laity in what is strictly speaking the duty of the hierarchy, namely, an apostolic care for the whole" (Chanoine Glorieux).[2]

Workers' Catholic Action, for example, is responsible for the spread of the Church among the working classes: it has both the mission and the means to this end. Certain priests still believe that in this regard the Church is merely using a convenient, though laudable, stratagem; they apparently think that the Church entrusts the direct Christianization of certain environments to the laity because priests are scarce and are unable to go everywhere; besides laymen generally have greater success in their immediate environment. However, Catholic Action is no mere temporary relief measure because of a shortage of priests. Even in countries and regions where priests are sufficiently numerous, there are Catholic Action movements. This is because the Christian life is essentially apostolic (cf. Part I, chap. VIII), and this apostolate is organized in the Church of today in the various forms of Catholic Action. That is why, for example, Canon

---

2 *L'Eglise à l'oeuvre.*

Cardijn, the founder of the Young Christian Workers, speaks so insistently of the irreplaceable mission of young workers.

2. **The Priest's Mission.** The primary preoccupation of the priesthood of the Church in this twentieth century is that of awakening the apostolic awareness of the faithful, of nourishing them with the word of God and with the riches of the sacraments for their missionary task. Priests have at their disposal all the riches of Christ and His Church, and these riches will make real apostles and Catholic Action militants of the faithful. These in turn will carry the living, active presence of the Church into all the concrete situations of their daily life. Pius XII reminded us of this recently in an address to the Young Christian Farmers: "Let them never forget their mission is to be the *living and radiating presence of the Church* in rural life." They will everywhere form communities animated with the life of Christ and radiating His love so as to spread the Christian life, and first of all, to make it possible and desirable for all men. There is a hierarchy of values in the priest's life. His besetting concern should be to build up the Church within the dimensions of the real world, and to do this he must raise up and animate an adult and responsible laity living the life of Christ in his priesthood.

III. The Fundamental Attitudes of Catholic Action

We are going to reconsider all these main ideas in a more concrete way by showing what ought to be the preoccupation of Catholic Action apostles.

The first essential is to feel our responsibility until we suffer from it; to understand well the Church's mission and our place in this mission, the immense needs of the world on the one hand, and those of Christ and the Church on the other. This awareness of the task which lies before us should summon us to holiness. Catholic Action, like the apostolate of the Apostles themselves, is first of all a summons to follow Christ: "Come, follow me." Catholic Action is a gift of ourselves to Christ and the Church so as to realize the mission

216

we just defined above. It demands real holiness of us. Let us try to specify some of its fundamental attitudes.

1. We must be "part and parcel."

Too often we Catholics stand "over against" or "on the side lines"; for example, on the side lines of the labor movement. This movement was born and became of age outside the Church. If the Church ever succeeds in baptizing it, it will be an adult baptism. We have done the same for other natural human communities and for human society as a whole which is now more than ever "one world."

Only too often our apostolate consists in withdrawing men from their natural solidarities in order to shelter them in falsely isolated positions. But if Catholic Action has any meaning, it is that of inviting us to be with and in the real world and its natural solidarities, not to one side of them; we are to be *leaven* in the dough, *salt* in food, *light* in the world.

Our task in Catholic Action is not to produce fermentation under test tube or hothouse conditions, but in real life, in the market place. We don't have to go looking for Catholic Action activities: in a sense we have only to accept the natural solidarities springing from our surroundings, our work, etc. The highest form of love consists simply in being part and parcel of a given human situation, in sharing loyally the same destiny as others. The great temptation consists in escaping from such situations, in looking for alibis.

We must be a "part" and not "apart" and so imitate the Incarnation of the Son of God Who made Himself one with all human existence, including the consequences of our sins and death. But it is precisely this example of Christ which invites us to be a "part" in a Christian way.

2. Be a "part" in a Christian way.

It does not suffice to be a "part" simply. If we are just as pagan as our surroundings, our presence will be of no service to them. For our presence to be an evangelical witness, our life must be at once like that of those who surround us and yet different:

—*Like*, or there will be no common meeting of minds;
—yet different in that very resemblance; we share the life

217

and trials of others, yet we react differently even as regards our sins, for we do not choose to remain in them: we suffer from them, we disavow them and we strive to be purified of them.

"Being a part in a Christian way," therefore, demands that we live by faith and live in our real life.

—**Faith** is not a series of religious acts on the side lines of an otherwise pagan life. It is life renewed in all its aspects. It is in some way the vision of Christ grafted on our own so that we may see all things with Him, like Him, in Him. For a Catholic Action Christian, nothing is simply profane. He sees his work through Christ's eyes and comes to regard it as a collaboration in creation, a participation in the mysteries of redemption. He sees his companions with the eyes of faith and comes to regard every man as a member of Christ, a brother for whom Christ died, a brother with a Christian vocation of which he may be ignorant, but which he may come to know through Christian witness and apostolic contact.

—Nor is **Love** just a series of acts of charity added on to an otherwise egotistical or indifferent manner of life. It is a complete change, a transfiguration of all human relations. For a Catholic Action apostle, love is the heart of Christ given us so that we may love with Him, like Him, in Him, all persons of every walk of life.

—This Christian presence in the market place is not easy. Catholic trade-unionists experience this fully during the course of a strike, for example. But the Incarnation of Christ is a redemptive one; Christ saved the world not just by sharing our human condition to the full, but by dying on His cross, and by rising again. Similarly, our presence in real life contacts will be a redemptive incarnation; like Christ we shall only save the situation with which we are burdened through sacrifice.

3. **Be a "part" with the Church.**

What Christ and the Church expect of us is not that we each go our own way, with our own program for holiness, reform and sense of dedication, but that we do this with the Church. Sometimes we meet up with Christians who say:

"I believe in Catholic Action, but it is more the spirit than anything else which counts. I don't want to commit myself to any definite Catholic Action group."

Now it is true that Catholic Action is a spirit transfiguring all our activities, but it is also a *"body."* The Church entrusts an apostolic mission to Catholic Action movements, not to individuals. If we want to work with the Church in re-Christianizing the world, we have to work with Catholic Action as the Church proposes it to us, that is, with its national, federal and local organs.

What we are looking for in Catholic Action is neither personal success nor just any kind of apostolate. Rather we are seeking to advance the Church in the world. What matters is not that religion appears attractive in certain persons or priests, but that the Church be present and active in all domains of human existence, for example, among workers and employers.

If we want to work with the Church, we have to accept the discipline of the Church and the movement. Sometimes we may get the impression that this slows us down. We may be tempted to quit these mandated organizations in order to join other movements where we could work more effectively than in Catholic Action. But this is an illusion.

Only the Church, and only the apostolate rooted in the Church, have promises of life. We have to think and work in union with Christ and the Church. When we do so, our Catholic Action activities will take on their true dimensions, truly becoming missionary acts of the Catholic Church destined to redeem the world.

4. Raise the environmental level.

Catholic Action not only proposes to love all men but to awaken them to love. It knows that a wealth of love and dedication lies dormant or is badly used in every man.

Our faith, love and concerted Catholic Action efforts will open up ways for the coming of grace. When we invite someone to love, when we furnish him an occasion of serving his neighbor, we make him ready for the operation of grace. Love is thus a bonfire spreading other flames. This active presence of the Church in specific environments

219

through Catholic Action apostles permits all men to live in a Christian manner.

5. **Christianize our brethren.**

Our ambitions are as universal as Christ's orders: "Go into the whole world and preach the Gospel to every creature" (Mark 16:15). We want the Christian life to be possible for all men everywhere, in factories, in offices, on farms, during their leisure moments, in all real life situations.

We want the Christian life to be desired by all men everywhere, through the presence of the Church, the community of love, and the example of authentic Christians. We are confident that it is not by minimizing the demands of Christianity that we shall render it desirable. Its real attraction are its heroes and saints. (Just think of the influence exerted by a film like *Monsieur Vincent*).

Before the greatness of the task and the fewness of workers, we might feel tempted to discouragement. But to finish in an optimistic key, it must be recalled that any revolution is the work of an active minority. The Communists are a living example of this truth. But it is also Gospel teaching: a little leaven raises the whole lump, a little salt seasons much food, one candle lights up whole areas of darkness.

The united activity of the priesthood and Catholic Action, an "active minority," is at work in the world, in order to accomplish the Church's mission.

6. **Make the Church Really Live.**

We must not only collaborate in the mission of the Church in the world but also strive to make this visible society which is the Church conformable to its real nature as it was described by Peter: "You are a chosen race, a royal priesthood, a holy nation, a purchased people; that you may proclaim the perfection of him who has called you out of darkness into his marvellous light." (I Peter 2:9).

This Church which confronts civilizations and temporal institutions of the world like a city set on a mountain is something much more than a mere human society of Christian inspiration—for example, Christendom. Because this is so this Church must bear striking witness to a spirit of religious community and brotherhood in a world which does not apply the principles of justice and charity in social life and which refuses to recognize the universal kingship of God and His Christ.

PROJECTS

1. What are the various Catholic Action movements in your parish and diocese? What are their reviews or other publications?

PRACTICAL ATTITUDES

1. Is the Church really known in our environment?
2. Is the Church really present in our environment?
3. Judge where the Church is absent in our environment:
   (a) Persons for whom, in practice, the Church is absent;
   (b) Problems and crossroads of influence from which the Church is, to all practical purposes, absent.
4. How can we by working together assure an active presence of the Church for these persons and centers of influence?

The Nature of the Church

Chapter 34

THE CHURCH: THE BODY
OF CHRIST

This image comes from St. Paul and is a complex one like that of the Spouse. It designates what unites the Church to Christ and what functions the Church has in relation to Christ.

The Point of Departure: St. Paul

1. Texts.

In the great epistles (Romans 12 and I Corinthians 12) the idea of *unity* is paramount: he wants to point out the unity and cohesion between the groups and members (Romans 12:4-5; I Corinthians 12:11). It is only in a secondary fashion that Christ is presented as the Christian's source of life. Christ appears as the principle of life and organization in the same way that the body is as regards its members (the head as well as the other members of the human body: I Cor. 12:21).

In the epistles of the captivity: Ephesians, Philippians, Colossians, the chief idea is that all life flows from Christ as the Head (Ephesians 4:15-16). Here Christ is no longer the body, the principle of organization, but the head, the principle of the vital influx governing the whole organism: Eph. 1:23.

2. What these texts contain:

(a) *The faithful are united* and interdependent *like the members of a body:*

—Diversity of vocations, gifts and graces (Romans 12:4-5; I Cor. 12:18; Eph. 4:7).

—In order to complement one another (Eph. 4:15-16).

—They are members one of another (Romans 12:4-5; Eph. 4:25).

—All these gifts are conferred upon them as members of the whole, just as much as they are for their own sakes (Eph. 4:7; 4:12).

(b) *This body which they form is* in some way *identified with the Body of Christ,* with Christ Himself:

—Romans 12:4-5: "We, the many, are one body in Christ."

—I Cor. 12:27: "You are the body of Christ, member for member."

—Eph. 1:23: "The Church, which indeed is his body."

—Eph. 4:12: "For building up the body of Christ."

(c) *Christ is the principle of unity and organization for this body* made up of the mass of the faithful and with which He is in some way identified: Eph. 1:23; 4:15-16: He assures the harmonious growth of the whole Body which is in the process of being built up through the personal contribution of each of its members.

The Expression "Mystical Body"

1. This expression and image was at first applied to the Holy Eucharist. But now we understand by it that, on the one hand, the personal Christ, considered as Head, and, on the other hand, the mass of the faithful considered as the Body of Christ, go to make up one, single mysterious body, the Mystical Body, Christ not being complete except when He is considered with all His members.

2. St. Paul does not speak of the "mystical" Christ. Christ for St. Paul is the personal Christ. "In Christo" means in the personal Christ, in the life of Christ or under the influence of Christ. St. Paul does not speak of the "mystical" Body, but of the Body of Christ. The Church is called the Body of Christ, not the Mystical Body.

3. The Church is identified with the body of Christ.

Recent exegetes have brought out the real thought of St. Paul. He did not represent the Body of Christ, as later tradition did, in the following fashion: A mystical whole composed of the personal Christ as Head and the Church as body. On the one hand, the Head; on the other, the body, the whole being the mystical Christ, the complete Christ.

For St. Paul, as Cerfaux [1] has so clearly shown, there is only the personal Christ, and not a mystical Christ of whom the personal Christ would be a part. The mass of those who live in Christ are bound to one another as are the members of one body and are *mystically identified with the body of Christ,* either His eucharistic body (I Cor. 10:17) or His glorified body.

Certainly Christ is the head, the source of grace, and the principle of unity and organization; Christians as a whole, all of whom live the life of Christ, are united like one body; but St. Paul did not (as Tradition did) superimpose the two images, and say that the personal Christ and Christians form one mystical body of which Christ is the head and the Christians the members.

There is only one body of Christ, the personal Christ, but the mass of Christians, this body which they form, is mystically identified with the body of Christ. This is so because the same life circulates in the body which Christians form as in the body of Christ.

The body of Christ is the "pleroma" (receptacle) of His divine life; the body formed by Christians is the "pleroma," the receptacle of divine life transmitted by Christ, communicated in Christ. Consequently, the body made up of Christians is in some way identified with Christ's body.

4. The Church is Christ made visible. We may even say that it is identified with Christ. Indeed, as Malevez [2] remarks, in rabbinical literature the body ("basar") designates the whole man existing corporeally, or even better, it is the very person, but manifested and made visible.

By referring to the Church as the Body of Christ, therefore, we mean that it is Christ made present and visibly manifest in time. Indeed, the "Body of Christ" **is not an invisible reality,** a "soul": rather it is **made up of men,** united to Christ, gathered together in Christ. Here below men exist

---

1 *La théologie de l'Eglise selon Saint Paul.*
2 *Rech. de Sciences religieuses,* 1944; Nouvelle revue theologique, Jan. 1946.

in a *mortal body*. But later on they will not be reduced to the state of "soul." Rather they shall rise at Christ's return and exist in a *glorious body*. Thus, the "Body of Christ," the Church, undergoes the same two stages experienced by Christ in His Incarnation: the lowliness of the earthly life, the glory of the risen life.

The Bond Between Christ and the Church

The unity formed by the mass of the faithful, which is elsewhere presented as the unity of a people, a vine, is here presented as the unity of members in a single body. And the union of the faithful with Christ, which is elsewhere presented as the union of spouses, is here presented as the union of Christ with His own body. No other image points out so vividly **the union of the faithful among themselves,** and **the union of the Church with Christ.**

The Fathers made great use of this image.

St. Augustine abounds in such texts: "When you love Christ's members, you love Christ.... Extend your charity throughout the whole world if you want to love Christ, for the members of Christ are spread abroad throughout the whole world. If you love only a part, you are divided; if you are divided, you are no longer part of the body; if you are no longer part of the Body, you no longer depend upon its Head. You are like a man who would kiss you on the head and crush your feet... What would your tongue say?: 'I suffer.' It does not say, 'My feet suffer,' but 'I suffer.' " [3]

St. John Chrysostom uses the same comparison: "The Church is a body with eyes and head. If a thorn enters the heel, the eye, which is one of the members of the body, casts a glance towards the ground. It does not say: 'Noble as I am, why should I take care of those lowly members?' Rather it lowers itself; inequality gives way before sympathy, all is equalized on the level of charity. You must do likewise. Let the eyes look out for the heel. If thorns bother it, put yourself on that level and rid it of that thorn." [4]

---

3 *Tractatus in Joan. Epist.* 10, 8; P.L. 35, 2060.
4 *De Lazaro Concio* 6, 4; P.G. 48, 1032.

But this image also points out the Church's function as the organ of salvation in relation to Christ.

The Church's Relation to Christ

The Church is not just Christ's institution. Christ continues Himself visibly in this institution. In it He continues His visible presence and activity; in it He continues visibly His redemptive Incarnation. He even likens it to the Incarnation itself, for Christ is the Incarnation of the Word in human nature; Christ is the Word in His state of incarnation. The Church is the incarnation of Christ in a visible society. The Church is Christ in His present, earthly state of incarnation.

We have seen that Christ is not an intermediary whom we must surpass in order to find divine life, but that it is in Him that divine life is communicated to us, precisely because He is the Incarnate Word. Similarly, the Church of Christ is not an intermediary which we must surpass in order to find Christ, rather it is in it that Christ gives Himself, for Christ is incarnate in His Church with all the riches of life He desires to bestow upon mankind. The Trinity is in Christ; Christ is in the Church.

That is why the mystery of the Church **continues** the mystery of Christ. The Church is Christ continuing His presence and redemptive activity on earth. We agree completely with the opinion of a Protestant:

"For Catholicism the Church is the continuation of the Incarnation, the extension of Christ's person and work. Because of this fact it is infallible, the depository of divine grace, and the mediator of salvation." [5]

Yes, for Catholics the visible mediation of the Church continues and prolongs the visible mediation of the Incarnation. Just as Christ once sanctified by contact with His body, so now He sanctifies us by **contact with His Church.** The Encyclical *Mystici Corporis* makes this comparison clear: "For if the Word of God wished to make use of our nature to redeem men through His sufferings and torments, He likewise makes use of His Church during the course of

---

5 *Protestantisme français*, p. 508.

the ages to perpetuate the work He began." Indeed, since His Ascension Christ is absent, not spiritually but only visibly and corporeally.

It is from this point of view that the hierarchical and apostolic organization of the Church continues Christ and represents Him sacramentally "somewhat as the eucharistic species serve to make His corporeal presence visible and localized." [6]

First of all there are **sacramental things:** obviously the seven sacraments hold pride of place in this regard and stand as the very foundation stones of the Church. Yet the whole Church built up upon them is sacramental. The entire liturgy is in some way sacramental: it represents the life of Christ and confers a special grace for each mystery. (A sacrament is an efficacious sign: what it signifies exteriorly, it produces interiorly.)

Then there are *sacramental persons:* The *Pope,* is the sacrament of Christ, the Church's Head, for the whole Church. The *Bishop* is the sacrament of Christ, the Church's Spouse, for his diocese. The *priesthood* is the sacrament of Christ in its powers of order and jurisdiction.

This is why the encyclical on the Mystical Body reminds us that "We must accustom ourselves to see in the Church Christ *in Person.* Christ lives in His Church; through it He teaches, governs and communicates holiness; He also manifests Himself in the various members of His society."

It is because the Church is the Body of Christ that it is One and Holy.

PROJECTS

1. Study this theme of the Body of Christ in St. Paul's Epistle to the Romans, chap. 12, and in his first Epistle to the Corinthians, chap. 12.

Show what is taught in these passages concerning Christ, the Church, and the union of Christ and the Church.

2. Do the same for his epistles to the Ephesians, Colossians and Philippians.

3. Show how St. Paul relates morality to the mystery of our incorporation in Christ (I Corinthians).

---

6 Congar, *Esquisse du mystere de l'Eglise,* p. 49.

Chapter 35
UNITY OF THE CHURCH

It was to Peter, the Apostles and to their successors alone that Christ entrusted His mission, word, sacraments and powers. Consequently, there can be but one Church: the one, Jesus chose as His "visible body." Since any other Church is merely a human society, it cannot transmit the life of Christ.

I. The Religious Meaning of Unity

Sacrament of Living Unity

The visible unity of the Church is the sacrament of its invisible unity: it expresses and realizes this unity.

1. **It expresses it.** There is only one Church because there is only one Christ and only one body of Christ. Now the interior reality of the Mystical Body is a life of charity, a *life of communion*. Consequently, the Church's visible unity is the sacrament of this life of communion, of this community of love. In Christ this love is a participation in the love which makes up the life of the. *Trinity*. That is why Jesus gives as the model of the visible unity of His Church, the unity existing between the Father and the Son: "that they all may be one, even as thou, Father, in me and I in thee" (John 17:21).

Such a life of union must necessarily express and translate itself visibly, take body; if it does not do so, it is not sincere and therefore does not exist.

2. **It realizes it.** The whole organization of the Church has as its aim the realization of this unity, of this *community of*

love. For example: the exercise of authority in the Church is the exercise of charity. That is why the Church demands "perfect charity" from its bishops. The life communicated by the sacraments is a life of love.

A Family Unity

The life of the Trinity is given us in Christ and in the Church. The life of the Trinity which "humanizes" itself, so to speak, in passing through the heart of Jesus becomes "maternal" in passing through the Church, His Spouse.

In order to come to us the Word became man, became our brother; in order to reach us effectively He drew even closer to us: **He became maternal.**

Each one of these "stages" intensified our unity and love: we are united among ourselves, not just by being the many sons of one common Father, but in a much more intimate fashion within the unity of the Only Son made flesh (Sons in the Son). And finally the Church's maternity adds a family bond to our unity; we are all children of one and the same mother, the Spouse of Christ.

Unity and Catholicity

These are but two aspects of a single reality. Catholicity may be defined as "diversity in unity." Unity may be defined as "unity in diversity." The life of Christ communicated to us by the Church produces neither levelling nor confusion; for unity is not uniformity, and catholicity is not dispersion. We are dealing with a **life of communion,** a life which is both *personal* and therefore as variegated as the persons who go to make it up, and *communitarian,* because it is a community of thought and love. These facets may be expressed and realized within the unity of the Catholic Church. Unity and catholicity are equally universal because the Church has the mission and power for gathering together within herself the whole world. She is the focal point of unity for restoring all things in Christ.

II. The Traditional Images of Unity

The Eucharist

It is in the Eucharist above all that the Church sees both the image and the cause of its unity. "Because the bread is one, we though many, are one body, all of us who partake of the one bread" (I Cor. 10:17).

And St. Augustine continues: "Christ would have this food and drink to be understood as meaning the fellowship of His own body and members, which is the Holy Church... this is why, even as men of God understood before us, Our Lord Jesus Christ delivered His body and blood to us in those things which from being many are reduced to some one thing. For a unity is formed from many grains of wheat, and another unity is formed by the flowing together of many grapes."

"This is what the Lord has taught us by the eating of His flesh and the drinking of His blood, that we should abide in Him and He in us. But we abide in Him when we are His members, and He abides in us when we are His temple. But that we may be His members, unity joins us together." [1]

The Eucharist is partaken of together as a family, in the house of God, just as in times past the paschal lamb, the figure of the Eucharist, was eaten "family by family and house by house."

"The sacrament of the Passover contains nothing else in the law of the Exodus than that the lamb which is slain in the figure of Christ should be eaten in one house. God speaks, saying: 'In one house shall it be eaten, neither shall you carry forth of the flesh thereof out of the house' (Exodus 12:46). The flesh of Christ and the body of the Lord cannot be cast outside nor is there any other home for believers but the one Church. This home, this household of unanimity, the Holy Spirit designates and points out in the Psalms, saying: 'God, who maketh men to dwell with one mind in a house' (Psalm 67:7). In the house of God, in the Church of

---

[1] *Tractatus in Joan. Evang.* 26, 15; P.L. 35, 1614; *Tract.* 27, 6; P.L. 35, 1618.

230

Christ, men dwell with one mind, and continue in concord and simplicity" (St. Cyprian).[2]

The Church is the Seamless Robe

"This sacrament of unity, this bond of a concord inseparably cohering is set forth in the Gospel where the coat of the Lord Jesus Christ is not at all divided nor cut, but is received as an entire garment, and is possessed as an uninjured and undivided robe by those who cast lots concerning Christ's garment, who should rather put on Christ.... He cannot possess the garment of Christ who parts and divides the Church of Christ..."

"As the twelve tribes of Israel were divided, the prophet Ahias rent his garment. But because Christ's people cannot be rent, His robe, woven and united throughout, is not divided by those who possess it; undivided, united, connected, it shows the coherent concord of our people who put on Christ. By the sacrament and sign of His garment, He has declared the unity of the Church" (St. Cyprian).[3]

St. Augustine saw in the division of Christ's garments a sign of both catholicity and unity:

"The garments of the Lord Jesus Christ parted into four parts symbolized His quadrapartite Church spread abroad over the whole world, which consists of four quarters... But the coat for which lots were cast signifies the unity of all the parts, which is contained in the bond of charity."[4]

The Church Is the Sole Ark of Salvation

It was prefigured by the ark of Noe (II Peter 2:5), for "the sinner leaves it like the raven once left the ark" (St. Hilary).[5]

"Noe's contemporaries would not believe his warnings as he was building the ark, and so became fearful examples for all posterity. Christ our God is now building His Church as

---

2 *De catholicae Ecclesiae unitate*, c. 8; P.L. 4, 506.
3 *De catholicae Ecclesiae unitate*, c. 7; P.L. 4, 504-505.
4 *Tractatus in Joan. Evangel.* 118, 4; P.L. 35, 1949.
5 *Tractatus in Psalm.* 146, 12; P.L. 9, 874.

an ark of salvation and calls upon all men to enter it" (St. Augustine).[6]

This image of the **ship** had great vogue and was enriched with all kinds of secondary themes:

For St. Hilary the Church is the ship "into which Jesus enters with all His faithful followers." Or again it is the ship "out of which it is impossible to understand the divine word, for Jesus spoke from the boat to the people who were gathered together on the shore." Finally, it is "Christ's boat battered by the winds and waves of the world and tormented by impure spirits." [7]

St. Ambrose gave this image an unexpected extension. The Church is "the boat in which Christ sits and from which the crowd is taught. By the breath of the Spirit, which swells the sail of Christ crucified, it passes unharmed through the waves of this world. And Peter, sitting in this boat fishes sometimes with a hook and sometimes with a net." [8]

"Although this boat is often battered by the waves or tempests, it shall never suffer shipwreck, for Christ crucified is its mast, the Father directs from the poop, the Holy Spirit holds the tiller and twelve sturdy rowers bring it into port through the narrow straits of this world, that is, the twelve apostles and a like number of prophets." [9]

III. Some Aspects of Unity

The Pope, "Sacrament of the Church's Unity"

He is both the visible expression and the guarantee of the Church's unity. There is only one Pope because there is only one Church. The Church's unity is rendered visible and tangible in the person of the Pope.

"When a Christian kisses the pope's hand, he kisses all his brethren, who are joined together into one in the person

---

6 *Sermo* 361, c. 22; P.L. 39, 1611.

7 *Commentar.* in Matt. 15, 39; P.L. 9, 1007; *Commentar.* in Matt. 13, 2; P.L. 9, 993; *Commentar.* in Matt. 7, 9; P.L. 9, 957.

8 *De Virginitate*, c. 18; P.L. 16, 297.

9 *Sermo* 46; P.L. 17, 607.

of the pope. His heart broadens out into the heart of all Christendom, of the unity in fullness. Moreover, the pope himself teaches, acts, strives, suffers only in the name of this unity" (Karl Adam).[10]

Communion with the Pope is the criterion of unity, the sign of our union with the universal Church.

Practical Religious Attitude

We have to develop an appreciation of the Pope's position and significance. It is Christ and the Church as a whole that we venerate and love in him. He is Christ's visible representative, the Vicar of Jesus Christ, the visible expression of the Church's unity, the bond of Catholic communion. We should not only pray for the Pope (notice the importance of this prayer in the liturgy), but also pray with the Pope, sharing with him his "solicitude for all the Churches": "one with thy servant our Pope."

The Pope is always associated with the Church just as the Church is associated with the Pope: "together with the flock committed to his care" (Collect for the Pope).

Notice the liturgical feasts (the feasts of St. Peter are also those of the "Cathedra Petri," of the See of Peter, and therefore of the present Pope): Jan. 18: chair of St. Peter at Rome; Feb. 22: chair of St. Peter at Antioch; June 29: Sts. Peter and Paul; Nov. 18: Dedication of the basilicas of Sts. Peter and Paul; the Mass for the Pope.

The Bishop, Sacrament of the Diocese's Unity

He is the visible expression of the unity of his diocese, the witness in his diocese of the unity of the whole Catholic Church. He is the center of unity for his diocese: apostolic commissions, the priesthood, every power stems from him by way of participation.

Since the Bishop is the common love of all personified and their center, it follows that whoever is united to him is in communion with all, and whoever is separated from him has

---

10 *The Spirit of Catholicism*. New York: Macmillan, 1930, p. 39.

withdrawn from communion with all, and no longer belongs to the Church. Consequently, this center is so necessary that without it no common bond is realizable; and a Church may therefore be defined as 'a people united within its bishop.' Two bishops within one community are as hard to conceive of as two centers within a single circumference; only one of the two can be the true Bishop (St. Ignatius, St. Cyprian).[11]

Practical Religious Attitude

We have to develop an appreciation of our Bishop's position and significance; in him we love and venerate:
—*the immediate representative of Christ* (like Christ he is called the Church's Spouse), the father of our diocese,
—*the visible expression of the unity of the diocese,*
—*the witness of our communion with the Pope* and the whole Church: "Tu es petrus" is sung for him.
It is in this sense that we should understand the marks of respect and veneration of which he is the object.
Notice the Bishop's place in the liturgy: prayer for the Bishop, prayer with the Bishop, communion with the Bishop: "one with our Bishop."

IV. Some Problems of Unity

"Ecumenism"

This is the term given to the problem of the Unity of the Church,[12] that is, of the return to the Church of the separated Christian Communities, notably, the Orthodox Community and the various Protestant Communities.
1. In separating themselves these churches kept some elements of the Catholic Church which are like stepping stones towards reunion:
—the very organization of these churches, inasmuch as they kept the hierarchy and the sacraments (the Orthodox);

---

11 Moehler, *Op. Cit.*, p. 172.
12 See *Divided Christendom* by Congar.

—Holy Scripture;
—the majority of the articles of belief;
—the principal prayers: Credo, Pater;
—the liturgies.

2. We must apply what we already said concerning the problem of the Missions to this problem of the separated churches.

—The authentic religious values these churches have are good. Consequently, it is only normal that these churches have the desire and will to preserve and defend their own proper riches. A return to the Church would not only permit this legitimate desire but would even develop these riches and bring them to fulfillment within the unity of the Catholic Church and to the greater benefit of the entire Church;

—Consequently, they would have to renounce nothing positive; they would have only to enlarge, **complete,** and drop their negations. It is to be noticed that the older form of abjuration has been replaced by a profession of faith by a declaration of the Holy Office of 1936.

—This return to Unity would, be the actualization of the Church's Catholicism as well as the fulfillment of the religious values thus incorporated. For example: the return of the Eastern Orthodox would bring about great liturgical enrichment.

3. The unity of the Church demands unanimity in essentials, in what is of divine institution, but it permits legitimate human diversity. It is like a family in which all members bear a common surname, but in which each individual also possesses a distinguishing Christian name.

Outside the Church, No Salvation

This is the *traditional* formula stemming from the first ages of the Church. In every context it is clear that what is meant is the Roman Church.[13] Nevertheless, equally good tradition has it that "none will be condemned save he who

13 Denzinger, *Enchiridion Symbolorum,* 247, 423, 468, 714, 1647, 1677.

sinned against the light." Those who are invincibly ignorant of the Church *can be saved.*

How can these two affirmations be reconciled? If those
who are saved, although apparently outside the Church,
really belong to the Church, how do we conceive of this belonging?

It has been said, that such men would belong to the soul
of the Church, and not to its body. The soul of the Church,
then, would be the Mystical Body; the body, the exterior
organization of the Roman Church. But this is not a happy
distinction, for the Roman Church *is* the Mystical Body, both
body and soul. One cannot, therefore, belong to the soul of
the Church without in some way belonging to its body. What
then is this belonging to the Roman Church, Christ's earthly
incarnation?

1. Solution for the Separated Churches.

(a) In the first place, as Karl Adam reminds us, in order
to understand the real meaning of this dogma, that is, the
meaning as the Church understands it, we have to see it in
its origins and in its entire dogmatic setting. Now this *dogma*
is aimed first of all at communities separated from the
Church:

> "It is certain that the declaration that there is no salvation outside
> the Church is not aimed at individual non-Catholics, at any persons as
> persons, but at non-Catholic churches and communions, not so far as
> they are non-Catholic communions. Its purpose is to formulate posi-
> tively the truth that there is but one Body of Christ and, therefore,
> but one Church which possesses and imparts the grace of Christ in its
> fullness. Stated otherwise the declaration would run: Every separated
> Church which sets itself up against the original Church of Christ stands
> outside the communion of Christ's grace. It cannot be a mediator of
> salvation. So far as it is a separate and antagonistic church, it is essen-
> tially unfruitful as regards the supernatural life. So that the spiritual
> unfruitfullness which is predicated in the doctrine is not to be affirmed
> of the individual non-Catholic, but primarily of non-Catholic com-
> munions as such" (Karl Adam).[14]

Only the Church possesses Christ's mission, Christ's sacraments, Christ's word and Christ's powers. To the degree in
which other churches are separated from it, they are sterile.

---

14 Adam, *op. cit.,* 164.

(b) But they are not completely separated: they have all taken with them and preserved a part of the Catholic Church's treasure.

Whatever, therefore, is fruitful in these churches comes from what they have taken with them and preserved of the Catholic Church. They are fruitful to the degree in which they are Catholic; sterile to the degree in which they are non-Catholic.

—Thus the spiritual fecundity of these churches really comes from the Catholic Church. "The Church gives us to understand that some men can receive its baptism even outside her, but that no one can either receive or possess salvation outside her.... She is the one only Spouse holding and possessing all the power of her Spouse and Lord; she has the conjugal power of bearing sons even through handmaidens" (St. Augustine).[15]

—By what is best in them, therefore, the faithful of these churches are already within the Catholic Church without knowing it. Baptism administered in these churches incorporates such persons, not only into Christ, but also into the Catholic Church. This is the Church's traditional teaching.[16]

St. Albert the Great, in commenting upon Psalm 84:4: "Even the sparrow finds a home, and the swallow a nest in which she puts her young," applies it to the sacraments performed in dissident Christian communities: "The Church's nest is the sacraments, and these nests do not belong to heretics; that is why when they lay their young in them, they put them in the Church, not outside it."

—That is why the members of these separated churches, insofar as they are of good faith, belong not only to the invisible Church, but belong "invisibly to the visible Church." But because such religious life stems from and tends towards the Catholic Church, it will only blossom fully when reunited with the Catholic Church; cf. the encyclical *Mystici Corporis:* "With persevering prayer to the Spirit of love and truth We wait for them with open arms to return not to a

---

15 *De baptismo contra Donatistas,* lib. 4, c. 1; P.L. 43, 154-55.
16 Council of Trent, *Canon De baptismo,* Denz. 696, 860.

stranger's house, but to their own, their Father's house" (no. 118).

2. Solution for the Human Community.

For humanity as a whole there is no salvation outside the Catholic Church:

(a) *The Church, mankind's sole means of salvation.*

Mankind is not made up of isolated souls like atoms, but forms a unity. It is in Christ and in Christ alone that the Trinity quickens mankind. In his turn, it is in the Church and in the Church alone that Christ desires to apply, extend and realize the fruits of redemption.

The whole order of grace comes, not just from the Word, but from the Incarnate Word; similarly, the effective application of redemption, the accomplishment of the restoration of all things in Christ, will come, not just from Christ, but from *Christ incarnate in His Church.*

"Outside Christ, the Incarnate Word, no salvation." But Christ is incarnate in His Church, and, therefore, we must add: "Outside the Church, Christ incarnate, no salvation." This does not say: "Outside the Church, no grace," as the Jansenists claimed (a condemned proposition). But it is through the Church that grace is present in the world, for it is through the Church that Christ is present and active in mankind. "Although grace may act outside the bounds of the visible Church, its presence and activity is no less involved in the visible Church, since God connected the salvation of the world with the constitution of a Church" (De Montcheuil).

We shall see how every outpouring of grace comes from the Church and tends toward the Church.

(b) *Every outpouring of grace comes from the Church:*

The normal way foreseen by Christ for receiving His grace is through the sacraments. Even those who do not receive grace visibly through the sacraments still receive it by reason of the sacraments of the Church, particularly because of the *Eucharist.* All grace issues from Christ's sacrifice; but this sacrifice, in the present economy of salvation willed by God, is destined to bear fruit through the masses celebrated in the Church, which are its sacramental renewal: the two are inseparable. Without the Cross, the Mass would be only an empty ceremony; but without the Mass, the Cross would be only a sealed fountain. Without the sacrifice of the Mass offered by the Church there would be no grace poured forth on mankind. All the graces conferred upon redeemed humanity are due to the sacrifice offered by the Church. The distribution of graces in the world is dependent not only on the sacrifice of the Mass, but also on the Church's prayer, her maternal intercession in favor of mankind.

(c) Just as all grace comes from the Church, *so all grace tends toward the Church,* for there alone will it blossom forth in all its fullness. Sometimes we hear the following objection. Since salvation is possible in Protestantism, Buddhism, etc., why not leave such persons in good faith rather than risk damning them by preaching a faith which they might refuse?

We may answer such an objection by the following comparison. A family from Lille lost one of their children in the south of France during the collapse of France in 1940. They later learned that their child had been taken in by a good family who gave it shelter and even affection. Do you think that the parents, on hearing this news, asked themselves: "Shall we go get our child? Do you think we have good reasons for doing so?" You can be sure that such questions never entered their heads. They simply went for their child, because they were its parents, because it was their child, because they felt it could not reach its full achievement except in its *true home.*

Similarly, the Church is missionary minded because every one of Christ's members is its own child, and because these children will not reach their full achievement except at her maternal breast. "Other sheep I have who are not of this fold. Them also I must bring, and they shall hear my voice, and there shall be one fold and one shepherd" (John 10:16). The Church would cease to be the Church if it ceased to be missionary minded, just as parents would abandon their basic instincts by abandoning their children to strangers.

3. **Some Conclusions.**

(a) *"Invisibly in the visible Church."*

We may say of all those who, although apparently outside the Church, are in the state of grace, that they belong "invisibly to the visible Church," and that it is this belonging that will save them. We may also say that they are in the Church "by desire." For they are truly disposed to follow the light of grace, to face up to its demands in such a way that if they recognized the need to enter the Church, they would correspond, not by a new act, but by the very movement already animating them. If they refused, they would do so only by revoking the purpose which up till then had justified them, and they would, therefore, lose the state of grace.

(b) *Priesthood and kingship.*

The sanctifying and maternal activity of the Church is, therefore, much vaster than is visibly apparent. Père Congar in *Divided Christendom* remarks that this tendency to drift apart prolongs and manifests a previous one existing in Christ between the two prerogatives which He possesses to an equal degree, but which He does not exercise equally: His priesthood and His kingship. "Christ the Savior is truly king, but His royal prerogatives are, as it were, hidden, in favor of His priestly function of Saviour through the Cross. Although the adoration of the world and the obedience of its elements were His by right, He came not to be served but to serve, in the form of a slave, not a conqueror. Here below Christ saves more than He reigns."

Here below the Church is the body of the crucified Christ; and that is why it "saves more than it triumphs and incorporates more members than it numbers subjects."

(c) *Degrees of belonging to the Church.*

A final source of difficulties remains to be considered and resolved. The Church is not a simple thing. Men belong to it to a greater or lesser degree, and they are justified to the degree in which they belong to it.

—The normal state is that of belonging to it *visibly and perfectly,* not only by baptism and faith, but by grace.

—Ignorant persons of good faith and righteous life belong to it *invisibly* and *incompletely.*[17]

17 See *L'Eglise du Verbe incarné* by Charles Journet, Vol. I, pp. 43-55.

—Bad Catholics belong to it visibly but imperfectly. "How many that are not ours are yet, as it were, within; and how many that are ours are still, as it were, without" (St. Augustine).[18]

Two consequences can be drawn from this:

The situation of the bad Catholics in the Church is a precarious one. He will not stay in it forever; either he will adhere fully and pass over into the eternal Church, or he will not adhere fully and will not pass over into the eternal Church. "The slave does not abide in the house forever" (John 8:34). Such is the lesson of the parables of the kingdom: the weeds among the wheat, the net.

The paradoxical situation of the righteous who are "outside the Church" should make us understand Christ's longing and urge us to bring it about: "Other sheep I have who are not of this fold. Them also I must bring, and they shall hear my voice and there shall be one fold and one shepherd" (John 10:16).

It Does Not Suffice to Be Baptized in Order to Be Saved

We must, in addition, really live according to the demands of our baptism. St. Augustine explains that the word faith (fides) is made up of two words: do and say; faith, he says, consists in doing what we say.

On the other hand, God knows His own, even those outside the Church, or rather He recognizes as true members of the Church some persons who are not visibly in the Church. St. Augustine often reiterates his notion: "How many wolves in the sheepfold; how many sheep outside."

Bad Catholics are already outside the Church spiritually, and at Christ's return they will be outside the Church corporeally. At present, they are in the house, but not of the house; consequently, at its Dedication they will be shut out.

"They that are not ours, who are within, when they find an opportunity, go out; and they that are ours, who are without, when they find an opportunity, return." [19]

---

18 *Enarratio in Psalm.* 106, 14; P.L. 37, 1428.
19 *Enarratio in Psalm.* 106, 14; P.L. 37, 1428.

"What is so near as two men in one Church? What is so distant as iniquity from righteousness? For where there is agreement, there is fellowship. Two men are handcuffed together and brought before a judge; one is a robber, one is merely in bonds; the one wicked, the other innocent, bound with one chain but far from one another. How far are they from one another? As far as wickedness is from innocence. Behold these are far from one another! One robber perpetrates his crimes in Spain; his nearest neighbor is the robber who does the same in Africa. How near? As near as crime and crime are joined, as near as robbery is to robbery." [20]

Thus Augustine can conclude: "If you love your sins and continue in them, you are contrary to Christ. Whether you are within or without, you are an antichrist; you are chaff. But why are you not without? Because you have not yet fallen in with a wind to carry you away." [21]

PROJECTS

1. In St. John pick out the theme of unity. Show what is taught regarding:
   —unity as a distinctive mark of the Church;
   —unity among Christians;
   —the model of this unity, etc.
2. Do the same in St. Paul.
3. Show how the Eucharist is the sacrament of the Church's unity by studying the liturgy of Corpus Christi and by comparing it with the references given (I Cor. 8-11; John 6).

PRACTICAL ATTITUDES

Are we concerned about the problem of Church unity?
Do we really try to know the separated churches and their members?
What should be our attitude toward efforts for unity?
Resolution: take part in the Church Unity Octave (Jan. 18-25).

---

20 *Enarratio in Psalm.* 128, 8; P.L. 37, 1693.
21 *Tract. in Joan. Epist.* 3, 9; P.L. 35, 2002-2003.

Chapter 36

HOLINESS OF THE CHURCH

It is not merely a question of *de facto* holiness. But before giving the exact notion of holiness, we shall begin by noticing the presence of both saints and sinners in the Church.

Presence of Saints and Sinners

1. Presence of Sinners.

There are sinners in the Church not only among the laity but even among members of the hierarchy. Our faith and love towards the Church does not rest upon ignorance of its weaknesses nor upon a refusal to recognize its present and past miseries. "The existence of a Christian who can say: I have confronted all the scandals of the Church's history; I know anything that you can bring up, and yet none of these things hinders me from saying with full conviction, every time I recite the Creed: 'I believe in the Holy, Catholic Church...' is a fact which ought to cause unbelievers and those shaken in their faith at the sight of such weakness to reflect" (De Montcheuil).

It is to be noticed that this presence of sinners in the Kingdom was foreseen by Jesus: the parables (weeds, the net); Judas among the twelve apostles. In Christian ages the faithful in their works of art often represented members of the hierarchy and monks of all kinds in purgatory and even in hell; such representations astonished no one and did not shake men's faith in the Church. (Cf. Chartres: the central bay of the South Portal.)

It is also true that besides sinners there are numerous saints in the Church.

2. Presence of Saints.

We have to be as honest about the existence of saints in

the Church as we just were about the presence of sinners. Even during the darkest periods of its history, the Church produced great saints. (Here we could develop the themes customarily found under the headings of Apologetics: the real holiness of the Church, its activity in the world, etc.). But our faith in the Church's holiness is not based upon this kind of opposition.

True Notion of the Church's Holiness

Just as the Church is in itself essentially Catholic, Apostolic and One, so it is also essentially Holy. The Church is Holy because it is the Body of Christ. In order to grasp this point we can employ the kind of argument St. Augustine used against the Donatists.[1]

1. Holiness according to the Donatists.

Diocletian's persecution of the North African Church brought about some defections among the Catholics. Certain of them, for example, handed over to the pagans the sacred vessels and books. They were called the *traditores*. Once the danger was over, these persons re-entered the ranks of the Church.

It was then that the Donatists separated themselves from the Church because of this readmittance of sinners into its ranks. They founded the "Church of the Saints," admitting only the "pure." They claimed that the Catholic Church in tolerating sinners in itself had lost its holiness and could no longer sanctify its faithful. For example, baptism administered by one of the *traditores* could not confer grace upon the one baptized. "It is by the conscience of he who baptizes that we are to judge whether or not he can purify the conscience of he who is baptized," said the Donatists.

2. Holiness according to the Church.

---

1 See particularly:

Ad catholicas epistola contra Donatistas, vulgo, *De unitate Ecclesiae;* P.L. 43, 391-446.

Contra Cresconium; P.L. 43, 445-594.

De unico baptismo contra Petilianum ad Constantinum; P.L. 43, 595-614.

Contra epistolam Parmeniani; P.L. 43, 33-108.

De baptismo contra Donatistas; P.L. 43, 107-244.

Contra litteras Petiliani Donatistae; P.L. 43, 245-388.

St. Augustine refused to debate on the grounds of personal sanctity, that is: Which Church has the most saints. For God alone is holy.

"None is good save God alone. He came for those who were sick. Who has no need of His healing?" We are all sick, and we all need the physician. He simply remarks that the efficacy of baptism cannot come from the personal holiness of its minister. "Do you believe that it is your perfection, no matter how real it may be, which causes the Lord's grace to descend upon the baptized? What importance do you accord the sacrament itself if man's power can corrupt it?" God alone is holy; God alone sanctifies. One man cannot make another man holy.

St. Augustine situated the problem on its true basis: the Church is not holy because of its members; the sacraments are not holy nor productive of grace because of the personal sanctity of their ministers; it is not the holiness of the preacher that causes faith, but the word of God transmitted by means of the Church's preaching.

(a) **But the Church is holy because of Christ, because it is His Body.** It is the true Body of Christ. That is why it alone is the true and holy Church. "Christ is the real priest. He who officiates is merely the representative of the one Priest without fault." Similarly, the whole Church gets its holiness from Christ alone.

(b) The Church's **sacraments** are holy because they are Christ's acts. In consequence, it matters little whether the bishop or priest is a saint or a sinner, since he is not the mediator between God and his people. He merely represents Christ, the real Mediator, and there can be no shadow of iniquity in Christ Who offered Himself for us and Who is our Mediator in heaven. The ministers of the Church have nothing to do with purification or justification, as these words of the Apostles give us to understand: "Neither he who plants is anything, nor he who waters, but God who gives the growth" (I Cor. 3:7).

Nevertheless, although these sacraments are always holy because they are Christ's sacraments, they only serve to condemn those who administer or receive them unworthily. The ministry of a sinner profits others but not himself.

(c) Similarly, the efficacy of **God's Word** does not depend upon the holiness of the preacher but upon Christ Himself Who confers grace and faith on those who hear it. As St. Paul declared: But what of it? Provided only that in every way, whether in pretense or in truth, Christ is being proclaimed; in this I rejoice, yes and I shall rejoice" (Phil. 1:8). "The word of God cannot be bound."

With Père de Montcheuil we may conclude:

Faith teaches us not to see the Church as the result of the men who compose it. The Church is the organ by which divine charity is implanted in mankind to raise and transform it. The Church is Redemption at work, in action. Consequently, we must expect to find in it the divine force which purifies and sanctifies, and the mass to be transformed and sanctified.

If we separate the two, there is no longer any Church. There would only be, on the one hand, a divine force without influence on the world, and, on the other, a mass given over to sin with no leaven to transform it. There is a Church because this divine force contacts sinners through the intermediary of visible and sensible instruments, the hierarchy which teaches and administers the sacraments.

But these two elements are not of the same order. We cannot weigh them in the same balance. Actual Christian holiness represents what has allowed itself to be transformed and sanctified. Sinful members or what remains of sin in those who have begun to let themselves be gripped by grace is like the untransformed residue, it is the evil which resisted or still resists the power of grace. The actual holiness of members of the Church is not the holiness of the Church itself. It is the effect, the manifestation of this essential holiness which belongs to the Church.

The holiness of the Church's members is the sign, the revelation, the **expression of the Church's holiness:** "It is that part of the holiness and sanctifying power of the Church which Christians permit in themselves."

Thus the Church is the "Pleroma" of Christ's holiness: in

the diversity of its children, its spiritual families and its ethnic groups, it unfolds before the world the astonishing riches of Christ's holiness. It is in this way that we are to understand the Church's many schools of spirituality, the extraordinary diversity of its saints, its various liturgies, its many forms of dedication, its various religious orders.

A Holy Church and Sinful Members

Thus it is not contradictory to affirm at one and the same time that the Church is holy but that its members may be sinners. The Church's Word is holy because it is the very Word of Christ Himself calling us to holiness. The Church's Sacraments are holy because they are the very acts of Christ Himself giving us life. But the Church's members can refuse to conform their life to the holiness of this Word and these Sacraments. No one emphasized this presence of sinners in the Church more than St. Augustine, and because of the Donatist error. "Is it surprising to find bad Christians among so many?"

We have to put up with sinners in the Church until the last day. Perhaps the grace of Christ will some day win them over. To leave the Church because it contains sinners is to cut oneself off from Christ.

St. Augustine excuses himself to his hearers for returning so often to the same refrain (Haec semper contavimus...):

"Let us recognize that Ark which prefigured the Church; let us be the clean beasts in it, yet let us not refuse to allow the unclean ones to be carried in it with us until the end of the deluge.... Consequently, whenever anyone, because of the alleged uncleanness of some, leaves the gathering of unity, which is an ark carrying the clean and the unclean during the deluge, he shows that he is rather the sort of creature that flies away (like the raven)." [2]

In its present state the Church is a threshing-floor in which both grain and straw are to be found. At Christ's return the

---

[2] Epist. 108, 20; P.L. 33, 417. Trans. by Wilfred Parsons, *Letters of St. Augustine* (N. Y.: Fathers of the Church, Inc., 1953), V. II, pp. 236-37.

good will be separated from the bad like the grain from the straw, for no sinner can enter the coming Kingdom.[3]

At present, however, there is no distinction made between saints and sinners. Both seem to be alike in all things. Only at the time of judgment will the holiness of some appear and the sin of others.

"Therefore, brethren, now we are the same as other men: just as they are born, eat, drink, are clothed, pass their life, so also do the saints. Sometimes this resemblance deceives men into saying: 'There is one who has become a Christian; has he lost his headache?' or: 'Because he is a Christian, in what way does he differ from me?'

"O dead vine, you see near you a vine that is bare indeed in winter, yet not dead. Now during the winter weather the fruits appear not on the stock; you observe, so to speak, dead trees during the winter. He who cannot see truly thinks the vine to be dead. Perhaps there is one near it which is really dead; both are alike during the winter; the one is alive, the other is dead, but both the life and death are hidden. When summer comes, the life of one shines forth, the death of the other is made manifest. . . . Thus summer will come, the Lord will come, our Splendor, that was hidden in the stock" (St. Augustine).[4]

Previously, the Shepherd of Hermas had compared the present Church to a winter forest in which the just are not distinguishable from sinners; and the world to come to a summer forest in which the just will bear fruit.[5] These different images, therefore, remind us not only of the fact of sin and the presence of sinners, but also of the necessity for holiness.

Necessity of Holiness

1. For the success of Redemption.

Christ really entrusted the responsibility of redeeming the world to the Church. To it He has transmitted His mission and pastoral charge. And just as Christ did not bring

---

[3] *Contra Cresconium*, lib. 4, c. 59; P.L. 43, 587.

[4] *Enarratio in Psalm.* 148, 16; P.L. 37, 1947.

[5] *The Shepherd*, parables 3 and 4.

about the Redemption of the world by His ministry alone, but also by His sacrifice, so, too, He entrusts the mission of sharing in His sacrifice to the Church. In the present order of providence He has made the progress of the Kingdom dependent upon the ministry of the Church and, in consequence, upon the holiness of its members. If the Church grows lax, evangelization slows down, holiness diminishes, souls are no longer directed, prayer and sacrifice no longer ascend towards heaven in constant appeal for divine grace for humanity.

In order to reassure ourselves we often repeat: "The Church is eternal"; "the gates of hell shall not prevail against it." But these promises mean simply this:

"God gives His Church the absolute assurance that it will not perish, but that is the only absolute assurance He gives it; all other assurances are conditioned by the virtue of Christians. The Church cannot die, but it can decline; it can become decadent and corrupt. Christ acts through the Church, but His activity can be hampered by the infidelity of Christians. The absence of holiness in any one of us is a corruption of the Church. Christ needs the holiness of each one of us, for He can act in the Church only insofar as He finds in it souls who are docile before His activity. The Church can be at death's door for great periods, souls can be lost and whole peoples await the truth in vain if we Catholics are unfaithful" (J. Leclercq).[6]

We must not forget Jesus' warnings: salt must not become corrupt; we should not hide our light under a bushel; the leaven must leaven the whole lump. Time is given us so that we can build eternity: the Church Militant builds the Church Triumphant. Each passing day is of incalculable importance for eternity, not only for ourselves, but for the whole world. The coming of the Kingdom of God depends on us; it depends on our prayers, for God planned that we should petition Him for it; it depends on our holiness, our Christian witness, our evangelizing efforts.

2. For the progress of the Church.

Few pages are harder on the abuses and failings of the Church than those written by St. Peter Damian or St. Bernard. But the great reformers always burned with the Church's own flame when attempting to renew it. Whether

---

6 *La vie du Christ dans son Eglise*, p. 48.

it was Gregory VII, the flowering of the mendicant orders under St. Dominic and St. Francis of Assisi, the founders of the Counter-Reform or those of the Christian renewal of seventeenth century France, it was always the same method which was used. They found a remedy for the Church's evils in the Church itself, for it is only in the holiness which it possesses that there can be found a remedy for the sin which afflicts it. A great lesson to keep in mind.

We may, we even must, suffer from the mediocrity of its members, from their sins, from the Church's lack of real contact with the world, from the unawareness of so many Christians in face of the moral problems presented by the modern world, from the little they do to remedy such situations, from their inertia, timidity and cowardice. But it would be madness to quit the Church because of such things. This would be to leave the fountain of holiness, the only one from which it can well forth, under the pretext that it does not make its effects felt strongly enough. Rather, we must begin by drawing from this source of holiness ourselves, and cause it to spread by our own efforts, and it will begin its work of transforming the world.

When enough Christians become aware of the fact that the Christian world is not what it should be, that its hold on the modern world does not suffice, and when they decide to make their own lives the means of spreading the Church's holiness, then we can predict a magnificent Christian renewal. We do not have to look elsewhere to transform the world (de Montcheuil).

Many "apostles" today, aware of the great problems of the world and the present amplitude of the Church's mission in this world fast becoming one, suffer from what they call "the Church's slowness, the inadaptability of its apostolic methods," and desire to "reform the Church" in one point or another. But they speak of the Church in the third person as if it were a stranger and exterior to themselves.

Rather, we should always speak of the Church in the first person, for we are in the Church. And we must always begin by seeing in ourselves the defects or delays with which we reproach the Church in general. Then we shall be able to reform it efficaciously and immediately at the very spot in which we can attain and transform it, namely, in ourselves.

PROJECTS

1. From the Kingdom parables show that Jesus foresaw the mixture of just and unjust in His Church.
2. Show that the existence of sinners in it is merely temporary (the judgment scenes in these parables).
3. Show the holiness expected of the faithful according to one of the following texts: John 14-17; Epistles of St. John; the Epistle to the Hebrews 10-13; Jesus' discourses in one of the Gospels; the first Epistle of St. Peter; the Epistle of St. James.

Conclusion

We have now arrived at the end of our study. Before concluding let us sum up briefly the ground we have covered.

In the introduction we learned the need of seeing the Church with the eyes of faith, of contemplating it from within, as a mystery. This mystery appeared to us as complex: the Church was founded by Jesus Christ and yet existed in some way before the coming of Christ, just as it will continue to exist after the general resurrection at the end of time when the present structures, such as the sacraments and the hierarchy, will have disappeared.

In the first part of the work we studied the fundamental reality which endures throughout these changes. The Church thus appeared to us as God's loving design for "restoring all things in Christ."

In the second part we studied the various states in which God's plan is realized, following the essential stages of the history of salvation.

In the third part we studied the principal aspects of the mission and nature of the Catholic Church, the present stage in the realization of God's plan. We called it the Church of the New Testament in order to situate it between the Old Testament stage and the stage to come at Christ's return.

In the conclusion, therefore, we shall be able to specify in what the mystery of the Church consists, of which the Creed says: "I believe in the One, Holy, Catholic and Apostolic Church."

251

Chapter 37

THE MYSTERY OF THE CATHOLIC CHURCH

In the Catholic Church there is:

—*an enduring and eternal element* which is both *Christ,* the source of life for all mankind, and *mankind,* united to and incorporated in Him;

—and *a transitory element:* the present means of salvation by which and in which Christ gives us His life and gathers together mankind into one; this is the hierarchical and sacramental structure of the Church.

Until Christ's return these two elements are inseparable. The Catholic Church cannot be reduced to its enduring element alone. Such is perhaps the temptation of certain syntheses concerning the "Mystical Body" understood as the "soul of the Church." We have already pointed out how contradictory it is to say that the body (mystical) is the soul of the Church.

Nor can it be reduced to its transitory element alone. Such is perhaps the more current temptation in manuals treating of the Church; they often reduce the Church to its salutary function, to its means of salvation, even when they do not reduce it to its merely juridical organization.

The Catholic Church has both an enduring and a transitory element; or more correctly it is the enduring element in the transitory one, understood as we explained it in the third part, namely, that it is by reason of these passing structures that the People of God are being formed here below. In order to throw some light on this point, we shall recall some traditional images.

A Building Project

This image goes back to the Shepherd of Hermas.[1] The Church is, as it were, a temple in the process of construction. It is neither the *temple* alone which is being built (the enduring element) nor the *scaffolding* alone (the transitory element) by whose means the temple is presently being constructed. Rather it is the whole building project, that is, both the temple and its scaffolding, or more exactly,

—the temple contained in the scaffolding

—and constructed thanks to the scaffolding.

When the temple will be completed, when God's plan will be realized in time, that is, at Christ's return, then the scaffolding will be pulled down as no longer necessary, this scaffolding being the hierarchical and sacramental organization of the Church. Only the temple will remain in all its splendor. "For the Lord God almighty and the Lamb are the temple thereof" (Apocalypse 21:22).

But so long as the temple is not completed, the edifice itself is hardly distinguishable from its scaffolding. The building is masked, hidden, disfigured by this framework which contains and supports it.

Similarly, the external framework of the Catholic Church runs the risk of hiding from us the eternal Temple which it contains and constructs. Yet those who wish to enter the eternal Temple have to pass through the instrumentality of this framework (cf. Outside the Church, no salvation). Those who want to live forever with Christ in the completed Temple must enter the Temple now under construction.

Again, so long as the temple is not complete, we have no way of knowing whether or not such and such a timber or beam or brick will definitely be part of the finished building. Similarly, in the building up of the Church there are stones which will go into the eternal Temple and there are others which will be excluded from it (cf. parable of the net). At present, however, they are indistinguishable.

St. Augustine often employed this image: "The house which is now in building will only be dedicated later. For

---

1 *The Shepherd,* parable 9.

now the house, that is, the Church, is in building; only later will it be dedicated. In the dedication will appear the glory of the Christian People which is now hidden." [2]

But St. Augustine employs a much more graphic image to explain this union of the Church's two elements, one durable, one transitory.

The Limb in the Cast

"The physician binds up your bruises that you may attain complete soundness, until that which has been broken and bound up may be firmly knit. What are these means whereby He binds? The sacraments of this present life. The means whereby He binds up our bruises are the sacraments of this present life, whereby in the meantime we obtain our comfort: and all the words we speak to you, words which sound and pass away, all that is done in the Church in this present time, are the means whereby He binds up our bruises. For just as, when the limb has become perfectly sound, the physician removes the cast; so in our own city Jerusalem, when we shall have been made equal to the angels, do you think that we shall receive there what we receive here? Will we then need the Gospel read to us that our faith may abide? Or the laying on of hands by any Bishop? All these are means of binding up fractures; when we have attained perfect soundness, they will be taken off." [3] So long as the fractures have not knit, the limb is contained in and supported by the cast.

At present, mankind is broken and dispersed by sin. "The name of Adam signifies in Greek the whole world. . . . Adam, therefore, has been scattered over the whole world. He was in one place and fell, and being thus reduced to dust, he filled the whole world. But the mercy of God gathered together the fragments from every side, and forged them by the fire of love, and made one what was broken." [4]

At Christ's return wounded mankind will appear as cured

2 *Enarratio in Psalm.* 29, 6; P.L. 36, 219.
3 *Enarratio in Psalm.* 146, 8; P.L. 37, 1903-1904.
4 *Enarratio in Psalm.* 95, 15; P.L. 37, 1236.

and unified in Christ. But here below it is in the "bandages" of the sacraments and the Church's ministry that wounded and dispersed humanity finds its unity and salvation.

The Kingdom in Formation

There are still many other such images which could be employed, for example, *the parables of the Kingdom.* It is in the Church that the Kingdom is to be found in its phase of growth and mixture, and it is through the Church that the Kingdom grows and develops. Or to put it more exactly: the Church is this Kingdom in its earthly phase of growth.

It is in the visible structures of the Church: dioceses, parishes, different localities, organized charities, that the mystery of salvation is communicated to us, the faithful, and proposed to the whole world by a collective witness. Union with God is symbolized by the very material structure itself of the Church whose façade sometimes bears the inscription: "This is the house of God," and whose steeple lifts our gaze towards heaven.

The Church lives on earth, and it is the earthly aspect of this visible society which we should recall at the conclusion of this study of the mystery of the Church. All members of the Church, both priests and faithful, are called upon to give life to these visible structures which sink their foundations so deeply into the material universe; they must guard them from the contamination of evil, and they must keep them in harmony with the mystery of salvation and open to all those whom the Church's mission leads to the threshold of the mystery of the Church.

These considerations will permit us to understand what we mean by belief in the Church.

Chapter 38

BELIEF IN THE CHURCH

When we profess our faith in the Creed: "I believe in the Holy Catholic Church," the object of our belief is neither the enduring element alone nor the transitory element alone, but properly speaking, the synthesis of these two elements.

In order to come to grips with this problem, let us consider the following propositions:

1. Our act of faith in the Church is similar to our act of faith in Christ.

2. Belief in the Church is included in belief in Christ; it is not an additional act of faith.

3. Our adherence to the Church is not a consequence of an already acquired salvation, but it is precisely this adherence which justifies us.

4. Adherence to the Church is the sign of our adherence to Christ.

Similar to Belief in Christ

Our act of faith in the Church is similar to our act of faith in Christ.

1. **Belief in Christ.**

We must grasp what faith in Christ meant for His contemporaries. This act of faith did not consist in saying: "I believe in God." For in this case the object of faith would not be Christ, but the God of the Old Testament. "I believe that this man exists." They saw Him, they knew His family, perhaps they had even met Him when He was twelve years old on the occasion of His pilgrimage to Jerusalem.

Their act of faith consisted in the following synthetic judgment: "I believe that this man whom I know is God." We can hardly conceive how difficult this extraordinary act of faith was. We are sometimes led to imagine that Christ's contemporaries adhered to Him spontaneously by reason of the fascination of His words and miracles. Such was not the case; even the Apostles frequently misunderstood Him.

2. Belief in the Church.

Today we have the same attitude towards the Church that Christ's contemporaries had towards His person.[1] Belief in the Church does not consist in saying: "I believe in mankind's vocation; I believe that the Blessed Trinity loves us and desires to have us participate in Its divine life." For in this case the object of faith is not the Church, but an aspect of God's plan. Nor does the act of faith consist in saying: "I believe that the Catholic Church exists," nor even: "I believe that Jesus Christ founded the Catholic Church." Any unbelieving historian could determine that.

But the act of faith in the Church consists in a synthetic judgment analogous to that made by Christ's contemporaries with respect to His person: "I believe that **this Church,** Catholic, Roman, and Apostolic, which I see, **which I know** in history and by personal experience, I believe that this Church is **the Body of Christ** and the meeting place of God and the world." The synthetic judgment about Christ was hard and difficult for the Jews of His time. The whole Old Testament told them that God could not be represented; they were forbidden to make images of God and, later, even to pronounce His name, Yahweh. And now a creature of flesh and blood calls Himself God. . . . It was a scandal. And yet the object of faith was Christ in person, the very Son of God, visible surely, but holy, poor—going about doing good.

For us the Church is Christ in a human society which includes even sinners. Consequently, if faith in Christ was difficult for the Jews, faith in the Church is even more difficult. We should not be surprised that unbelievers hesitate and that even those within the Church sometimes have temptations against the faith.

The act of faith is, therefore, this synthetic judgment: "I

---

[1] St. Augustine often stressed this notion: the Apostles saw Christ and believed in the Church; we see the Church and believe in Christ. See, for example: *Sermo* 116, c. 6; P.L. 38, 660.

believe that this Church in human form which I see is the Body of Christ; I believe that it is in this Church that communion is realized between mankind and the Trinity."

Included in Belief in Christ

Belief in the Church is included in belief in Christ; it is not an additional act of faith. What follows is very important and often lies at the root of many critical decisions. We must believe in Christ, that is, we must adhere to Christ and to all that He is: to all His will, to His entire work, to His whole being; consequently, we have *to adhere to Christ in His Church* which is His will, His work, His being. The Church is the will of Christ; the formation of the Church is His work; the present being of Christ, between the time of His departure at the Ascension until His return, is also the Church. We either must believe in Christ in all that He is and accept Him completely, or not accept Him at all. We cannot divide Christ and choose what we like of Him; that is, we cannot choose His person to the exclusion of His will and His work, or choose Him as son of Mary to the exclusion of His body which is the Church. St. Augustine, speaking of Donatus, the first great schismatic, constantly repeated: "Everything in Scripture having to do with Christ can just as well be applied to the Church." Such is the foundation of his exegesis and his whole theology.

What right have we to set ourselves up as judges and say to Christ: "I believe some things you say, for example: 'I am the light,' but I do not believe others, such as: 'You are the light.' I believe in you when you say: 'I am the Good Shepherd,' but I no longer believe in you when you say: 'Thou art Peter...Feed my lambs, feed by sheep.'"

But let us examine two concrete examples of this:

1. **Faith and Baptism.** The prime necessity of faith appears clearly in the New Testament and was already indicated in the Old. "He who believes is saved, he who does not believe is condemned." It is faith which justifies. But if it is faith which justifies, wherein lies the necessity of the sacrament? Think of the baptismal service. The person to be baptized is

258

asked: "Do you believe?" He makes an act of faith and is then baptized in the name of the Father and of the Son and of the Holy Spirit.

Philip the Apostle said to the minister of queen Candace of Ethiopia: "If thou dost believe with all thy heart, thou mayest be baptized." And he answered and said: "I believe Jesus Christ to be the Son of God" (Acts 8:37).

In the final analysis, what justifies, faith or the sacrament? The answer is simple: the sacrament is part of faith. To the degree in which *faith includes the desire for baptism* it justifies the believer.

Christ demands total and unconditional faith, and this faith includes Christ's will, His work and the means He established. "I believe in Christ, in His will and in the means He instituted for us to go to Him and for Him to come to us."

Since men are justified to the degree in which their faith includes the desire for baptism, if a catechumen were to retract his desire for baptism after having made an act of faith, he would not be justified.

2. **Contrition and the Sacrament of Penance.**

If a perfect contrition remits sin, why do we need the sacrament? The answer is analogous to the one above: "The sacrament is an essential part of perfect contrition." Belief in the Church is, therefore, included in belief in Christ, and is not an additional act of faith. Belief in the Church is a part of belief in Christ just as desire for the sacrament of baptism is a part of justifying faith, as *desire for the sacrament of penance is part of the perfect contrition which remits sin.* The faith which justifies is faith in Christ, including faith in the Church.

It Justifies Us

Adherence to the Church is not a consequence of an already acquired salvation, rather it is this very adherence to the Church which justifies us. The Church is our Mother, not only because she fosters her children's faith and life, but above all, because she engenders us unto divine life. Christ wills to communicate with us in His Church. He wills to give us faith by means of the apostolic message of His Church; He wills to give us life by means of the sacraments of His Church. Total faith, therefore, contacts Christ where He wills to give Himself: in the Church. We are justified to the degree in which our faith contacts Christ in His Church. If our faith does not extend this far, that is, to Christ in the Church, we are not justified.

It is not we ourselves who give the Church existence by our gathering together in a body; the Church is given us by Christ Himself **Who chose the means of communion** between Himself and us; it is Christ Who gave the Gospel to the Church to deliver to us; it is Christ Who chose the sacraments as the means of communicating divine life; it is Christ Who chose the means His Church employs. Entry into the Church, therefore, comes first: "He who has not the Church for Mother cannot have God for Father."

It is sometimes said that what characterizes the Catholic as distinguished from the Protestant is precisely this adherence to the Church. For the Protestant, such adherence is a consequence of salvation; for the Catholic, a required condition for salvation. But we must go further and say that what characterizes the Catholic is *total, complete, unconditional faith in Christ,* and that this belief includes faith in the Church, His Body, and in its role in our faith, our divine life, our education.

Sign of Our Faith

Our adherence to the Church is the sign of our belief in Christ. This last affirmation results from the preceding points. Since total faith in Christ, that is, the true faith, includes adherence to Christ in the Church, belief in the Church will be the proof, the clear sign, the guarantee, the seal of true faith in Christ.

Think back on what we said concerning the justifying faith of baptism: baptism is the seal of authentic, justifying faith. Justifying faith is expressed in the sacrament of baptism which is both the sign of this faith and its *efficacious* sign.

The cause of our difficulty may lie in the fact that the act of faith and the reception of baptism, of necessity, belong to two successive moments of time so that at one moment the catechumen is asked: "Do you believe," and at the next he is given the sacrament of faith. In fact, however, they do not succeed one another, but are included in one another, united on a superior, spiritual plane. Baptism is an essential and integral part of justifying faith; baptism is the physical expression of real belief in Christ; baptism is the efficacious sign of real faith in Christ.

Requirements of Our Faith in the Church

"He who believes and is baptized shall be saved" (Mark 16:16). Such is the normal way of proceeding envisaged by Christ: faith being an adherence to the Gospel propounded by the Church, and divine life being given us through the Church's sacraments. (It is always through the Church that Christ sanctifies mankind, either visibly as in our case, or mysteriously through the hidden influences of the eucharistic sacrifice and prayer.)

We Catholics have the great joy of believing in Christ fully and completely, that is, of believing in Christ in the Church, but we must maintain the following attitudes:

1. Absolute certitude as to the truth of the Catholic Church.

2. Personal humility.

1. **Certitude that our Church is True.**

The Church is Christ's only Spouse, the Mother of all mankind, the sole Ark of salvation. To non-Catholics these claims appear unbearable and scandalous, yet the Church refuses to make any concessions on this point. As the ecumenical movement grows among other Christian communions, the Church becomes more intransigent, even at the risk of checking the movement towards reunion. We have to have absolute certitude as to the truth of the Catholic Church.

2. **Personal Humility.**

Although a Catholic may lay claim to such prerogatives for his Church, he cannot do so for himself personally, for

261

no one Catholic makes up the whole Church all by himself. The Church is a complex reality to which we belong to a greater or lesser degree; we are saints to the degree in which we submit to the Church, sinners to the degree in which we do not. No Christian succeeds in fulfilling all the requirements of the Church to the point where he can mirror its perfections wholly and perfectly in his own person. The imperfection of its members expresses the Church's own inner contradictions in that it is both the body of Christ and a body composed of sinners; it is the parable of the Kingdom in which the weeds grow among the wheat until harvest time.

The more we are aware of the truth of our Church, its holiness and its extensive demands upon us, the more we should be personally humble. Only this humility permits any kind of dialogue between ourselves and Protestants and Orthodox, or with those who do not share our faith. Our Church is holy, but we cannot lay claim to the privileges of such holiness for ourselves. Protestants may well be holier than Catholics if these latter are unfaithful to their vocation and to the Church's requirements.

3. **Reconciliation of these Two Attitudes.**

How can we reconcile these two apparently contradictory attitudes? First of all, let us make an important observation both from a personal and a pastoral point of view. Only too often, belonging to the Church is presented as a kind of easy road to salvation for those privileged enough to have the faith. Most of us were baptized as infants and so became the children of God unknowingly, while the pagans will perhaps be obliged to bear witness by the baptism of blood. In the sacrament of penance, imperfect contrition is enough to save us, while for those outside the Church only perfect contrition remits sin and restores God's favor.

Now in this context are we not tempted to put most of the emphasis on the efficacy of the sacraments, on their "ex opere operato" aspect? However, because it is more traditional and more in accordance with the Gospel, we have to say that membership in the Church is not so much an easy way, but above all, a greater obligation to sacrificial love and holiness.

To be a member of the Church means having the true light and this advantage brings with it definite responsibilities: we must not keep this light to ourselves.

To be a member of the Church means having at our disposal because of all the riches of Christ greater possibilities for holiness and love, and, consequently, greater obligations to holiness and love. "To everyone that has, shall be given" (Luke 19:26).

Christ did not promise a wide and easy road. He came to bring love, that is, an invitation to greater and greater dedication. In this perspective the sacraments established by Christ are meant to offer us greater possibilities for holiness and the apostolate.